SEAN FARQUHAR

Under the Baobab Tree

A New Life in Africa

Rosemary Long

Eric Dobby Publishing

Published by Eric Dobby Publishing Ltd, 12 Warnford Road, Orpington, Kent BR6 6LW.

First published 1993
Reprinted 1993

A catalogue record for this book is available from the British Library

ISBN 1-85882-003-0

Typeset in 10pt on 12pt Palatino by Origination and printed by BPCC Wheatons Ltd, Exeter.

Contents

Foreword

No-one was more surprised than I when I fell in love with a Gambian. But I like surprises. What follows here is the expanded, unabridged version of many months of INTO AFRICA columns in the Glasgow Herald – or The Herald, as it is now called.

Within these pages I change from being a Glasgow journalist to being a Gambian wife (known to my neighbours as Mariama Faal), occasional cook, bottle-washer, landlady and unsuccessful banana-grower.

None of it would have happened if I hadn't come to the Gambia on holiday and fallen in love with Relwan (Ray) Faal. He still surprises me every day. You could say this book is my way of thanking him, and the people of the Gambia, for changing my life.

ROSEMARY LONG

Goodbye
to All This

'It's surely not true that you're . . .'

'I heard that you were . . .'

'Marrying a prince . . .'

'Opening a safari park . . .'

'Going to South Africa . . . Timbuktu . . . Zambia . . .'

'Away wi' the fairies . . .'

When a middle-aged, divorced, Merchant-City-dwelling, cat-loving, theatre-going, pension-fund-contributing, Marks-&-Spencer-card-holding journalist (and grandmother of three) announces to her friends, colleagues, family and readers that she's going to 'throw it all away' and live in the Gambia, the phone never stops ringing.

Especially when the woman in question has let it be known that she has fallen in love with a young, black, Wollof-speaking village-dweller in Africa's smallest democracy, and is abandoning the Culture City, the poll tax, glass shopping centres, plastic money, Kylie Minogue and Terry Wogan, CDs and VDUs, car phones and crinkle-cut chips, and people who call you darling because they can't quite remember your name but think you might be useful to them one day . . . to MARRY him; shock, horror, murder, polis!

'Rosemary, please think what you're doing.'

'Dear, don't you feel you're being a bit impetuous?'

'Darling, don't go!'

But here I am, passport in pocket, suitcase crammed with essentials, eyes red from a series of tired-and-emotional, sloppy, searing, incredibly painful goodbyes (no-one ever said such nice things to me till they knew I was leaving; it's like reading your own obituaries!) arms and bum aching from innumerable jabs (tetanus, typhoid, cholera, hepatitis A, yellow fever, meningococcolus, since you ask, but nothing that innoculates you against sentimentality).

My goods and chattels are somewhere on the high seas, due to arrive in Banjul early in 1990, God willing. A piece of red, palm-fringed earth awaits me, five minutes from the sea and a million emotional miles from the place that's been home for nearly half-a-century.

'What a step to take!' people have gasped.'How brave! Won't you miss the arts, the telephone, the TV, the microwave, the hairdresser, the delicatessen, your family, your friends?' To which, of course, only the last two elicit a resounding YES.

As to the rest? Come on now, you cannot be serious?

I think perhaps, for the benefit of those who see me cowering in a mud-hut living on sorghum and pining for Pirandello and pop-in-the-oven, garlic-and-thyme-stuffed boneless chicken breasts, I should say this:

They're right; it is a piddling little Third World country with erratic electricity, 90% female illiteracy, malnutrition as a primary cause of death among infants, female circumcision still widespread, appalling roads, rampant malaria, corruption in high places, gruesome sanitation and no TV station.

But there are compensations. I won't do a Mills & Boon testimonial to the man I'm about to marry, because it would embarrass him. But suffice it to say that after one marriage, I maintained for nine long eventful years that I would NEVER, NEVER get married again. And he made me change my mind, which surely says it all.

And what about his forebears, and the gloriously daft, delightful ever-exploited-but-always-resilient history of the place?

How about Gonga Moussa (circa 1307) ruler of the Mandingo empire, who made a pilgrimage to Mecca accompanied by 60,000 retainers, carrying eighty sacks of gold, preceded by 500 slaves carrying a gold ingot apiece? Does he not make your twentieth-century, white, gold-card-carrying, Porsche-driving Glasgow yuppie look downright wimpish?

Or consider Captain Diogo Gomez, who, around 1458, got Chief Nomimansa so plastered on Portuguese plonk that he begged to become a Christian? Or look askance at the noble white adventurers who, in the eighteenth century, found, according to Francis Moore, that (sic) 'the Girls would have People think they are very modest . . . but take them by themselves and they are very obliging; for if you will give them a little Coral or a Silk Handkerchief, you may take what Liberty you please with them . . .' This, you'll note, is very much the same philosophy as that pursued by twentieth-century Glasgow man in his own happy hunting grounds: 'See her? Gie her a couple of Courvoisiers and lemonade and she's anybody's.' I mustn't let this develop into a history lesson, but it's smashing stuff, absolutely begging to be made into a much better novel-and-TV-series than Arther Hailey's embarrassing Roots.

So, how about the geography? My own small portion of it is by a forest which is a clutter of mahogany and other trees, laced around with tangled underbush, in which colobus monkeys with bright black eyes in pert white faces congregate in family groups and gibber the days away in the yellow-and-brown striped shadows. Birds bustle in and out of the bushes like handfuls of rubies and sapphires. Lizards, indigo and purple, with indignant elbows and haughty faces, jitter on the rocks. Past the forest, down a steep, scratchy path, is a soft platinum-coloured beach washed by giant foamy rollers. The temperature hovers between 80° and 95°F all year round, and the sea-water is as warm as bath-water.

This portion of mine is merely a patch of cleared bush, where butterflies flounce on dry ochre weeds and a five-foot high termite hill like a giant traffic cone had to be hacked down where the wall will be. There is a standpipe nearby, a leaky tap in a muddy corner next to the cattle. Our house, we hope, will be built by January . . . or February . . . or March. One day, who knows, we may have electricity. Or then again, maybe we won't, but does it matter?

There are no supermarkets, Macdonalds, Miss Selfridges or building society offices, no theatres and no multi-storey car-parks. The sprawling town of Serrekunda (with 80,000 people it is twice the size of the capital, Banjul) is a vast, vibrant shanty town, made of mud, concrete blocks, corrugated iron roofs and fences, glimmering at night with candles and oil lamps outside booths selling nuts and bolts, chillies and lucky charms, kebabs cooked over charcoal in rusting oil-drums, flip-flops, enamel basins painted with flowers, dead fish and live chickens. In the sports stadium in Bakau, famous African and West Indian bands have played and in June, in Banjul, the conference of the Organisation of African Unity was held. This toty wee insignificant gutsy country is the headquarters of the African Centre for Human Rights. There is, I rather suspect, too much to be written, about the people and the customs and the bloody awful roads and the backhander system and the beggars and the mangrove swamps and the bright smiles and calls of 'Hullo, welcome, how is de morning?' which spill over adoptive Gambians such as me, like sunshine, warm and enveloping. I may suffer from a surfeit of visual and aural sensation and write too much, too often, wallowing in an overdose of new experience. Be tolerant with me. I have to haul myself back to the here and now. A wet November in Glasgow and an empty house.

But my mind keeps wandering. A wedding has been arranged. The registry office in Banjul is what we plan. My son to give me away (which we both find hilarious). A host of new relatives. Wollof to be learned. Yes, of course Ray speaks English; it is the *lingua franca*. He also speaks pretty competent German and a smattering of Swedish, French and Finnish. But Wollof is his mother tongue, a language that spreads through Senegal and down to Guinea, and I'm damn well going to try and learn it . . . eventually.

Now let me ask you this: Have you ever sat in a mud-hut drinking treacly Chinese gunpowder tea with a ninety-year-old village headman and haggling over three-quarters of an acre of baked scrubland? No, I don't suppose you have.

Let me tell you, it's an exhausting and exhilarating experience. Doodoo Faal, alkalo of Bijilo village and some sort of great-uncle to my husband-to-be, is illiterate but sharper than a Surbiton stockbroker. He wears a long white nightie and an embroidered cap and he speaks no English. His son interprets. We ask after each other's health, circling each other like newly-introduced rottweilers, and verbal battle commences.

Bargaining is an art form in the Gambia. You do it when you go to market to buy a handful of herbs. You despise and mistrust the foolish, unadventurous person who says, straightaway: 'Yes, that's fine; I'll pay you what you ask.'

I reckon I did OK. I offered x. He demanded y. I eventually settled on buying the land for $x + \frac{1}{2}(y - x)$. The smart word is, it may be a bit of scabby red earth on the outskirts of Bijilo village but it's due to become the Kilmacolm of Kombo South . . . once they build the road, maybe a couple of new hotels, and a few more bungalows near ours. The pity of it is, I like it as it stands, surrounded by isolation, empty spaces spiked with palm-trees and sung to by weaver birds and sun-finches. But that's progress for you.

So we've bought the land, planned the nuptials, broken the news to kith, kin and colleagues, and I've resigned from the job as feature-writing Woman's Editor with the Glasgow Evening Times where I was, as they say, in with the bricks and expected to remain so till they pensioned me off.

Just like that. Simple. Nothing to it.

Oh, but yes, there is a lot to it. For a start there are the reactions, briefly touched on in the first few lines of this splurge of self-indulgent true confessions. These were among the kinder comments. There were also the ones that went: 'You must be absolutely mad.' Or: 'How can you possibly marry a black man? They're not the same as us, you know.' One ungainly, red-nosed colleague whispered to another: 'It's a long way to go for a bit of black nookie.' Another sniggered: 'It must be the menopause.' Bets were taken that I would change my mind. I took courage from an experience recounted by a friend, who had a Greek boyfriend, one with skin as warmly golden as his heart. In an eaterie in the 'hospitable' north of Scotland, she was asked: 'Could you no' at least huv got one of your own kind?' My friend looked at her hostess who had posed the question, and then at the host, beer-gutted, blotchy-skinned, balding, beery-breathed and well past his sell-by date. 'You mean one like him?' she enquired sweetly. 'No, thank you.' Enough said about that.

I can handle all that stuff. And most of my friends have been real friends, genuinely concerned for my wellbeing. What I can't handle so easily is all the other stuff. Like these jabs for every nasty disease known to mankind which, in a couple of cases made me hallucinate, break out in a cold sweat and throb with pain from ear to ankle. Tourists need not panic; it is only intrepid emigrants to the White Man's Grave who need wall-to-wall protection. I lay in bed wondering if we might have to arrange a funeral for the week intended for our wedding.

I had barely recovered from that when the shipping people arrived to take me apart and pack up my life in a series of giant paper pokes labelled 'books', 'pots and pans', 'kitchen sink'. You're never going to believe this but I *am* actually taking a stainless steel sink, bought in Paddy's Market, and I don't want any smart-ass remarks about it, so there!

There are labels saying 'china cats' and 'flat-pack table' and 'cushions'. The shipping people drink coffee from one cracked mug and one stray sugar-bowl, because everything else is packed, or given to Oxfam, or stored in the lofts of friends, along with winter clothes, granny's china, high-heeled shoes and an assortment of wooden and wally elephants. You can take a kitchen sink to Africa, but you can't take elephants; it wouldn't be right, somehow, I feel.

As the furniture goes, the stains and splodges and savage indentations in the carpet begin to dominate. As the pictures go, white rectangles stand out against the murky walls which, just a day or two ago, looked clean.

I sob a lot over old photographs, and cards which say 'We'll miss you', and 'Haste ye back' and 'Here's to my favourite old battle axe!' (It's strange how touching even insults can be at a time like this!)

I panic about things I might need and still have to pack. Tin openers, Tampax, typewriter ribbons, Nescafe, tomato seeds, a wine cooler, Wet Ones, spare dental plate, Mozart tapes, Eddie Chisnall posters, an inflatable mattress. Last time I was in Bijilo I slept on a straw-and-sacking bed and it's something I'd prefer not to do again. It was like sleeping on someone's rockery.

Only the day before I was a footloose fancy-free back-packer. Suddenly, I was a jackdaw. Throw everything in. You never know when you might need clothes-pegs, cup-hooks, Evostick, nail varnish, maps of Wester Ross. The shippers shrug and get more brown paper.

Meanwhile, I am cutting off arteries one by one. Goodbye, telly and video-recorder. Goodbye, telephone. But not before a dozen more calls saying: 'Are you sure . . .?' 'Must you really . . .?' Goodbye, my cats. Be happy, Rusty and Chou-chou. I will miss you achingly for I have loved you dearly. But you wouldn't be happy in Africa. You'd miss the Whiskas and the Axminster.

There are farewell lunches and dinners and drinks and I get more and more maudlin with each passing hour. Not at the going, but at the leave-taking, if you can understand what I mean. I try to read out some of the cards and letters to my mum and my voice breaks up into a slobbery rattle and I sob on her shoulder instead. Oh, mum. How am I ever, ever going to say goodbye to *you*?

I raise my glass to toast close friends and my confident smile turns into a puckered whimper.

I sit, for the very last time, at my word processor in this big hi-tech building in Albion Street where so much of my life has been spent and I think, maybe for the moment, I should stop writing. Because the watery-eyes syndrome is starting again.

Wish me luck as you wave me goodbye.

The next bulletin will be dry-eyed and full of sunshine. At least, it should be. But everyone cries at a wedding.

For a Handful of Kola Nuts

The kola nuts were cracked and dispensed, big fat purple conkers, tasting bitter to me, but maybe I'll acquire the taste.

'Are you married now?' whispered Liz.

'I suppose so,' I said, bemused. 'Where's Ray?'

My new husband was in the village square, under the baobab tree, dispensing *dalasi* coins to the locals, smoking, and exchanging coarse comments with his friends. He was wearing a torn Snoopy tee-shirt and shorts. At a Gambian wedding, it's the woman who goes through the ceremony.

Forget all about morning coats and champagne and Crimplene dresses with flowery hats. Forget funny telegrams and frilly bridesmaids. As for the bridal car, it's a battered Peuguot of indeterminate age, painted green with Rasta yellow and red stripes along the sides. It dips alarmingly to the left, and when I alight from it into the hot orange sand of the square, where chickens scratch and dogs sleep, the door falls off with a long, reverberating rattle.

We are having a Muslim blessing on our union. Ray has been given a thorough going-over by the Imam, an unbearably handsome young man with broad high cheekbones and wide, humorous eyes. Ray's cousin is whispering a translation to Liz. Liz Kristiansen is a Scottish Television continuity announcer and also my best friend. She has taken a week's holiday to watch me plight my troth in Africa. She is trying not to giggle.

The Imam, she told me later, was telling Ray that he must give up his bachelor ways, devote himself to my welfare, say his prayers and teach me to say mine, give up drinking alcohol and never go off with the boys and leave me alone at home. Sounds fine by me.

It is 6.15 in the evening, 20 November, 1989, in the village of Bijilo in the Kombo South district of The Gambia. The population numbers almost 2000 and almost all of them are related to the groom, Relwan S M Faal . . . my Ray.

Most of them are in the street around the mosque, which is a low tin-roofed building with peeling whitewashed walls. The women wear vivid cotton skirts. Their babies hang on to their teats or bounce on their backs, tied like bustles over their buttocks with strips of fabric knotted firmly under their breasts. The young men strut in Levis and tee-shirts extolling everything from Coca Cola to Scottish Television. Liz has been magnanimous with her gifts. The children giggle and tumble, impervious to the elders' roars of wrath.

I arrived at Yundum International Airport exactly ten days before. Yundum International Airport is small patch of baked yellow earth under a single control tower, with a terminal roughly the size of a small British railway station. There is no carousel for the luggage, which is dumped in heaps near the trestle table of the customs inspectors and fought over by porters while the owners wilt under the flat-iron heat.

I have two huge suitcases. They contain my African survival kit. Typewriter ribbons and tampons, photographs of my mother and packets of Paracetamol, malaria pills and Nescafe, cotton knickers and kitchen knives, books and brassieres, sheets and lavender wax polish, towels and frying-pans. Marks & Spencer underpants and socks for Ray. Pictures of my Glasgow cats. Two folding canvas chairs.

Ray has a friend in airport security and somehow I am swept past queueing holidaymakers and through passport control and hordes of Gambians asking for newspapers, dalasis, my address; and I am beyond the wire fence and there is Lamin, Ray's brother, in a car like a crushed shoebox, and we are driving into my new life.

I haven't seen Ray for six months. We feel shy. We keep looking at each other and laughing and crying and the world outside the car windows is a blur of corrugated iron roofs and cows, mango trees with leaves which are khaki from the dust and people selling little plastic bags of red water flavoured and coloured with ginger and chilli pepper.

And now I am being married. I am on the verandah of the little tin-roofed mosque, seated on a very low armchair, surrounded by the old men, the village elders, who sit easily in the lotus position, fingering their beads; wrinkled black faces under knitted woollen caps. We are all barefoot. They are unlikely to be impressed by the fact that I am wearing an exclusive ivory silk frock made for me by Glasgow designer Lex McFadyen, with matching French knickers and a dolly-bag concocted by Lex's mum. Just so long as my legs are covered. Thighs, in Africa, can, it seems, stir base reactions in a man.

I have loaned Liz a pareo to wrap round her suntanned nether regions. She looks very elegant.

I sweat into the silk. I have uttered loudly my Gambian vows. My son David, in cut-off denims and bare chest, sits cross-legged with the elders, looking solemn. I asked him earlier if he ever wished he'd had a normal, conventional mother. He said no. Ray's Uncle Assan acts as interpreter. It was he who acted as middleman when I bought my land from the Alkalo, or village headman, earlier in the year. He is wearing a bright scarlet shirt.

'You must promise you will encourage your husband to say his prayers five times a day and abstain from alcohol,' he says, straightfaced. Earlier that day, he was with us in Banjul, downing pints with practised gusto, but he looks suitably virtuous now under the handsome holy eye of the Imam.

I nod demurely. 'Waow,' I say ('Yes.')

There is a lot of stuff about washing after sex and before prayers, which embarrasses Assan more than it does me, and then he says: 'Now you must choose an adopted father.' I blink. Which of these old men would I want to call Daddy? I pick the village headman the *alkalo* because he's the only one I really know. His ninety-year-old face remains chiselled from ebony; then he says, with a glint in his yellow eyes, that this must not be just words, for the ceremony, but that I must visit him in his compound, as his daughter. Another wrinkly has been nominated as Ray's sponsoring parent. Dignified haggling breaks out between them. Will the alkalo accept one hundred dalasi for his daughter? Certainly not. I sit in a dream, half-listening to it all, the bartered bride. In the end, I fetch three hundred and fifty dalasi, about £23.50. And to think that once, in Morocco my mother refused 500 camels for my hand in marriage!

The *griot*, a kind of town-crier and repository of village lore, bellows out speeches on behalf of the old men, long, pompous homilies welcoming me to the village community, trusting that I will be a diligent and obedient wife, and that Allah will heap prosperity on us both.

A crumpled brown paper parcel is laid in front of the alkalo and the kola nuts, bought by Ray in Serrekunda earlier, are exposed and distributed, half to the men of the village, half to the women.

I am led to Ray's mother's house, where each of the women comes in and shakes hands. Little girls curtsey. Grandmothers guffaw and say that I have stolen their boy away from them, therefore I must give them dalasi. Ray's mum, who is the sister of the Imam, and has the same fine cheekbones and splendid eyes, hugs me. 'Mariama. *Da ma kontan!*' ('I am happy -')

Mariama is the name I was given halfway through the ceremony. I am pleased at the name, which is that of Ray's mother and his small sister. It is better, I think, than Haddy, which sounds like a fish, or Bintah, which sounds rude, or Fatou, which sounds . . . fat.

'Where is Ray?' I whimper, overwhelmed. Lex's expensive silk is soaking, clinging to my back like a wet rag. It has all been very emotional. I start to cry. 'I'm only crying because I'm happy,' I croak at the women. I'm also exhausted. The day hasn't gone quite the way we planned it.

At eight o'clock that morning we set off for the Kombo Beach Hotel to change our clothes and pick up Liz, and my son David, who had trudged grudgingly along the sand from his hotel, muttering about this being the middle of the night.

Ray put on his Marks & Spencer trousers, shirt and tie. My white shoes pinched. People in the hotel looked curiously at us. Some of the staff had heard what was happening. 'Congratulations. That is good. Welcome. Welcome to the Gambia. We are very happy.'

We set off, with Uncle Assan and brother Lamin, to the courthouse in Serrekunda. A criminal lawyer and his clients squabbled with an official on the next bench. Half of the plasterboard roof had collapsed. Another official snarled at Liz when she tried to take pictures.

'You cannot have a civil wedding here,' we are told. 'You must go to Banjul, to the Ministry of Justice, give them all your details, swear an affidavit, then your application will be sent to the President's office for approval. It might take a week . . . or two weeks.'

Consternation all round. Liz is going home on Wednesday and David on Friday. Are they to be cheated out of a wedding?

We pile into our two rickety Renault taxis, sticking to the plastic seats. Make the jostling, suspension-shattering drive to Banjul. 'We want to be married,' we tell a lofty African lady with straightened hair and a shiny lilac dress. 'But you cannot be married today. There are formalities. You must get approval from the President.'

Uncle Assan saves the day. 'We *will* have a wedding,' he says, like the good fairy in a pantomime. 'I will arrange it. Come.' That's how we came to have Muslim nuptials in Bijilo village, how I came to be called Mariama, and acquire a headman as a surrogate dad.

This morning we went to the Serrekunda Courthouse again, wearing jeans and tee-shirts, and picked up our Gambian marriage certificate. It says things like 'amount of dower which was paid at time of marriage', 'whether bride is adult or otherwise', 'name of guardian of bride'. There are two copies, one for Ray, one for me, with our photographs at the top, my face obscured by a purple official stamp.

And at least the reception went ahead as planned. It was held in Uncle Dembo's, an African bar near the Senegambia Hotel. The tables and chairs are of wobbly metal and the beer comes without a glass. The donner kebabs would blow your head off, and the toilets have no running or flushing water and are alive with ants. But they strung up flags for us and played Gambian and Senegalese music that set the blood racing. Amadou, our lawyer, turned up, with a girl on his arm who he swore was Mrs Samba.

The boys from the taxi rank and the market were there, and some of the village girls, and Liz and David.

Our health was drunk in Julbrew, the Gambian-bottled beer, or in Sprite, Coke or Fanta. Our cake, made by Glaswegian Christopher Reece Bowen, and brought out by Liz, was cut and handed round. Liz reveals that, at Manchester Airport, she accidentally left the cake-box in the loo and started a security alert.

The cake was a wee touch of home, under a black African sky. Now all we have to do is live happily ever after. Watch this space.

Watching the
Occra Grow

Well, well. Here we all are then.

Watching the tarmac dry.

It's 3 pm and the sun is blasting all its big guns. Trucks bounce past full of African labourers turned pale biscuit-coloured by the dusty sand.

This is the Banjul-Serrekunda Highway, or at least it will be. They've been making it for years. It is an obstacle course of deep furrows and small hillocks. The labourers work in a desultory fashion. Some of them are sleeping, in wheel-barrows, on top of bags of cement, standing up.

'You are a big fool, you driver. You are the son of a prostitute. You have coos-coos instead of brains, huh?'

Marie-Thérèse is getting tore in. She is voluptuous, nay, gargantuan, her fuschia and yellow skirts and bodices billowing around her like an angry sunset, her white teeth snapping, her round eyes rolling, flashing thunderbolts, her vast bosom heaving and shuddering in indignation, a volcano about to erupt.

Her victim is the driver of our bush-taxi. He is small, skinny, sullen under the onslaught of her wrath. His vehicle may once have been a fourteen-seat Mercedes Benz. Now it is a fourteen-seat heap of clattering metal, bursting upholstery, rattling gear-box. The floor is covered with cracked kitchen linoleum patterned in yellow flowers.

In obvious pain, a wheel has self-amputated, halfway between the capital city of Banjul and the seething clutter of Serrekunda. We are in the midst of a long, lugubrious roadworks. The locals call it the M1. No-one can quite remember when it was started. No-one believes it will ever be finished.

One small section glistens. It is blue-black, steaming, still wet from the roller.

The driver and his boy lie down under the van, with a spare wheel, a couple of bricks and some strangulated pieces of metal. For a while there is silence. Possibly they have fallen asleep.

We, the passengers, clamber over the red earth to look at the tarmac. We exchange pleasantries about its appearance, its texture, its resilience. I tell everyone it was a Scot who invented the stuff and they look at me politely, unimpressed but nodding sagely.

This is almost as exciting as watching paint dry. I know this, because the next day, in a yard full of cassava – yams – and rooting ducks, that's just what I did. But more of that later.

Back to the M1. Marie Thérèse has her second wind. She spits venomously on the tar and launches a second offensive. 'Your vehicle is like a peanut, ready to crumble if someone touches it with one finger. You are a homosexual.' 'And you, madam, you are a lesbian!' ripostes the driver with sudden courage, brandishing a tyre-lever experimentally. The passengers cheer both sides in turn.

Voices reach maximum volume. Insults are hurled faster and faster. Ray is providing me with a simultaneous translation from the Wollof. Now I know what 'Aitcha!' means. It means '**** off!' and comes out as a fine, satisfying crack like breaking timber.

Then, suddenly, just as I feared blood might be spilled on the brand new asphalt, both protagonists and all the passengers burst into great, gritty squawks of laughter. Tears of mirth stream down their dusty cheeks. Marie Thérèse's bosom heaves so energetically I wait for it to explode in a shower of fuschia and yellow like bougainvillaea flowers. This, I begin to discover, is how Gambian arguments are conducted: with vigour, relish, ferocity then, finally, guffaws in celebration of a battle well fought.

The wheel had in fact been loose when we left Banjul. Passing drivers yelled warnings. Marie Thérèse bounced up and down on her broken-springed seat like a blancmange, shouting curses, demanding reparations, but the driver bore on, implacable, trusting to Allah to hold everything together. Inevitably, we ground to a grating, lopsided halt.

Still, it wasn't such a long wait. Not by Gambian standards. If patience is a virtue, then the entire population, me included, will one day be canonised en masse.

I am already a dab-hand at doing nothing for long periods of time, while things seem not to happen, seem indeed to be going backwards but, in the end, somehow miraculously manage to come to a surprisingly satisfactory conclusion. Well, mostly they do.

Let me tell you, for instance, about our bed.

We are ready to move into our 'self-contained' – three empty whitewashed concrete-floored rooms in a compound on the outskirts of Serrekunda, along a bumpy lane flanked by tin-roofed shacks and tufts of palm, thorn and maize.

This is our home until our bungalow is built. We share a shower and toilet with other families in the compound, smiling women squatting before charcoal stoves and huge tubs of washing.

There are flocks of children who cluster round me chanting 'Tubab! Tubab! ('White man!') In the times that follow I am going to become very familiar with this word. It is shouted by toddlers who can hardly stand, by schoolgirls and grannies, usually followed by 'Any dalasi? Give me pen!' At first I smile and give coins, or shake my head apologetically.

Then I realise that this is silly. I live here. If some little brats in Bellgrove or Busby shouted 'Give me money!' I'd send them packing. So later I stop being patronising and treat them like real kids. 'Hey, you come here! Does your teacher know you go around begging? You are very rude. Stop it at once!' They apologise in a giggling gaggle. 'Sorry, missus. Sorry. You are right. We will not do it again.' They do, of course.

In the compound the children gradually get used to me. 'Mariama!' they call. 'Nanga def?' ('How are you?')

My furniture will arrive, we hope, in a month's time, by ship. Meanwhile we need something to sleep on.

In the first carpenter's yard we are quoted prices of optimistic enormity. Ray mouths the Wollof equivalent of 'Away an' bile your heid, you greedy, double-dealing git,' and we flounce off, shaking our heads, waving our arms, offers of compromise following us as we go.

We repeat this performance in several establishments. One of them sells beds of such fabulously appalling vulgarity I am almost tempted to buy one. Headboards of plump shiny satin the colour of tinned salmon loom over dreadful bedside cabinets of cheap laminated wood with shiny squiggles. Each bed costs more than two months' rent. We back away, blinking.

We arrive at the shop of Mr Secka. It is made of corrugated iron, filled with the perfumes of sawdust and glue and sweet mahogany. Ancient tools tumble from drooping shelves in wild profusion. In the yard, ducks check out the soil under the cassava plants, between rows of occra. Occra is one of the Gambia's staple foods. It is used to make stuff called *sooppa*, viscous and greeny-brown, spooned over rice like something leaked from a boil.

Outside Mr Secka's shop, four beds are lined up lasciviously. Two of them are padded in puce velveteen, but two of them are handsome edifices of heavy carved wood, varnished to a burnished copper.

We choose one. Maybe you think that's that? Pay, uplift, depart? Hey, this is the Gambia, folks. In Wollof we say 'Fie Gambia-la.' It means only 'This is the Gambia', but is usually said with a lifting of shoulders, a quirking of eyebrows, to imply many hidden meanings of unpredictability, complication, prevarication and utter frustration.

We go into the yard to debate, discuss, deliberate. Mr Secka tells me his life story. The diplomatic tensions between Senegal and the

Gambia, which wither and sprout with the seasons, are dissected assiduously. Mr Secka has heard of old Gambian ladies being strip-searched at the border. Ray shakes his head and curses all Senegalese. Two of the junior assistant trainee carpenters are Senegalese, but they just grin.

There is a small matter of fifty dalasi difference in the price Mr Secka desires and the price Ray is prepared to pay. They circle each other verbally, parrying and thrusting, and breaking off to light more cigarettes. I settle back on a wobbly chair and watch the occra growing and the ducks ageing and allow the cadences to flow over me. These are two world-class hagglers. This will take some considerable time. I know already that the figure reached will be somewhere halfway between the asked and the offered. They know it too. It is always thus, but the joy is in the jousting.

In due course, the matter of price is settled. Thereafter, the bed has to be dismantled and various spars and struts and screws removed or inserted. One screw proves hostile, recalcitrant. It breaks inside the wood. Five Gambians study the situation intently, attack it, severally and individually, with screwdrivers, chisels and foul oaths in five tribal dialects.

We go off to buy a foam mattress from the Lebanese foam factory in Kanefing. There is two-inch foam, three-inch, four-inch, five-inch, six-inch, covered or uncovered. The spring interior mattress is virtually unknown, or unaffordable, in the Gambia. Most Gambians have vast sacking bags filled with dried grasses and stitched across. We slept on one in the guest house in Bijilo. It had lumps and craters and, I suspect, an insect population. So we buy a six-by-four chunk of four-inch foam, covered in bold candy-striped cotton.

It takes about an hour. It is a factory so prices are not negotiable. We push it into the back of a taxi and it sticks out like a giant lump of Blackpool rock. We go back to Mr Secka. The screw has submitted. Fresh varnish has been applied. We watch it drying. As the carpenter points out, reasonably, a yearning expression on his broad black face, if the Gambia had machine tools, reliable electricity, enough oil . . . maybe things would happen faster. As it is, the electricity seems to go off more and more frequently, for longer and longer periods, and endless queues form at fuel stations.

Photocopiers, disco equipment, battery-chargers, petrol-pumps and electric sewing machines are paralysed regularly. Our evenings are candle-lit. Even if the compound had electricity, which it hasn't, it would be cut off, like the water, for long periods most days. The Gambia Utilities Company is known as the Generally Useless Company, or Give Us a Candle.

You need patience to deal with this kind of thing. That is why a Gambian will spend an hour waiting for a stamp, squat on his haunches for three hours in his lawyer's office studying his Koran, buy his petrol a gallon at a time, see his woman walk a kilometre to the well or the standpipe for water. And why, after an hour at the roadside watching the tarmac drying, they can still laugh and trust in Allah to get them moving when he thinks fit.

Our bed may not be a contender for the British Design Awards, but it's every inch hand-made. So are the chair and table at which I type. They were made for me by Mr Secka, to my personal specifications, in a day and a half. Plus an hour to settle the price.

There are no sprung bases on Gambian-made beds. Instead, pieces of palm 'run' are balanced across the space between the shiny wooden sides, and a sheet of hardboard (known as cardboard here) is placed on top of them. Then the foam mattress. In time, the palm runs get dislodged and the hardboard and the foam collapse on to the floor. But it looks very handsome.

It was brought to the compound in pieces, in a taxi. It took several trips, and another couple of hours to re-assemble it in our concrete-floored, curtainless bedroom.

Afterwards, I stuck all our Wedding Greetings cards on the crumbling off-white walls, and bought some plastic buckets in which to do the washing at the tap in the yard. For three months, this will be home.

I use hard brownish-yellow locally-made soap to rub the towels and underpants. The children watch me critically, doubtful of the ability of a tubab to do her own washing. Early in the mornings I share the tap with a skinny girl of about eleven, who seems to wash all the previous night's cooking pots and eating-bowls for the people in the next-door compound. Sometimes the water goes off when we are in the midst of rinsing or scrubbing. We don't complain. We just sit on the step and watch the sky lightening and the sun getting bigger and brighter and higher in the sky.

Dusty Days and Dusky Maidens

This is no place for the houseproud. A film of reddish dust settles on my typewriter, over the radio, in my sandals, round the bed-posts. Every time I buff it off, it descends again within minutes.

The floor is concrete and creates its own constant cloud of dust, shedding its surface, making me cough as I clean. I brush it with a broom made from twigs tied together. I borrow this from the policewoman's mother who lives next door, or the landlord's girlfriend who noisily shares his room on the other side of the path from us. The broom is extremely efficient, whisk, whisk, whisk, although it involves a lot of bending and my back's beginning to suffer.

Anyway, the dust comes back, on our feet, on the breeze. It is in the air we breathe, which is why the Gambia has such a high incidence of respiratory disease. It paints the leaves of the trees, the roofs of the houses and the flapping canopies over the stalls selling betel nuts and cigarettes and black mints, everything a pale uniform fawn colour. Corrugated roofs start shiny silver or red oxide scarlet or elegant sage green, but they all end up fawn from the dust.

Most of the time I wear a length of cotton wrapped round and tied at the waist, a cotton top and flip-flops, the universal footwear of Africa. One day, on the beach, I see a huge sheet of what looks like pale grey lace. On closer inspection I find that it is thin foam rubber stamped out with the looping shapes of hundreds of flip-flop soles. I have several pairs of high-heeled shoes and stylish sandals bought in Argyll Street and Buchanan Street, but I can't bear to wear any of them. Too hot, too tight, too dangerous on these rutted red roads.

This morning, however, I decided to look brisk. We went to Banjul to try to arrange a civil wedding to set the official seal on our Muslim village wedding. I put on my Marks & Spencer walking shorts and 'K' Springer sandals and tried to look cool and crisp. After all the colour and confusion of the first wedding, we went to Serrekunda Courthouse to get our marriage certificates. A fat African sat at a large desk, chewing nuts and flirting with the girl who was cleaning the windows.

He gave me a long lecture on Islam and instructed me to come back next week and collect another certificate that would entitle me to enter mosques in Saudi Arabia, Iraq and other Muslim countries. I never went back for it, thank you very much. At the Ministry of Justice in Banjul, after the inevitable long wait, we filled in some forms and handed over some money, and they told us to 'come back next week'. Sometimes the Gambia sounds like a perpetual quiz show.

On the way back from Banjul, we stopped at Serrekunda market. Seething crowds examine giant slabs of sea-snail flesh, which looks like yellow rubber. Ray says it tastes disgusting and I'm quite prepared to take his word for it. There are ladyfish and grey mullet and red snapper and yams and live rabbits and chickens There are heaps of unidentifiable roots and herbs and dried leaves. The dried leaves of the baobab tree are positively packed with vitamins and minerals, but I still can't figure how to cook them. One of Ray's uncles sells us two sticks of warm, doughy bread, and an aunt has a stall selling corn and millet. I gradually realise that uncles and aunts are any slightly older people who are vaguely related to the nth degree.

The Food and Nutritional Unit of the Ministry of Agriculture is forever linking up with foreign aid agencies and drought control organisations to encourage Gambian women to cook with local cereals like sorghum and coos and maize, to decrease reliance on rice. Thousands of tonnes of rice are imported or donated every year, and locally grown fields suffer regularly from poor harvests, late rains, inadequate irrigation. I would like to cook *mbahal* and *chakiri* and *choo* and *benachin* but we have no cooking facilities in our 'self-contained' so I don't cook anything at all.

We live on bread and sardines, or bread and corned beef or street corner kebabs. The meat for these is basted in small pieces over an oil drum full of smouldering wood or charcoal. It is actually illegal to use charcoal now, part of the campaign to halt deforestation. There is a place where you can buy briquettes made of peanut hay, but I've never seen anyone use them. There is a thriving trade in black-market charcoal. The kebab meat is fingered by prospective buyers for tenderness and texture.

It scorches under the dust and the fumes from passing cars with engines which burn oil in clouds of black smoke and I suppose I shouldn't risk eating it, but it tastes terrific. The other roadside snack is hard-boiled eggs, split open and sprinkled with crumbled Maggi cube. When Mrs Currie & Co were bleating about salmonella chickens and dodgy eggs in Britain, many of the European rejects were dumped on Africa, so the Gambia had its own outbreak of salmonella poisoning, just like the trendy tubabs.

Along the sides of the roads in Banjul and Serrekunda are open concrete-lined ditches intended to catch the overflow from the summer rains. Instead they have become foul open sewers, full of slimy fluid and nameless floating things. When we walk at night I cling to Ray, fearful of falling into one and breaking a leg.

In Banjul, some compounds have soakaways – septic tanks – but many rely on the 'nightsoil men' who take their unsavoury cargo and dump it along the Bund Road – also famous worldwide as a birdwatchers' paradise. When we build our house, it will have a soakaway. Unfortunately it won't have running water to flush anything into it, as the GUC hasn't reached our part of the Kombos yet.

Yesterday we went to look at our land again. The foundations are laid for the house, a simple shape hooked round a long verandah, designed by me. I'm rather proud of my little diagram but the men in the Department of Physical Planning looked at it pityingly and provided a proper blueprint full of technical squiggles which Ray's uncle, the builder, can't understand. He still uses my wee drawing. Twelve Africans are mixing concrete to make blocks, shovelling and smiling. A herd of cream and white calves wanders over and stands under the baobab tree surveying the work.

The ground is as dry and hard as a coconut shell and covered with the tangled web of thorns, crackling grasses and stunted palm clumps known as 'the bush'. I used to think the bush was fine sprawling distances of yellow plains and forests. Here the bush is any patch of scrub that someone hasn't built something on. My skirt is peppered with small prickly burrs that cannot be removed without tearing the threads, and my legs are scratched.

One day, I tell myself, this will be a spruce white bungalow surrounded by tropical plants and lemon trees and bananas. One day. Bamboozled by our dreams, in a moment of wild abandon, we agree to pay about £750 for the neighbouring plot, complete with scrawny palms (not the kind that bear coconuts or palm-fruit or dates; all they ever grow is sharp pointed leaves which are used for roofing when you can't afford grass-thatch or corrugate), a termite hill, and more thorns and weeds. There are lizards everywhere, doing press-ups in the skinny shadows.

Now we have about an acre-and-a-half. We plan, lazily, languorously under the scorching sun, to build, one day, some little huts for adventurous tourists. We'll make them attaya (the Chinese gunpowder tea) and serve them cold drinks and all these local dishes I can't cook now because we don't have a cooker or even a single gas-ring. We'll entertain them under the baobab, and introduce them to

the calves and the monkeys in the forest which runs parallel to the
sea. The sea is seven minutes from where our gate will be. We pace it
out, trying to walk at tourist speed.

Now I am typing by candlelight in our temporary lodgings.
Night falls like a shutter at seven in the evening. I am listening to
Radio Syd. 'Tell us, Mr Jallow – you have been using your -----'s
wheel-barrow for ten months now. What do you think of it?' 'I am
very happy with my ----'s wheel-barrow, I can assure you.' The
adverts are great.

Ray has gone to Bijilo to pay for our latest acquisition of land.
Then he'll go to Sukuta to buy bunches of grass at two dalasi each,
and sheets of woven palm called *kirinting* to rebuild his beach-bar.
The big re-opening is planned for Friday. It's to have a new name, a
cunning combination of his English name and my Gambian name –
MaRAYama's. No-one understands it except us. I suggested doing
real Scottish breakfasts with tattie scones, but my daughter said she'd
never speak to me again if I did that. So we'll stick to fish and prawns
baked in foil over a wood fire. This isn't actually 'ethnic' either. No
ordinary Gambian could afford prawns, and the only fish they eat
regularly is the bone-filled bonga fish, costing a dalasi for two.

But with lots of chilli and garlic and the smell of wood smoke on
the wind, it's the beach-bar version of the taste of the Gambia.

The other night we had a different taste of the Gambia – the
finals of the Miss Africa Pageant, held in the stadium in Bakau. This is
a predominantly Muslim country. Women are supposed to keep their
heads and their lower bodies discreetly hidden from lascivious male
eyes. Village women wear long swatches of fabric firmly wound
round their waists, covering them to the ankle, topped by another
oblong with a slit for the neck which flaps gracefully round their
shoulders and torsos. Yet another piece is swirled round their heads
in intricate shapes like flower-buds or birds in flight.

Yet here we are, seated on the hard concrete steps which act as
seating, with local bands playing and spotlights turning the night pale
yellow, and we are watching fifteen girls trotting across the stage in
swimsuits cut to their oxters.

Chief Mueez Akande, the Otun Parakoyl of Abadanland in
Nigeria, whatever that may mean, in portentous purple robes,
declares the contest open. A very fat man in a white suit is the MC.
Lady Chilel, First Lady of the Republic, is guest of honour. They, and
almost all the eminent persons in the posh seats at the front, are
devout Muslims, but the Gambia seems to be able to adapt cheerfully
to any outside customs that make life more enjoyable. None of the
men in the audience runs amok at the display of thighs and buttocks
and cleavage.

The criterion for entry seems to be some sort of African heritage, however diffused, so the skin-tones range from pale gold to purple-black. Sadly, many of the girls look as though they'd used skin-lighteners. Real black is in the minority, fake tubab is predominant. They represent an odd assortment of countries – Guadaloupe, Wales, the Turks and Cacos, Martinique, France, Nigeria. There is, for heaven's sake, a Miss Scotland. She is blonde with only a faintly dusky skin, and has an accent which is slightly south of Manchester. She wears a very short tartan kilt and carries bagpipes. Miss Gambia is black and pretty and shy. She looks, perhaps, too African to be Miss Africa. Miss Bermuda takes the title.

I enjoyed the previous night better. We went to Eddy's, an African bar and nightclub in Serrekunda. The tables wobble and there is no lighting to speak of, and mosquitoes chew your ankles as you sit in the open air drinking Julbrew beer from the bottle. The toilets are execrable and there are lots of girls in shiny satin skirts who Ray says, pursing his lips and looking prudish, are prostitutes. Little boys climb on to the high wall at the back and sway to the music of Jamil Cham, the Senegalese master of the talking drums. He and his band leap and strut and roar and the drums talk like lovers sharing secrets. It is very erotic. The women in the audience, some of them as large and cushiony as sofas, jump up and gyrate their bottoms to the music, shrieking and sniggering and thrusting banknotes at the musicians.

Their dresses cover them from shoulder to instep in riotous colours of cotton. They are much sexier than the beauty contestants with their thighs and peerie-heels.

Not Quite Cordon Bleu

Perhaps there are a few folk at home who imagine me reclining, hour after hour, day after day, on a beach-bed set on silver sands, sipping something frosty and reviving. Golden skin round a small bikini, a bestseller on my lap, ripples of blue water licking my toes.

It's not quite like that. We opened the beach bar the week after the wedding. I wouldn't want you to visualise a place of tiled and metallic opulence where ex-pats relax on padded stools attended by dusky maidens pouring pink gins. Think instead in terms of wobbly posts of rotting palm trunk, girded and roofed with the sheets of woven palm known as kirinting. The floor is sand. There is some concrete underneath somewhere, but as fast as I sweep it out with my bunch of twigs, the sand blows back in, so I hardly bother now. The seats and tables are long spines of crumble-edged concrete, which we covered with cheap plastic curtaining, held down by large apricot covered shells for ashtrays. There are dishes of peanuts just to show that we're a cut above the other beach-bars. I did consider olives, but that's going too far.

The cooking is done in another corner, behind more kirinting. There's a dilapidated table for cutting the onions and things on, some cardboard boxes full of potatoes and tomatoes and plastic cups and various beetles and ants which take up squatters' rights. A square of bricks with a space in the middle is where the twigs and driftwood are set alight, topped with a rusty iron mesh, on which Bacofoil parcels of fish, lobster and prawns are cooked with their garlic, chilli, tomato and crumbled Maggi cubes. No-one in the Gambia makes stock with Maggi cubes. They crumble them into rice, on top of hard-boiled eggs, on bread, and into their baked fish. Very tasty they are too.

Tourists in the know ask for *benachin*, the sort of savoury rice dish with fish. It's what the Wollofs eat at home and, as my old grandpa used to say, it fair puts a lining in your stomach. We serve Julbrew beer. I understand that, once upon a time, Colonel Gaddafi offered to pour a lot of Libyan aid into this country, if only, as good

Muslims, they'd close down their brewery. Beer won over booty.

We also sell Coke, Sprite and Fanta, and, when asked, cheap whisky or gin from the supermarket. Sounds OK, eh? Working on the beach, meeting lots of interesting people, cooking the natural way. But it doesn't just happen. We rise at 7.30 am and plod up the lane from our compound. We do this to a regular fanfare of calls: 'Mariama! Tubab! How are you?' I am the only white person in the whole area, so I'm a bit of a celebrity – or a freak, I'm not sure which. We head along the dusty main road towards the market, dodging bush-taxis and bicycles and deep gutters full of stagnant water and floating debris. We carry the ghetto-blaster for Ray (who pretends it's to entertain the customers), a pack of cards, cartons of cigarettes which we buy at the supermarket and sell at a profit, cassettes, pens, pads, extra crockery and cutlery. Also my bikini, which I've never had time to wear yet, and sun-oil. The sun-oil is not for me; it's for Ray, whose beautiful black, satiny skin needs oiled every day or it goes greyish and cracked like old crazy paving.

We stop at Rauchie's. She sells drink in crates of twenty-four bottles, trade price. We put the crates into the back of a local taxi, held together by wire and faith in the Almighty, and inch through the traffic to Kanefing to buy ice. The factory is called the Iceman, but it cometh not to us. We go to it. We buy a large block of ice, which melts furiously as we make our way back to the beach. Sometimes Ray buys bread, the long hot baguettes, which are delicious, and goes straight to the beach before the ice melts completely, and I stay and plunge into the salubrious sprawl of the market to fight fiercely over ladyfish and onions. 'Du ma tourist!' I bawl confidently, 'I'm not a tourist!' It halves the prices.

I take a bush-taxi to the beach, and trudge along the sand with my shopping, stray dogs sniffing at the fish and the fruit ladies trying to sell me mangoes. I cluck about the beach-bar, wiping up last night's tomato stains, wrapping the bread in clingfilm, poking the prawns to see if they're fresh, muttering romantic sweet nothings to my husband, on the lines of: 'Why the hell can't you put the sharp knife back where you found it?' He retaliates with 'Mariama, I'm trying to fillet this fish; don't nag.' All marital dialogues sound much the same, be they in Shettleston or Serrekunda. I love him passionately, but he's a man, and remarkably like all other men in his habits.

I peel potatoes, slice onions. 'Sidi, for God's sake go and smile at these tubabs – maybe they'll come in for a beer.' 'Ibrahim, don't give them the bread for nothing. We have to pay for it.' 'Alieu, please don't put the melon in the same bag as the barracuda!' 'Ray, why is Ida sitting on her bum while I'm up to my elbows in onion skins?'

Oh yes, we have a staff. In fact, we have more staff than we have customers, most of the time. It's very hard to say no when people come pleading for work and offering – or so they tell you – devotion, loyalty, skills of a standard that would stun the Savoy. Alieu whispers to me: 'Ladyfish just tastes like barracuda, and it's cheaper. The customers won't know the difference.' I am shocked, but tempted to try it all the same. Ibrahim, from the village, carries tubs of water on his head and rakes the sand and gathers firewood, knowing that, at the end of the day, he'll get a bowl of rice and fish and enough money to buy some cigarettes. This is because we've explained to them that until we get customers we can't pay properly. Our takings range from zero to about £15 on exceptional days from which we have to buy the provisions, the beer, the ice, the peanuts, pay the night watchman and pay for the local taxi to bring us to the beach. No, we can't walk. Serrekunda is about four miles away, too far to carry crates, fish and ice, even if we had the energy. So if we earn, the staff earn. If we starve, we all starve together.

Sidi is very handsome, with flashing teeth and wonderful biceps. We pay him, really, to flash both at impressionable Swedish girls in the hope they'll come in and eat. In between times he may change a cassette, or wipe a table, very slowly. Mostly he sits in the sun. Ida was brought in because Ray said a female employee would attract the male customers. I have doubts about this. Yesterday she came to work wearing a plastic shower cap and an old butcher's apron wrapped twice round her. She takes ten minutes to peel one potato. But she's a sweet girl and we exchange stilted chat about menstruation and men and the price of fish.

Ida has a baby son, who stays with her mother and sisters when she's at work. The father is alleged to be in England. If she has to work late, she dashes home to feed Matthew, then comes back. Not surprisingly, her breasts become engorged and she gets abscesses. Most Gambian women have this problem, since the idea that breast-feeding is something you do regularly or not at all seems to have escaped them. Sturdy two and three-year-old infants munch coos-coos and rice all day, but still expect a wee sip from mummy's tap at night.

I should tell you more about Musa the watchman. He is about 70, and weighs about seven stone with his overcoat on. He sleeps on the concrete kitchen floor through the night, wrapped in the coat, after kneeling behind the woodpile to pray. He is Fula, so we can only nod and smile at each other, and occasionally he clutches my hand and bows over it in a deferential manner which makes me feel terribly embarrassed. Yesterday, using Ibrahim as interpreter, he indicated that he required a cutlass. 'Pardon?' I said. Maybe 'kutlus' is Fula for torch, or thermos flask? But Ibrahim explained. 'He must have a cutlass to protect himself. All the watchmen have a cutlass.' Yesterday, in Banjul, we bought one. The thought of dear little Musa hobbling across the sand after some gang of armed raiders, waving his cutlass, worries me occasionally, but Ray says he'll be fine.

Every household here has a cutlass, for hacking coconuts open, splitting wood, chopping lumps from the carcass of a newly-slaughtered cow. Small boys carry them between their thighs when they shin up coconut palms. When the other fruit is ripe, the large green palm-nuts, they hack them down by the dozen and split them open to suck the bitter-sweet flesh. From these, too, comes the palm-oil used for cooking, which gives a gingery-gold hue to the rice and a flavour far different to the mild nutty groundnut oil.

As for the cutlass, Musa sleeps with it under his pillow of old sacks. Would he ever hack at a thief with it? I prefer not to think about it. Instead, I think about marketing. State-of-the-art advertising in the Gambia means I spend hours with coloured felt pens making cute little menus, extolling the virtues of our prawns and the cheapness of our beer. Or typing out 'flyers' for Sidi to hand out on the beach. I have no carbon paper, so can't even do two or three at a time.

Sometimes I get desperate and go myself, plodding along the edge of the sea, smiling gamely at tourists and waving a leaflet under their noses. They back off suspiciously. I say: 'Why don't you come and have a free beer, and maybe you'll want to order a meal?' Sometimes they look puzzled and respond in Swedish or Finnish. I sneak into the Senegambia Hotel and leave our menus scattered on the vanity-shelf in the ladies' loo. I fume at the fact that so many visitors are loath to leave the security of the hotel's toasted sandwiches and hamburgers.

A friend of Ray's painted our sign for us in shiny red and black on a yellow background, with a fish at one corner and a glass of wine at another. It won't win any art prizes but it looks nice on the beach. I just wish more people would stop and sample our cooking.

Those who do are invariably likeable, the kind of people who leave the phoney Europeanism of the hotels and venture out into the world, Gambian-style. When they've come once, and realise we serve wine, pasta and coffee, as well as the ubiquitous foil-baked fish, and that we dispense such things as paper napkins and side-salad, they come back. They are intrigued by us. 'Er, I hope you don't mind us asking, but how did you, er, actually meet Ray?' they'll ask shyly, and I find myself recounting again the Great Romance of the Century story, embellishing it a bit to make them stay longer and drink more beer. 'Oh,' they gasp, 'you're so brave!' Brave? What do they mean? Here I am in the sunshine with a man who is nuts about me and whom I love most tenderly. What's brave about that?

It's the days when no-one comes in to eat or drink that are a drag. It's pleasant on the beach, and I've reached page 225 of Nicholas Nickleby, but I'd rather do some business. Or how will we pay Musa and Alieu and Ibrahim and Sidi and Ida at the end of the month?

Sometimes, as I juggle ladyfish and barracuda, and haggle to get the very cheapest garlic, I feel like Mrs Wackford Squeers. When four amiable Swiss ordered lobster yesterday, Ray and I did a secret jig in the kitchen, from happiness at the thought of actually covering the day's expenses.

Nevertheless, we do better than some of our neighbours. Because I'm a tubab, some tourists come just to have a look at me, the strange Scottish woman who married a Gambian. But there's no animosity from the competition. We wave to each other, and they buy fish from us and borrow beers when they can't afford their own. 'We all have to help each other,' they'll say, watching sadly as the Europeans stride past, eyes averted, back to their burger and chips. If only they knew what they were missing.

Friends and Neighbours

Big Bintah next door is at the yard tap washing her chickens. Large, lanky beige birds which she kills at the back door, plucks, then chops into pieces and cooks outside her front door over a wood stove. She takes them to the pub up the road and sells them on the porch, daubed with a venomous chilli sauce.

The noise of the chickens getting the chop used to upset me, but you get used to it. It's a very noisy compound altogether. Apart from the chickens squawking and the neighbours shrieking and roaring at one another (this is normal social intercourse in these parts) there are the folks across the road. One lot are very religious and amplified calls to prayer bellow into the black air at 5.30 am wakening the chickens and me as well as the truly faithful. They have a lot of what seem to be prayer meetings or holy concerts, and their speaker system is very powerful.

It isn't quite as powerful as the other lot's. They are into disco and reggae music, played at a pitch that makes your brains rattle in your head till around three or four in the morning.

Bintah works topless, as all the women do, whether planting in the rice-fields, washing clothes at the standpipe or brushing out their houses. Tits don't titillate in the Gambia. Another neighbour is a buxom young policelady whose enormous mother looks after her baby when she's on duty. The baby wakens at five every morning and howls, possibly in anticipation of the call to prayer.

There are a couple of other young mothers and a scattering of young men and toddlers. The policewoman hasn't got a husband but a succession of men seem to spend time with her. It's hard to tell which men belong to which women and which children are whose. They all shout 'Na ka suba sie, Mariama?' (How is the morning?) and I shout back 'Suba san fie rech!' (The morning's just fine!) as I brush the path with my little bunch of twigs and wash Ray's Glasgow's Miles Better tee-shirt.

Olla, the landlord's brother, who was supposed to be in charge of the place, has gone and I miss him very much. Ida was, you might say, his bidey-in. He had a face like a tranquil cherub, nut-brown and innocent under a bashed straw hat.

We would sit with him outside the compound gate on a pile of sand that had been dumped in the lane, brewing up gunpowder tea as thick and sticky as molasses but with an extra tang from some secret herbs of Olla's, playing Crazy Eight, that fast and wicked card game at which I'm becoming quite a dab-hand. It is pitch dark in the lane, and only the light from the hot charcoal flickers on the cards and on the eyes and teeth of the players. London Corner is supposed to be a den of iniquity inhabited by foreigners and thieves, and the police raid homes there regularly, but I like it. All the furniture we have is a bed and a table and we eat sardines and bread because we've no cooking facilities, but I'm happy here.

Olla was a reprobate. One night Ida came home from her late-shift job at the bar where Bintah sells the cooked chicken, and found him in bed with another girl, a bemused Brikama lass he'd met at a party. There were loud crashes as Ida smashed in the window because Olla refused to open the door, curses, whimpers. The next morning she chased him remorselessly round the yard waving a large walking stick with which she whopped him, missing his back by inches and screaming a torrent of epithets after him as the straw hat bobbed up and down and the pink soles of his feet rose and fell. His face was crumpled and crestfallen. But not for long. Olla was always good for a laugh, jaunty, unputdownable, even by Ida, who was what might be called a big hairy, if this was Glasgow.

One night he beckoned us mysteriously into his room, where any furniture there was had disappeared and a large bundle was packed ready to hoist on to his shoulder. 'I'm going to Dakar. Maybe I'll get taken on by a ship as a deckhand and leave Africa. Maybe I'll go to Barcelona. I'm fed-up with this place, and Ida's a fat whore. I'm going. Goodbye, my good friends. May Allah make you have long life and prosperity.' With a sibilant hiss to keep us quiet, he slunk off into the lane and we never saw him again.

Later, we discovered that the reason we had no cooking facilities or individual toilets in the compound was because of Olla.

There were small closets at the back with holes for plumbing to come through, but they were empty, filled only with the scuttling sound of rats and the drip of water. The landlord had given brother Olla the money to buy the fittings but Olla had spent it and sold off what sinks and lavatories were there, and the beds that were supposed to be provided for the tenants. 'He is a filthy criminal pig!' bawled the landlord. I suppose he was, but we liked him a lot.

He could be right about Ida. We met her in the pub next evening. She was wearing a short satin skirt in a remarkable shade of fluorescent purple, a lot of lipstick and very high heels. She was wiggling her shiny satin bottom to a suggestive Senegalese pop tune. Later she went off, giggling, with a wall-eyed Wollof called Paps. They were both carrying bottles of Guinness. It's that kind of pub. Most of the pubs are that kind of pub, small, with peeling walls and stools that wobble and sometimes collapse, and very loud Gambian, Senegalese or Guinean music with a beat like an orgy. The girls come in giggling and shrieking and their buttocks and bosoms are tightly encased in lurex or polyester. People disappear into back rooms from time to time.

We met Uncle Assan in our local the other night. He's stopped going to the one round the corner because his girlfriend, who worked behind the bar, got fired for fiddling the till. He was with his other girlfriend, who was three months pregnant. I asked him how his wife and children were and he said they were fine. As I've told you before, Assan is the alkalo's righthand man in the village, sort of unofficial town clerk, and translated our Muslim wedding ceremony for me, looking devout and virtuous. A holy Wullie, with an unholy lifestyle. He has a fruity laugh and a penchant for Guinness, and I like him a lot too.

The reason, it has been explained to me, that Gambian men go with the girls of the night, or – sometimes simultaneously – seek white wives and girlfriends, is that some African girls are a greedy, shallow, acquisitive bunch who marry not for love but for money, and who, from the moment you start wooing them, demand gifts, clothes, food for their families and constant attention. This is how it was explained to me; I have no idea if it's true.

Possibly it IS true of the city girls, or some of them. Mostly the women I know are those of the villages, slender, graceful, hard-working, swathed discreetly in the traditional dress and headdress, babies nestling into their backs in their bright fabric slings, the mothers carrying massive burdens on their heads. They seem to me more beautiful and more worthy of attention than the floozies in the Serrekunda bars with their short tight skirts and blue eyelids.

My circle of friends and acquaintances grows. Doris had a Cockney husband who used to beat her up because he thought she was flirting with the customers in the bar they ran in the tourist area. He pushed her out of their car one night while it was bouncing along a dirt road. She wiped away the tears and dirt and walked several miles to the compound of their gentle, dignified Fula driver. She lives with him now, but is obsessed with seeking vengeance on her legal spouse. A few days after she left, he wangled an instant conversion to the Muslim faith and married a pretty young African girl. The marriage would not be legal in Britain, as Doris frequently reminds us with sparks flashing from her eyes. She has tried to have him thrown out of the business so that she can take over, but so far it hasn't worked. 'It was my money that started that bleedin' pub,' she says, gnashing her teeth. 'I worked me guts out for 'im.' But his name's on the deeds.

Father Mike was down from the mission in Farafenni. He flip-flops along the beach, belly wobbling over his shorts and all the beach-bar staffs shout 'Fadda! Fadda! How are you?' He is unfazed by the fact that I, born Episcopalian, one-time Wee Free, long-time virtually agnostic was married by the Imam in the mosque. So far as he's concerned, we're all God's chillun.

Janet and Moya went home last week, crying their eyes out. They both fell in love with Gambians and told me to keep an eye on them and see that they remained faithful until their next holiday. I wasn't too happy about the responsibility. One of the boys is OK but the other one will be off after another tubab before Moya's plane touches down at Gatwick.

Last night Ibrahim invited us to his sister's compound in Latrikunda for tea. We all sat in the parlour decorated with Islamic texts and old Christmas tinsel. A plethora of photographs and ornaments was lined up on the shelves of a remarkably ugly display cabinet, the pride of the household. The sister, several cousins, and innumerable nephews and nieces all crammed in beside us. The brother-in-law appeared in flowing white robes. He's a used car dealer by profession and the yard was full of venerable Peugeots, Mercedes and Opels.

We moved outside under the inevitable mango tree and Ibrahim brewed the attaya and told his prettiest cousin to speak to me. She spoke no English. My Wollof only covers Hullo, how are you? I'm hungry, I'm tired, I love you. So we smiled shyly at one another and said nothing. Words were pouring out all around me like waterfalls of sound and I felt I was drowning in ignorance. Ray translates occasionally for me, when he remembers, but usually he forgets and I feel as though I came from outer space.

There was a Fula programme on the radio the other night and I asked Ray what the commentator was saying. 'How should I know? I'm Wollof; I don't understand Fula,' he said. 'Now you know how I feel,' I girned. I should be learning Wollof. I should be writing a blockbuster novel. I actually started one in the Merchant City a million light years ago, before I learned to eat rice with my hands, to pee behind a bush without feeling embarrassed and to spend twenty minutes bargaining for a bunch of bananas.

But other things distract me. Sitting in the sun rubbing soap into shirt collars. Pouring soapy water over the floor of the compound shower because no-one else ever seems to think about cleaning it. Paddling in the sea to wash off the smell of fish. Haddy the postmistress, a stunning girl with a different dress on every day is going to take me to her tailor. She says he'll run up an exclusive little number for me for about a fiver. I stroll hand-in-hand with Ray through the Serrekunda night-time, picking up gossip and watching the old men selling kebabs from braziers of burning charcoal.

There are the menus to write for the beach-bar and Ray wants us to run a disco in the village on Saturday night. He plans to charge three dalasi entrance and make a profit on the sale of soft drinks (and beers round the back where the elders can't see). I'm supposed to sell the drinks while he works the cassette player. I panic. It will be dark and I won't recognise anyone, and if anyone orders more than three drinks at a time I'll mess up the change. Benna beer, ngarr beer, nyetta beer . . . I practise in my head.

Then we hear that someone else had a disco last week and some gatecrashers came from another village and created havoc. The elders have vetoed such sinful gatherings, at least for the time being. I am secretly relieved. Maybe on Saturday night I'll really get down to the Wollof lessons. 'Da ma kontan. Da fa suma kerr.' I'm happy. This is my home.

Wheels Within Wheels

High noon in Banjul. The sun slaps the faces of hustlers and hagglers, illegal money-changers and blind beggars. Banjul is the oxter of the universe.

They say once, when it was Bathurst, it was beautiful, with wide clean avenues, refuse collection, drains. There was a department store where the British bought their plum duff and marzipan at Christmas. It was against the law to allow standing water on your land, because it encouraged mosquitoes.

There are times, in the rainy seasons now, when Banjul is almost ALL standing water, a fetid, festering, muddy morass. Someone has produced a postcard of Banjul for the tourists, and someone has even recorded a pop song, 'Banjul, capital of the Gambia', sung in French and English in the kind of mournful meaningless chant usually reserved for the Finnish entry in the European Song Contest.

Anyway, wet or dry, it is not a good place, nor is noon a good time, to have your car impounded by the police. My temper is not so much frayed as ripped to shreds. Streamers of rind lie in windblown heaps in front of the orange-sellers and a man wants to sell me Lucky Strike at twice the supermarket price. I snarl at him in my only Wollof swearie-word and he says: 'Oh, you are a Gambian. Welcome, welcome.'

One small yellow car, a Deux Cheveux of impeccable pedigree, is breaking my heart and I might strike a policeman any minute and end up in jail. I might end up in the same cell as the African girl who attacked a bemused European girl with a razor when she found her in bed with her Gambian boyfriend, but that's another story.

Here is a health warning. Never try to import a car into the Gambia. It will make you mentally, physically and emotionally ill. Or if you must, make sure your shipping company is more clued-up than mine who neglected, somehow, to send the bill of lading – without which it is impossible to retrieve anything from a port – so that my little yellow car huddled on the quayside, growing dustier and more battered by the minute, for day after day after day, peering at me, puzzled and forlorn, through its cracked headlamps.

And day after day I pleaded for its release, by phone, by fax, by telex and temper tantrum. 'Can I speak to Mr. Bloggs?' I would whimper into the grubby phone in Gamtel's Banjul office. 'Eh, ah, Mr – er – Bloggs. Aye, yes. Just give me a wee minute till I see if he's available,' came the slow Scottish voice, disappearing into oblivion while I screamed: 'Tell him I'm phoning from West Africa. Tell him it's an emergency. Tell him this is costing me an arm and a leg . . .' Silence. Crackling. Whispers and creaks. 'Er, hullo there, is that you? Yes, well, er, actually Mr Bloggs is with a client just at the moment. He wonders if maybe he could phone you back?'

'I'm in a ****ing telephone box in ****ing Banjul,' I roar. 'Tell him to pick up his ****ing phone. I'm sure his ****ing client will understand . . .' There is more whirring and crackling and the line goes dead. I bang my head on the wall of the booth and several Gambians shake their heads disapprovingly at my display of tubab temperament. Each telephone call costs me about £25. Telexes and faxes disappear into the same heedless void. 'If you don't remove your car by Thursday,' says the official at the port, 'you must start paying rental.' I weep.

And even that was just a mere hiccup compared with what happened next. Let me pull myself together; this is bringing me out in spots. Let me tell it like it was.

The manifest of the good ship Maris stated clearly that my car was on board. We chuckled, and pictured it securely strapped down, bobbing across the waves towards its new life. No more anti-freeze, no more iced-up windscreens. Whoopee. For us, no more lugging fish and crates of beer surreptitiously through the sedate foyer of the Senegambia Hotel and staggering along the beach with the ice melting, the fish smelling and bottles clanking. What a treasure the 2CV will be, we told ourselves. It will change our lives. How right we were.

Let me try not to linger over the next eight, steaming, frying days in Banjul, reached by bottom-bruising bus and bush-taxi, worrying that the beach-bar would go bust in our absence, watching our small supply of dalasi disappearing in fares, phone calls, and faxes.

Tramping from Banjul Shipping Agency to the port, which makes Grangemouth look like Shangri La, waiting for hours in the Gamtel office, waiting for someone, anyone to acknowledge my deluge of demands for information. In the end, of course, the day came when we were allowed to extract the car from its pitiful position between a clapped-out lorry and a dessicated Audi which no-one had yet acknowledged. Auctions are held regularly of vehicles which have been abandoned thus by their owners, who find they cannot raise the import duty, sales tax and various other bits of bureaucratic rake-off. I sympathise with them.

Never mind the cost of shipping the car over. On top of that the aforementioned import duty and sales tax (sales tax? On my own three-year-old car?) comes to 47% of the value of the car AND the shipping costs. By the time we finally escape, my wee bargain buggy, one lady driver in Bearsden (if she could see it now!), 25,000 miles on the clock, has more than doubled its price – and that's AFTER we bribed a customs man to go easy on the duty.

'I told you you should have waited and bought a car in the Gambia,' muttered Ray. I snapped back like a cranky crocodile. He shot me a filthy look. I growled then burst into tears . . . I tell you, any marriage that can survive importing a car into Banjul has got to be forged out of tungsten steel.

From the port to the customs office, and back again. And again. Bits of paper to be exchanged for other bits of paper. Offices which suddenly closed their doors in front of our noses, officials who suddenly abandoned us in mid-sentence to deal with someone else. Finally, we got it. The port gates swung open and Lamin, Ray's brother, nudged us through swarms of Gambians along the Bund Road, past the mangroves and the Half Die prison, past the peanut-oil factory, and home. We washed off the thick layers of red dust and tapped out some of the dents, and told ourselves it was a sweet little car.

A mere three days of queueing and haggling and discussing and pleading later and the police had stencilled my new Gambian number rear and fore, issued a road tax and a licence, taken our cash and sent us on our way.

'Tra-la-la, here we are, in our car . . .' sang Ray, whose singing is as bad as his versifying. I still didn't dare drive among the chickens and goats and potholes and sandheaps and suicidal Gambians, who seem to feel that Allah will protect them as they walk straight under your wheels, chatting and smiling to each other. But Lamin will be our chauffeur. Fish and ice will bounce about in the boot, tomatoes and onions and Fanta and Julbrew and garlic will be safely stowed. No more fighting and clawing to get into the bush-taxis, squeezed between ladies with bottoms two-seats wide and spindly old men in cotton kaftans clutching chickens on their knees and balancing bowls of benachin on their heads. Now if a customer needs barracuda and we don't have any, Lamin can leap into the car, scoot into the market and buy one.

Happy motoring Hooray for the open road. For six days.

Suddenly, at noon in Banjul, a policeman – the very one who'd stencilled on our nice new number and given us our licence – leapt in front of the car, waved us down, and said: 'Give me your keys. We are parking your car. You are not allowed to drive this car here. It is illegal. This car has a right-hand drive.'

My knuckles are white, my eyes are red, and there is steam coming out of my ears. Of course it's a right-hand drive. I bought it in Britain. Did anybody there have a clue that some time in the recent past, some Minister of Something-or-other had decreed that right-hand drive cars should be banned from the Gambia? Did my shipping company know? Did the British government know? Did the people at the docks in Tilbury who loaded it on board ship know? If they did, they all kept it a pretty good secret. I stamp around the police station pushing queues of Gambians aside, demanding explanations, pleading to have my keys back. 'Be quiet,' Ray hisses. 'You're only making things worse.' I splutter and smoulder. 'Kindly keep your wife quiet. Tell her to behave. Have you no control over your woman?' a policeman asks Ray pityingly. Gambian wives do not behave thus. I shut up and snuffle in a corner while my husband takes control.

'It's very simple,' says the policeman. 'You must have the car converted to left-hand drive.

'We can do it in the police garage. It will only cost you . . .' I erupt again. I have a hysteria attack. All the patience and perseverance and faith in Allah that I have achieved in my first few months in my new homeland dissolve in a puff of smoke. 'Keep the blankety-blank car!' I yell. 'I'm going to buy a donkey and cart. Leave me alone. I'm going home.' The policeman raises his eyebrows and says: 'Tubab women can be very difficult.' Ray would like to agree with him but suspects I might do something violent, so merely shakes his head resignedly.

We go, back home in buses and bush-taxis, brooding, baleful, bereft. The car stays outside the police station for a week, once again shrouded in terracotta dust. Someone writes on its bonnet with a finger: 'Gambia No Problem.' Huh!

Machinations go on behind the scenes. There is an uncle who knows someone in the police. We visit this someone at his compound. He has just returned from the mosque, in flowing robes and a tall white hat. A baby is being named and all the women are resplendent in puffs and layers and loops of cotton, frilled at the shoulder, scalloped round the neck. I feel inadequate. I have decided to be a meek Muslim wife and leave the talking to Ray. I lower my eyes and call the policeman Sir. Three more days of wheeling and dealing follow. I go through it in a sullen dream, saying nothing.

In the end, £10 changes hands. I ask no questions. The keys are returned. We're back on the road again. Will it last? Who knows? There are several other right-hand drive vehicles around, in

Serrekunda, Bakau, Kololi and Banjul. Perhaps they too stay mobile by dint of judiciously placed tenners.

Goodbye principles. At least we're on the road. How else would we get to Brufut, the fishing village along the coast, to buy lobsters and barracuda for special customers? It's about five miles away, on a red rutted road flanked by fields of cassava and cashew trees, past the smelly commune of Ghana town, where immigrant Ghanaians dry malodorous sting-ray and shark and skate spread on tables under the sun.

'Can we have lobster tomorrow,' a jolly Swede or German or Brit will say.

'Certainly,' we say. 'No problem.'

In the morning we bounce along to Brufut and wait for one of the little lobster pirogues to go out and pull up the pots. Sometimes we wait one hour or two. Eventually, someone arrives with two or three wiggling crayfish – as near as you get to lobster here – and another hour of discussion follows over its price. We go into our friend Ibrahim's bar and drink cold beer while we wait, completely wiping out the small profit we might have made. But it's nice. The fishing boats, long narrow wooden craft painted blue and red and yellow, are surrounded by Gambian, Ghanaian and Senegalese women with sharp knives, cleaning the fish, angel-fish and catfish, shark and sometimes an illegal turtle or two.

Ray once used to walk here along the beach to buy crayfish. It took him about two-and-a-half hours each way. 'It's much better with a car,' he says comfortably.

I did mumble something about integrity and principles and fighting police corruption. 'Mariama, do you know how much these policemen are paid? If they didn't take 'gifts' they couldn't feed their families.'

Maybe he has a point.

Trouble and Strife

On Monday, old Musa the beach-bar watchman hovered around hopping awkwardly like a bird. His family's rice had run out, he told us. Could he have an advance on his wages? We gave him 150 dalasi, the price of a bag of rice.

On Tuesday, Ida's baby had to go back to the clinic again with respiratory trouble, which is endemic in the Gambia. The prescription for the medicine was to cost 75 dalasi. Could we help? We gave her some money, brooding over the fact that we now wouldn't have enough to buy urgently needed lemons and garlic for the kitchen. But when a baby is sick, what can you do?

Sidi has got a girl pregnant. 'I have a lot of problems at home,' he says, his handsome charming features arranged into a combination of sorrow and sincerity which I suspect is as ersatz as his 'Lacoste' tee-shirt. 'If you could just advance me ten dalasi . . .'

Alieu's little niece was taken to hospital. She has meningitis and doesn't recognise her family when they visit her. She cowers into the faded blanket – there are never enough sheets at the Royal Victoria Hospital – like a frightened rabbit. Can Alieu have the day off to help his brother and sister-in-law through their troubles? And maybe a few dalasi for anything they need . . .?

Last week Alieu took the morning off to go to a naming ceremony. 'I will be back at one o'clock,' he promised. In the end, he returned at three, apologetic but guffawing madly to himself. He explained the reason for his lateness:

'The father of the baby wanted to buy a goat from a man in Kololi. They discussed the matter for a long time. The father said he would consider the condition of the goat. The man from Kololi said he would consider the price offered. They separated. Later the father returned, having decided he definitely wanted this goat. The man wasn't there, so he took the goat with him, intending to pay later.' I raised my eyebrows sardonically, and Alieu shrugged. 'He definitely intended to pay later,' he said firmly.

'The man's wife discovered that the goat was gone and ran to the naming ceremony in a very angry condition. "Where is my goat?" she shouted. "Give me my goat!" But by this time, as you will understand, the goat had been slaughtered, and the guests were preparing to roast and eat it. The woman called the police. She was a very troublesome woman. The police said that the only way to avoid prosecution of the father of the baby was by paying for the goat. The chap didn't actually have the price of a goat at that time – as I said, he was going to pay later – so all the guests including myself had to dig into their pockets to keep the woman from making charges, and to make sure that the policeman went away happy.'

We all thought this was very funny. It made a good story to pass on to our customers. They are much more interested in this kind of thing than they are in the history and geography of the Gambia.

A few days after old Musa's problem with the rice, he didn't show up for work. Normally, we would see him tramping stolidly across the bush, hacking at the brushwood as he went so that he could light a fire in the chill of the night. His cutlass lay in its corner, with his blanket and his torch, but we watched in vain for his spindly little figure appearing from the evening shadows.

The watchman from the next beach-bar agreed to keep an eye on our beer and buckets and cooking-pots and cutlery that night, and the next, and the next.

Finally we drove out to Musa's compound in Bijilo. His wife and family were huddled outside the doorway. Inside three old Gambian wise men ('marabouts', whispered Ray) were squatting around Musa's scraggy body, murmuring soothing incantations. The old man watched them trustingly from his prone position and smiled weakly in my direction. An array of small white bones and other objects were laid out on the blanket. I patted Musa's shoulder and said comforting things in English, which, being Jola, he couldn't understand. The oldest marabout hauled him up to a sagging-sitting position and massaged and pummelled his back in what seemed to me a very competent manner.

I don't suppose the treatment was any worse for him than going to a 'real' doctor and being given expensive modern medications. I wondered, as we waved solicitous goodbyes, if you could buy Lucozade in the Gambia.

He hasn't come back to work yet. We miss him. He would bring us lemons and grapefruit and refused all our offers of food and drink, except the odd chunk of bread. 'He's a very devout Muslim,' Ray said. 'He's afraid you might have put alcohol into the food when you were cooking.'

Yesterday we fired Ibrahim. It was either that or he and Ray were going to tear each other apart. Ibrahim is a sturdy lad who works like an ox. But he grumbled all the time. Nothing pleased him. He scowled at the customers and contradicted everything we said. While a couple of Swedes nibbled at their prawns, war broke out in the kitchen. Smoke belched from the wood fire, sparks flew. Two people held Ibrahim back while another two held my husband by the arms. They were both snarling and hissing like angry dogs. I suspect Ibrahim had said something rude about me. That's what Ida told me later, anyway. It seemed like a good idea to pay him off. But he is the sole support of his family since his father died last year. I feel like a vicious Victorian mill-owner as I slip him some extra cash and beg him to leave before blood is spilled.

Sidi was three hours late for work yesterday. 'My clothes were dirty,' he smiles sweetly. 'I had to wash them.' Sidi is infuriating. His smile is stunning, and our tourists respond warmly to his cheerful, sincere conversation. Then they find themselves parting with their tee-shirts or their Walkman or their sunhats, because Sidi has gazed at them with pathetic yearning and said: 'Ah, how lucky you tubabs are. Me, I am so poor. These people don't pay me enough. If only one day I had some money, I would buy a Walkman like this.' It works like a charm. To my sure knowledge, Sidi has four at home already. We talk to him sternly, forbidding him to scrounge from the customers. He gazes back full of shame and distress and promises never to do it again. Then when our backs are turned we find him talking a tough German into giving him his Reeboks.

Ida brought her baby to work the other day, a pudgy placid eight-month-old, clamped on to her back and tied by a piece of cloth knotted at her waist and over her breasts. She began peeling potatoes, bending over the plastic basin on the floor, so that little Matthew tilted forward at a terrifying angle, wood-smoke swirling round his wee woolly head. 'Give him to me,' I wailed, dropping the prawns I was shelling. I thrust him into the arms of a sultry, shapely blonde who looks like a barmaid but is actually a highly qualified lawyer. She put down her glass of white wine and eyed Matthew cautiously. She tried a tentative cuddle, and he smiled calmly. African babies are used to warm bodily contact and lots of hugging. No-one ever dumps them into a playpen or a push-chair.

I went back to peeling prawns. Lately my culinary skills, such as they are, have been stretched considerably. A Finnish customer asked for pasta with tomato sauce. ('Can you make that?' hissed Ray urgently, 'He's a good customer. He always buys a lot of beer.') I boiled water for the pasta on the fire outside, jumping back and forward to simmer tomatoes, garlic and onion in a battered omelette-pan (we are very short of cooking utensils) over the inside wood fire. Smoke stung my eyes and I had to keep spooning cinders from the pan, and avoiding Ray, who was trying to bake fish over the same flames. The Finn said his meal was delicious. He drank six beers that afternoon.

Last week our American regulars from the US Embassy came in and asked if we could get pork chops for the next day. Have you ever tried to find pork chops in a Muslim country? There ARE pigs, small tough black-and-tan ones that root around in the lane outside our compound – but their meat is bought by the hotels for their Christian customers. The market stallholders looked shocked when we asked for pork. We searched Banjul and Serrekunda, using up enough petrol to have bought our own sow. It was Alieu who saved the day. 'I know a man in Kololi who sells pig-meat,' he said, and disappeared for an hour-and-a-half. He came back with a large chunk of pink meat with bones jutting out at odd angles. I hacked and squeezed and trimmed it until it arrived at what I hoped were vaguely chop-like shapes. I think the Americans enjoyed it. They're so cordial and courteous at all times it's hard to tell.

She is a vivacious little thing, with a mop of dark curls and golden skin. She looks Spanish but says she was born in Uganda. He is a big, amiable white, quiet American. They are unfailingly nice. I suspect if I gave them burnt hyena they'd smile and say 'Gee, isn't this just delicious!'

I wish I could be unfailingly nice. As it is, I nag rather a lot. 'Alieu, for pity's sake! Don't be so SLOW! Put the fish on the fire NOW!' Alieu tends to prepare fish in a loving, languorous way, stopping to eye it up like a sculptor admiring his own work, mixing up the tomato puree reflectively, oblivious to the fact that customers have been waiting for forty minutes. 'They want their lunch TODAY,' I thunder, 'not tomorrow!'

'Ida! Don't use the clean towel for wiping the dirty tables! Ray, I thought you were going to fetch some firewood? The fire's almost out! Ray, why does Alieu pour so much oil on the bloody fish? Tubabs don't like a lot of oil. Sidi! SIDI, stop ogling at these girls in bikinis and FETCH SOME WATER!' I suppose they'd all cheerfully string me up from the nearest palm-tree, but Ray reminds them, while frowning disapprovingly at me when they're not looking, that business is better since we 'have a tubab here'. For word has got around that we cover perishables with clingfilm, serve free peanuts, chill our drinks and even sell wine. We're not exactly inundated but we do have a steady stream of customers, who come back every day of their holiday and tell their friends about us.

This should please me, and it does, but it also makes me jittery and I nag more than ever, apprehensive that a hungry tubab might storm off because he's tired of waiting for his fish, or that someone might find an ant in the sugar for his coffee. So I continue to stomp about, muttering 'Burn the rubbish! Cover that tin! Wash that knife!

Peel the potatoes in advance!' By the time it gets to late afternoon, I'm exhausted, not by work but by anxiety.

That's when we all sit round a big plastic basin of benachin, with enough chilli to singe your intestines, topped with any fish that we haven't been able to sell. Ida, who prepares the meal in a big iron pot, also puts in the fish-heads, considered a delicacy. The rest I enjoy, and the tension eases and we all laugh and chat about our day.

The staff forgive me, for the moment, for girning, and I forgive them, for the moment, for their sloth and poor hygiene. We sprinkle crumbled Maggi cubes over the rice to make it even spicier. Ray has been eating rice like this since he was weaned. But it's cheap to make and we are poor. One day we'll have a gas ring and I'll cook him some Scottish food. But not yet.

Some tourists call a greeting as they take a late stroll along the water's edge. A kora-player is sitting on one of our stools strumming and singing. Ray brings me a glass of wine, no longer chilled, and I resolve to be sweeter-natured tomorrow. I just hope that old Musa gets better. And that no-one else asks for pork. And that Sidi remembers to come to work on time . . . 'Stop worrying,' Ray says. 'Everything's fine. And I love you.'

Black and White
and Boiling Mad

Most nights, we pack up and go home when the watchman arrives at the beach bar. After old Musa, who got sick and never came back to us, there was a young man who saw devils among the bottle-crates and the tables where we chop the onions and fillet the fish. 'They were here . . . big . . . evil . . . aargh!' he wailed to anyone who would listen.

So then we made an arrangement with the old palm-wine tapper. Like many of the palm-wine tappers, he is a Manjago, a sinewy proud figure, loping through the bush to his chosen tree then, using a tough loop of palm as a kind of sling, 'walking' up the trunk, leaning back at a precipitous angle to collect the sappy liquid that has dripped into a bottle under the spreading branches at the top. We agree that by day he will ply his trade and by night he will sleep in our beach-bar, wrapped in a blanket, his cutlass by his side. He fears no devils.

The other evening we walked along the beach as we always do, calling goodnights to the other bar-owners, sneaking through the plushy gardens of the hotel, carrying the bags with our books, the cashbox, my only potato-peeler, some bay leaves and chilli peppers for the policewoman's mum who is our neighbour in the compound. We ambled past the tourist-market and the taxi-rank to the bush-taxi stance. Before we reached it, two gendarmes advanced on us. The short ugly one shouted at Ray: 'What are you doing with this tubab?'

Gambia has an army and it has a police force. Both are under-equipped, under-paid and under-trained. But in between is the Gendarmerie, a paramilitary force introduced after the attempted coup of 1981, presumably to protect the President's back. They wear jungle green and carry guns and nightsticks and go around in Nissan Patrol vehicles looking tough. After some European holidaymakers complained (understandably) about the constant attentions of young Gambians around the hotels, the Minister of Tourism, with the President's approval, brought in these Senegalese-trained heavies to patrol the tourist areas.

The young Gambians can spot a new tourist at fifty paces, by his white-and-pink skin, the smell of expensive sun-oil, the nervous smile on his lips. That's when they move in, smiling, walking fast to keep up with their target, not with any sinister intention but in the hope of striking up a friendship that will yield a handful of dalasis, a surplus tee-shirt or training shoes before the holidaymaker goes home, a few free drinks in the local bars, or – and this is the Gambian dream – an invitation to go to England or Germany or Sweden, where the roads are surely paved in gold. They're a bloody nuisance, but dangerous they aren't.

So here we are, eyeball to eyeball with the protectors of the tourists. 'You, boy! Why are you with this white woman?' (Try to remember that this is a black democracy, not to mention the home of the African Centre for Human Rights.)

'She's my wife,' says Ray crossly. 'How do we know she's your wife; where did you get married? When? Don't give me any trouble boy or I'll lock you up.' The gun bulged at his hip like an off-centre phallic symbol and he brandished his two-foot long baton menacingly. Ray yelled 'Hey, she's my wife, I tell you. Leave us alone.' The gendarme shouted louder, holding Ray by the neck of his tee-shirt, pushing him and poking his stubby finger in his face. I stood there simmering, completely ignored. I HATE being ignored. 'Excuse ME!' I growled. 'Could you include me in your conversation?'

The gendarme looked at me briefly, blankly. 'It's not your business,' he said curtly. Not my business? What's the man talking about, not my business? 'It most certainly is!' I snapped, 'This is my husband. What is your problem?' I asked him for his name and number and threatened to report him to his commander, to the Minister of Defence, to the President . . . 'Do what you like! **** off!' he snarled. A crowd was forming round us. The lads from the market and the taxi-rank and all our cronies from Uncle Dembo's. There was no doubt whose side they were on. The gendarmes glowered at them all and waved their sticks. 'I can lock you up, beat you . . .', the wee ugly one was still blustering, while Ray got angrier and angrier and looked as though he was about to snatch the night-stick and wrap it round the gendarme's neck.

Fortunately, Uncle Dembo, one of the gentlest and kindest of our many Gambian friends, decided to intervene. He stepped between them, hushing and shushing, while I hopped around muttering about apartheid, and wasn't this supposed to be a democracy, and if he didn't like seeing black people and white people walking together, let alone marrying one another, maybe he should move down south? The taxi-drivers and stallholders cheered. I burst into tears. I had visions of Ray dumped in the Half Die prison. While I snivelled, the gendarmes, realising the size and sympathies of the crowd, backed off, grumbling. We boarded a bush-taxi and large African ladies patted my shoulder. 'Don't cry. That pig is just jealous because he hasn't got a tubab wife,' one of them said.

It's a sad sort of way to deal with civilians, it seems to me. Every so often truck-loads of gendarmes are deposited by the hotels to strut their stuff. If they find a local boy chattering to a tourist on the beach, they drag him into the bush and force him to do 'thee monkey dance', one hundred knees-bend squats, hands behind the head, in the hot sun, till his body aches. Or they beat them with their sticks. They will tell you it's to protect the tourists from bag-snatchers and molesters of women . . . but actual cases of theft and assault are tiny in number, far fewer than you'd find in Lido de Jesolo or Benidorm. Hotel security staff are slightly less heavy-handed, but even they have their bad days. Our friend Donal, an Irish priest, approached one hotel one afternoon with two young Ghanaian guests. Both of them were priests. 'Hey, you, boy!' grunted a security guard. 'Where you going?' It's odd to think that this kind of language comes out of the mouths of black people – the same kind of language that leads, rightly, to howls of protest when it comes from the mouths of white people in Alabama or South Africa.

The gendarmes often stroll past our beach bar, boots clomping through the sand, wearing black glasses and looking as menacing as they can manage. I call 'Good morning! How are you today?' and even give them an occasional beer. But I hate their presence there and I wish they'd go and direct the traffic or help some of their comrades in real crime prevention.

It was gendarmes who raided a compound in Kanefing the other day and made a one-ton haul of cannabis in a 'mini factory' operated by a drugs ring of Americans, Senegalese and Gambians. Nowadays the Turkish army seems to be training them in drugs investigation, which is fair enough. A lot of *ganja* grows greenly in discreet patches in the Gambian bush.

But as for the tourists, the presence of the gendarmes, and the warnings of the hotel couriers – 'Don't go too far from the hotel. Don't eat in Gambian places. Don't do this, don't do that' – is a real pain in the neck. Some visitors, sadly, huddle by the hotel pools, eating European food. The regulars – and many Brits, Germans, Scandinavians and others come back year after year – know that they can walk round Serrekunda enjoying the colourful chaos of the market and stroll along the beach sampling baked fish and Wollof rice in safety and friendship.

As to the beach-boys, 'the bumsters', as they are known to the locals, there are several ways of dealing with them. You can smile, say hullo, then firmly ask them to go and leave you to enjoy some privacy and solitude. You can do what one of my friends does, ask 'If you are a Muslim, why are you talking to women you don't know – especially women with their thighs exposed in bikinis?' Or you can say your brother-in-law is the commander of the gendarmerie . . .

But it's a pity to miss meeting the Gambians on their home ground. Regular visitors usually find that a friendship with one young local protects them from all the others. It also gives them the chance to visit his compound, perhaps attend a naming ceremony or a wedding, taste genuine village food and find out about life beyond the commercial tourist areas (though compared with resorts in Spain or the Italian Riviera, ours are positively tranquil!).

After the incident with the gendarmes, I wrote an indignant letter to the President, with copies to the Ministry of Justice, the Ministry of Defence and the Ministry of Tourism. I didn't receive even an acknowledgement from any one of them.

Never mind, there are consolations. And so many things to learn. You don't eat the fat round golden melons which grow like pumpkins in the scrubby bush behind the beach-bar. They're called snake melons, which is enough to put anyone off. You don't get too excited now if you see something that crawls. I opened up the suitcase where I keep my typing paper and a spider as big as a mouse birled out and went behind the chest of drawers. A month or two ago I'd have shrieked for Ray, now I just shrug and reckon that if it doesn't bother me, I won't bother it. The same goes for the geckos in the kitchen cupboard. I get irritated at the ants, but I am fascinated by long fluffy things like pieces of teased wool, which wiggle along the wall when I'm in the bathroom having a wash.

You learn to recognise a few of the five hundred or so species of birds in the country. Three black ones, with daffodil yellow tummies, settled on the back of one of the hungry cows which drift around the beach-bar disconsolately. 'Aw, look at the burdies!' I gushed. Ray jumped up and hurled stones at them with howls of abuse. 'These birds are very wicked. They live by pecking at cows and horses and drinking their blood.' Well, how was I to know?

You learn, too, about family solidarity. Ray had a fight (another one!) with his lanky, lazy brother Lamin who drives the car for us (sometimes I drive, but it still needs to be a real emergency before I'll face the heaving hordes around the market area). In between, he works in the bar with us, when he's not sleeping on one of the canvas chairs. I'm not sure what the fight was about this time, but Ray snapped: 'Give him his money. He can go!' Lamin slouched off in the huff. I said nothing – but had horrible premonitions about having to drive to market every day, mowing down old ladies and children and dogs in my nervous panic . . .

We brooded and sulked and muttered about the alternatives. Hire another driver? But who do we know who's reliable enough? Try to shop less often? But we have to buy the fish and prawns fresh every morning, we have no freezer – we have no electricity on the beach, even if we COULD afford a freezer. Ray – who's been scared to drive ever since he had a bad accident as a learner and spent three months in hospital – could go in bush-taxis, but that would take hours.

At that moment, there were voices on the verandah. Ray's dad and an uncle were there, with a sullenly repentant Lamin. 'Mariama,' said the uncle, 'We are all family. We must discuss this thing and settle it. Ray is your husband, but Lamin is his brother, same mother and father, so therefore he is your husband too.' (Eh, no-one told me this before!) 'If people see someone else driving your car, they will think there is trouble in our family. We would all lose face. We must talk and find a peaceful answer.'

So we did. Everyone talked, for about an hour, with simultaneous translation for me from the Wollof. In the end, peace was restored. Lamin works for us again. He and Ray have declared a state of truce. The family is very important in the Gambia. It's nice to be part of it.

Bawbee and
the Baobab

Her name is Bawbee. We thought at first she was a he and the Gambians think the name is Bobby. But it's Bawbee because, as dogs go, she is pretty small change.

Chocolate brown with three white slipperettes and one long white sock. We took her into the sea and rubbed sand and salt water on her fat white tummy to remove the lice.

We got her the same day we transferred from the compound in Serrekunda to one room of our still-under-construction house in Bijilo. We flitted in a cement lorry, with the bed and our clothes and our plastic buckets and my typewriter and several crates of Julbrew beer all clanking around tied with rope but not very securely. At Sukuta, a box escaped and spun on to the road, shedding papers and old birthday cards and paper-clips in the dust.

The workmen are still here, banging and plastering and yelling to each other in Wollof, their bodies grey with cement dust and striped with rivulets of sweat. Only the bedroom is finished, painted a searing lemon yellow distemper, all our wordly goods stacked around the bed.

I insisted on allowing Bawbee to sleep there the first few nights, curled like a hibernating squirrel on an old towel next to a pile of shoes. She is, after all, very young and there are rumoured to be hyenas and large snakes in the forest which runs a few hundred feet from our land.

Ray was appalled. Dogs live outside, he insisted. Dogs are unhygienic. Dogs smell. I said that was pretty rich, considering the pungent aroma of cattle dung which wafts in the windows from the herd of calves run by the International Trypanotolerance Centre next to the forest. As I'm sure you know, trypanotolerance is to do with tsetse-fly and sleeping-sickness eradication.

Anyway, I think there's something in the Koran that suggests I should, generally speaking, obey my husband now and then, so on the third night Bawbee slept outside on the verandah.

Or, rather, didn't sleep. Howled, yapped, squeaked, threw her small brown body against the steel door in an infant tantrum. Ray slept on. Ray would sleep on if a horde of hungry crocodiles were throwing their bodies against the steel door. I paced the floor and shouted Shhhh! and Aitcha! On the fourth night, she only howled for about four hours, and now she sleeps on a piece of sacking, like the baby she is, snuffling and dreaming of whatever puppies dream of.

When I emerge in the morning to go and fill a bucket with water from the standpipe surrounded by glutinous mud, taking my turn with schoolgirls and the watchmen's wives, Bawbee greets me deliriously and scampers round my feet tugging at the long wraparound skirt I wear and munching my ankles ecstatically. She reckons she's pretty damn lucky having a tubab mistress. Gambians don't make much fuss over dogs.

I brought quite few long skirts with me. I'd read all that stuff about legs being too erotic to be flaunted in public. Big Mary from Govanhill (who used to work in the Sheriff Court in Glasgow) fell out with her Wollof bidey-in and found herself a handsome Serahuli replacement. He gave her a telling-off for wearing a knee-length number over her sturdy Southside hips. She said, 'Listen, sonny. I'm a ****ing Glaswegian, no' a ****ing Gambian, and ah didnae come up the river in a ****ing banana boat.' They have a fairly torrid relationship, I believe.

Ray, on the other hand, looks disdainfully at my demure wraparounds and says 'Could you not wear your nice shorts?' But then, he's Wollof. It says in the book I once read about tribal history, that the Wollofs are a racy, immoral bunch. So when I go to the beach I wear my shorts. We Glaswegians can be pretty racy too.

The builder has been choosing colours for the rest of the house. I try tentatively suggesting a crisp white all over, but this upsets him. 'What about a nice pink? Or blue?' The choice of colours is extremely limited. The pink is a particularly lurid one, like cheap bubble-gum. On the whole, I got off lightly with the lemon yellow and it goes with the climate.

The mosquito netting over the windows is dark blue, giving a ghostly look to the outside world. All my papers and books and carbon-paper and photographs were bundled into plastic bags and boxes when we moved and I can't find anything. The family pops by with bags of grapefruit and oranges till the room looks like a Malcolm Campbell's storehouse. The oranges are green on the outside, sweet and juicy on the inside, full of pips. My blood is awash with vitamin C. The Gambians slice the top off, stripping away the outer layer of peel in long green ribbons, holding the fruit by its white pithy underskirt and sucking furiously until all the juice is extracted. I haven't got the knack, so I dribble a lot and keep swallowing pips.

I think it might be a good idea to market the Gambian Diet in opposition to the Cambridge Diet or the California Diet. Coos in the morning – millet ground fine with a giant wooden pestle by Ray's mum and eaten with soured milk and sugar. A share of the staff benachin in the afternoon around 5 pm – rice cooked with onion, tomato, chilli pepper, garlic and chunks of fish dried on the roof of the beach-bar. No other meals, just masses of citrus fruits and peanuts and the occasional coconut or papaya. I don't have an inch left to pinch. A friend in Scotland sees a recent photograph and tells everyone I must have had plastic surgery in London to get rid of my double chin.

I am simultaneously offended and flattered but I feel great anyway. When I finish typing in the mornings, I walk past the ITC calves and the mysterious forest, down to the beach, with Bawbee scuttling behind me, and tramp along the water's edge to the restaurant, about fifty minutes if you don't stop to have a conversation with friends on the way. 'Mariama, how is the morning? How is Relwan? How is the business? Nga ka kerr? (How are things at your compound?)'

'Aren't you swimming every day?' my daughter asks fussily on the phone. 'I hope you're keeping fit.' No, I'm bloody not swimming every day. Five fishermen drowned the week before last when their fragile pirogue broke up in the fierce Atlantic waves. The beach-guards at the Senegambia Hotel are forever dragging silly tourists out of the water, who have ignored the red flag and found themselves being pulled towards the Canaries by the undertow.

I'll swim when the sea settles down. Meanwhile, tramping back and forward with trays of fish and cold beers, sweeping the sand from the concrete floor of the beach-bar, shovelling fresh sand into the 'toilet' (a palm-screened corner we created for modest customers who didn't fancy going behind the nearest bush), fetching basins of sea-water to clean the ladyfish and butterfish and mackerel, and walking Bawbee along the shore keep me fitter than I ever was in Glasgow.

Mind you, when it comes to real fitness, Sidi's your man. Sidi of the rippling aubergine-coloured biceps and flashing teeth, who, when he isn't charming tourists into the bar for us, works out on the beach like a black Sylvester Stallone. Every afternoon, at exactly 4.30, he goes off into the bush with a bottle of water to 'post a letter', as he says. Sidi's bowels are as regular as the tide.

A minute later, the Air Europe flight sweeps in from Gatwick. I suspect the pilot looks out for Sidi to check he's right on time for his landing.

Every day, when we come home, smelling of fish and daubed with wood-soot, something new has been added to our house. The shower and toilet has no plumbing yet, but it's enormous, and it's tiled with the smooth golden-brown tiles I brought with me from Shawlands. Some of the tiles I bought myself; the rest were donated as wedding presents, a few square yards at a time, by friends like Darlinda, the astrologer, Sheila Davis, the model agent, Kitty Lamonte, and others. I write to them that every time I walk in and look down at the floor, I think of them with gratitude. I remember the constant cement-dust from the concrete floor in the compound flat in Serrekunda, and bless the fact that we have tiles, all the way from sunny Shawlands.

We wash in a bucket and the water dribbles down through a hole where the drain will eventually be. Other matters of a personal nature have to be attended to behind the baobab tree, with Bawbee sniffing cheerfully at our rear-ends. Soon, we will have a WC, I tell people who worry about such trivial matters.

We are situated ten minutes walk from the heart of Bijilo Village, where Ray's mum and dad live in a compound across from the tiny tin-roofed mosque where we were married. Behind us is Bijilo Primary School, and every day swarms of children, the girls in cornflower blue dresses with white collars, the boys in blue shorts, wander around the house en route to the standpipe. They carry empty bottles on their heads, fill them and carry them back, balanced immaculately, hands swinging by their sides as they chatter and skip, the bottles apparently glued to their tight black curls.

The cows mill around too, lowing and trampling over the heaps of sand and gravel, while the workmen shout and wave sticks at them. The house is still grey and unwhitewashed, its corrugated iron roof glinting in the sun, its windows, apart from the bedroom, empty black sockets. There are piles of blocks everywhere, made by hand in wooden moulds then tipped out and left in the sun to dry. None of it looks very pretty, but we burrow into our one room and make plans for a wall, a garden, maybe a roof terrace, maybe that bar area under the baobab tree.

In one of the giant suitcases under the bed are six frothy white ruched curtains made by my sister Pat as a wedding present. And Victorian plates to hang on the wall. And my big chunky Mexican cats from the shop at Kelvinbridge . . . Ray views all these tubab accessories with wonder. His home in the village had baked mud floors, no glass in the windows, no ornaments, and food was eaten from a communal bowl, everyone squatting round it on their haunches. People keep telling me I'm 'brave' leaving my life in Glasgow for something so different, but I have inherited some of my mum's Cancerian characteristics. I carry my home with me, my Mason's plates, my Wedgwood jugs, my Tron poster, my Habitat rugs. Maybe Ray's the one who's braver, who has to adapt and adjust.

At night, Musa our watchman brings his little charcoal stove and brews attaya on the verandah. Not old Musa from the beach-bar. Old Musa is still sick and we don't know if he'll ever come back to work. This is mad Musa, a lanky Senegalese with huge flapping hands and feet and a tiny wife who still lives in Gunjur with her family.

We sit in the dark and the heaps of grey crumbly blocks look like lumpy anthills under the enormous black shadow of the baobab against the navy-blue sky. We listen to Radio Syd, especially the adverts. 'National Sanitation! Ring us for all your sanitary and hygiene problems. We will empty your soakaway for a very reasonable charge!'

We sip the sweet green tea and watch the dull, illegal glow of the charcoal. Young men from the village come round to share the evening. I can't see their faces, just pale patches of moonlight on their cheekbones, or sudden gleaming smiles in the flare of a match.

The sea sounds like an express train coming in. Bawbee nibbles my toes and goes to sleep. I feel that now we have come home.

Some Local
Wild Life

'Bawbee's playing with a snake.'

'Mmmmm.'

'Is it OK?'

'What kind of snake is it?'

'I don't know. A long greenish-yellow thing.'

'Is it alive or dead?'

'Dead. Some kids killed it in the bush and I think they gave it to Bawbee.'

'Oh well. That's OK then.'

It was about four feet long with a dark herring-bone pattern and Bawbee had a fine time with it. But I got someone to chuck it into some thorns before she could try to eat it. She has, as it is, a very comprehensive diet. Yesterday Ray killed a mouse which was scuttling in a distracted way between the bookshelf containing the European history, politics and classics and the one containing the tatty paperbacks that we actually read. The mouse was just deciding between Ed McBain and James A Michener when Ray clobbered it with his shoe. He threw it outside. Bawbee ate it. There are other times when his breath smells like a Merchant City yuppie's, of garlic prawns left over from the beach bar. Penny the cat stays sleek and glossy and healthy-looking even though she long ago gave up eating the tinned cat food I was buying in the supermarket. I discovered that her principal source of protein is lizards, particularly in the lizard mating season which falls in early summer, when the lizard chaps dress up in purple and yellow waistcoats to attract the dowdy lizard ladies.

There are, to be sure, no lions and elephants in the Gambia. There are baboons, which you sometimes see loping across the road if you drive up-river, and I understand there are hippos though I've never seen one. There are crocodiles, some in the sacred pools in Bakau and elsewhere, and some living rough in the river. But these are curiosities.

What there is in profusion is a heck of a lot of small wild life with lots and lots of legs. 'Ray, I wish you'd do something about that spider,' I whispered at 2 am. I mean, OK, it was only a spider, but it was, I swear, four inches in diameter and looked like a black plastic toy from the joke shop in Queen Street that my nephew used to frighten his granny with.

I know I said I was getting used to beasties, but this was BIG.

My husband opened one eye. 'It's just a spider,' he grunted, and went back to sleep.

When we opened one of the packing cases to find some cups and cutlery, swarms of cockroaches clambered out from every crease in every piece of yellowing wrapping paper. That was in the back room of Uncle Njie's house, but their relatives have moved in with us in the bungalow, in the crockery, under my shampoo in the bathroom, in our shoes. They vary up to about an inch and a half long, black with a tinge of russet. They make a satisfying crunch when you stand on them. I once thought about being a Buddhist, many years ago. Not in the Gambia. Now I kill everything that moves and has more than two legs.

Well, not everything. There was a stick insect clinging motionless to the white wall of the house. I left it alone, because it neither slithered, crawled nor wiggled much. In fact it didn't move a muscle (do stick insects have muscles? I don't suppose so) for three days. It's the ants that really, er, bug me. There are the wee toty ones which are just THERE, like the dust (the last three days had the highest dust count for years, according to official sources; I think the Sahara is trying to swallow us up). And there are the big red ones which flock by the hundred towards the merest smell of sugar clinging to a coffee cup. One night I found an army of them marching across the floor from under the French door, up the side of the bookcase (which also acts as a dresser, a desk and shelving for the dishes) and into a cup which had been, I swear, washed, but had retained just a tiny dribble of sweetness.

At night, if we sit on the verandah under the stars, watching the black outline of the palms and listening to the sea, they throw themselves frantically at the hurricane lamp until they frizzle and die, writhing in self-inflicted agony.

There was a dead bat, about six inches long, under the car the other day, atrophied in the sunshine. The mouse that Ray zonked with his shoe, I forgot to tell you, had taken up residence inside the bed-settee; later we found bits of straw and droppings there. We open it up quite a lot, not for anyone to sleep on, but to show off to the villagers.

No-one's ever seen one before. The first day it arrived I demonstrated the method of unfolding the interior sprung mattress on its firm metal frame and Ray was spellbound. He opened and shut it a few times then called for Uncle Njie. 'Look. Watch this,' he said, like a conjuror with a flock of doves hidden in his handkerchief pocket. He opened up the sofa and Uncle gaped. 'I cannot believe it! It changes to a bed. Oh, the tubabs are clever.' Now other family and friends pop round shyly to ask if they can see the magic sofa. You can see that my ethnic period is fading just a little. Now we can cook on our little gas-ring and wash in the sink. The water still has to be carried from the standpipe, because we still don't have a supply of our own. We could be carrying buckets till doomsday, I sometimes snipe at Ray. But all the same, this ain't no mud-hut. There are Habitat rugs on the floor, whose terracotta tiles have a smooth, substantial sheen. Ray has begun asking for scrambled eggs or cornflakes in the mornings instead of coos. The light still comes from candles, though. From time to time we use our latest purchase, the hurricane lamp, but it chokes up with soot so fast and everything becomes covered with specks of black, just like at the beach bar when the wind blows the smoke from the fire all over the plates and glasses.

The bathroom is gigantic, owing to Ray's uncle the builder miscalculating something in the house plans. It has all the necessary bits and pieces, except they don't function because of the lack of water supply. I spend an inordinate amount of time pouring basins of soapy water and disinfectant and bleach down the loo. Especially lately, because we've been having guests.

The first was my friend Liz from Scottish Television's continuity department, who was, you will recall, the nearest thing to a bridesmaid I had at my wedding in the village. Her effect on the lusty male population of the Gambia has been a remarkable thing to watch. Like ants making for the sugar, they have come to the beach-bar and to the bungalow, scurrying and twitching, scenting something sweet and irresistible. There was Momodou who works at the watersports club, Paul who has a stall in the market selling jujus, Lamin who recalled once, eight years ago, catching a glimpse of her blonde charms and has, he says, pined for her since.

And Tom, Dick and Harry . . . or should I say Hassan, Ebou and Ibrahim. Liz began to wish she could buy a man-repellent on the same lines as the Bop insect spray we use to repel the termites. 'I just want to write my postcards,' she wailed, huddled on a beach-bed pretending not to see the gathering forces of passion. Ray got annoyed. 'These guys come here to look, not to buy anything,' he snorted, as yet another handsome black suitor ambled along the beach and took up an observation position. Liz smiled weakly at each newcomer and tried to concentrate on her postcards.

'There will be a fight,' Ray warned me. He told me about two rival boys, one of them the son of a very prominent local citizen, who were strung along coquettishly by a glamorous girl. The VIP's son lobbed a lump of concrete through the windscreen of the car driven by his rival and took the top of his head off. Ray himself recalled once asking a girl to dance at a local disco while her escort was in the gents'. When he came back he went for Ray with a broken beer bottle. No blood was shed in our beach-bar and the hopeful aspirants eventually gave up, but Lizzie will be remembered here long after the visit of the Princess Royal to our Independence Day celebrations is well forgotten.

Then there was Jamie Phillips, the Glasgow-born impresario who stages pantos at the Pavilion and the spectaculars at the Kings. He also produces lavish spectacles full of long-legged show girls dressed in feathers and sequins all over Europe, and has the biggest collection of Cinderella ball-dresses, panto villain outfits, Buttons' suits, feathered headdresses and lurex sheath-dresses in Britain, for hire to stage and TV companies. He came to the Gambia to get away from it all, and ended up sounding out a bunch of Fula acrobats as possible down-the-bill acts for one of his shows. But even he was surprised when he came to visit the beach-bar and chat over old times and found himself slicing up onions while I peeled the chips for an unexpected rush of customers.

It was because of Jamie that we later found ourselves having beers with the Fula acrobats, and for a little while, imagined ourselves as 'roadies'.

'Look at them! They're fabulous,' squeaked Jamie, as they tumbled and twirled, swallowed fire and walked on stilts on the stage of the Wadner Beach Hotel. 'I need them for my show!' (He gets like that, sometimes) 'Rosie, I leave it all to you. You and Ray chat to them after I've gone home. Find out if they have passports, whether they have family ties. Dates of birth . . . that kind of thing. Then I'll sign them up and you two can travel with them as their managers and interpreters. Simple!'

'What is your date of birth?' Ray said slowly in rusty Fula to the first of them (there were eight altogether). 'Yes!' smiled the acrobat. 'When were you born,' said Ray again. 'Ah, it was during Ramadan!' 'Very nice, but when? What year?' A blank look settled over the acrobat's face and he sipped on his beer. After about two hours in Fula, French, Wollof and English, we more or less ascertained that seven of the eight 'Gambian' acrobats, as they are billed, actually came from such places as Guinea Conakry. No of course they didn't have passports. Only two of them could make a stab at their dates of birth. 'We would take you to a big city called Glasgow. You would be in a big place called a theatre with nearly 2000 people sitting watching you,' I said. They all smiled. 'You would have to fly in an aeroplane to Britain.' They smiled even more widely. 'So you would need passports.' They all scowled.

I began to envisage weeks and months spent travelling to the Guinean Embassy in Dakar, pleading with the Gambian government to issue passports here, meetings with the British High Commission, the Ministry of Arts and Culture . . . checking on the acrobats' dietary needs, fixing their accommodation in Glasgow, trying to persuade them to cut their forty minute routine to eight minutes after the trick cyclist and before the boy singer. I decided I didn't want to be in show biz, thanks, and sent Jamie an apologetic letter. But we still bump into the troupe sometimes and they always smile hopefully, in case I might hand them eight passports and eight tickets to Britain.

Just before Liz arrived, I set fire to myself. Some eejit – I suspect it was Musa – put a full aerosol of insect repellent into the box we used for rubbish. When I set fire to the rubbish in the yard (no refuse collection here . . . not to mention no electricity . . . no phone . . . . no piped water. But I won't go on about the water again . . .) the can exploded, shooting flames into my hair and over my clothes with an almighty bang. Musa came running, then Ray's uncle arrived on his motor-scooter. Ray and Lamin – who drives the car – were at the beach-bar. Uncle tootled off to get them.

Musa dipped my head in a basin and tried to wash the burnt stubs of hair off with Omo. My arm, neck, shoulder and one side of my face were black, with blisters boiling to the surface. 'It's Saturday afternoon. We're shut,' said a nursing sister in Serrekunda clinic, when Ray, almost in tears, took me there. We ended up at the Medical Research Centre in Fajara, where they're more used to exploring the epidemiology of malaria and 'the interruption of hepatitis B transmission by the destruction of bed-bugs' and such tasty subjects. They cleaned me up and sloshed cream on my arm and told me my face would be fine and just to keep everything clean and dry. Next day my face was a mass of foaming blisters. It took a long time to clear up, and poor Liz almost fainted when she saw my arm, a multi-coloured mass of craters and scrofulous swellings. A relief map of Africa, in technicolour, from nostril to knuckle. Yukk!

Never mind, could have been worse, as the doctors kept telling me cheerfully. I think tomorrow I'll go to the beach-bar and see how things are. Check for ants in the sugar, lizards in the beer crates. And handsome black predators looking for Liz . . .

Growing Pains

Musa the watchman looks like the scarecrow in the Wizard of Oz. When he walks, his flip-flops perform onomatopoetically under his big splay feet. His knee-length trousers, like vast bloomers, flap under his tunic.

Musa is the worst mime artist in the world. His only European phrases are 'Mein Gott!' and 'Thank you'. Otherwise he shouts at me in earnest and incomprehensible Wollof, making frantic gestures and facial contortions. The mime which looks like 'I am practising for a bell-ringing contest' means 'I am going for a kip while the boss is away.' The pantomime which appears to indicate severe stomach ache indicates that he wants to plant more bananas for me.

He has a bit of an obsession with bananas. He has planted twenty-four which I feel is a nice round number. I rather fancy myself as a plantation-owner, but feel that twenty-four trees all laden with bunches of fruit (should that ever happen) is enough to satisfy even the most voracious banana-lover and ensure that we absolutely never get scurvy. Musa, on the other hand, envisages the entire compound filled with them. 'I really want to grow some onions, Musa,' I plead. 'How about lots of nice tomatoes? Lettuce? Parsley?'

'Bananas, nice!' he replies miming an aeroplane doing a crash landing. He has successfully killed off my tiny tender geraniums and the lemon balm seedlings, by dint of throwing buckets of water on them with terrific force. 'Ndoch!' he says happily (Water!). Being a watchman entails fetching water, helping the builder shovel cement, burning rubbish, keeping an eye on the place when we're not here (his cutlass is hidden under a mattress on the verandah) and, it seems, killing off small seedlings.

During Ramadan, he was very low of spirit. Keeping fast is no joke. Not that Ray would let me try it and I must confess, as I downed a glass of wine with my prawns and lit a cigarette with my coffee, I was profoundly grateful.

I tried to do these things well out of Musa's sight, for fear of depressing him even more. Sometimes I forgot the rigours he was enduring. 'Coffee, Musa?' I would say brightly, as he slumped on the verandah bed like an old bolster, banned even from turning on his transistor in case he heard any perky, profane disco lyrics. A vigorous mime which to me conveyed all the sinister menace and malevolence of Act 1, Scene 1 of Macbeth indicated that he was fasting, didn't I remember? No coffee, no cigarettes, no music, no sex. To make matters worse, his sprightly little wife Namjara and their baby son, whose naming day I had attended in Gunjur the previous June, had finally transferred from her mother's compound to Musa's, just at the very time he was required to turn his thoughts aside from carnal impulses.

Another activity obliterated from Musa's schedule during this month of self-denial was, of course, work. Not that downing tools is mentioned in the Koran, but a combination of lack of sleep, lack of food and the fact that even a sip of water is prohibited during the hours from sunrise to sunset gave Musa what he considered a valid reason to slouch on the bed all day scarcely moving a muscle.

He still managed, when he did move, to make a mess. Musa is the male equivalent of a slut. He leaves behind him a trail of Lucky Strike packets, old rags, empty cans, sticky puddles of sugar and water from his tea-making sessions which entice even more ants to gather round, and which stick to my flip-flops like toffee. I mutter about him a lot to Ray. 'I'll kill him. Look at the state of the yard. Look what he's done to my tomato plants. Why hasn't he burned the rubbish? I thought you told me he would collect some cattle dung so that I could start a proper garden?' Some couples argue over their children or their in-laws. With us, it's the watchman.

He carries the big blue plastic tub on his head, flip-flop, flip-flop, look, no hands. He manages to leave a trail of muddy footprints on the floor as he plonks his watery cargo down in the bathroom. He cannot, for the life of him, understand why one bucket shouldn't last us all day.

He clicks his teeth at me when he sees me sloshing buckets of soapy water down the loo to flush it, a strange tubab custom. Gambian loos are deep holes in the ground, in which the contents degrade naturally. All this stuff about U-bends and trying to kill off ninety-nine per cent of all known germs is beyond Musa's understanding. As for washing out tee-shirts, knickers and suchlike every day, he regards this as a culpable waste of energy and water. Musa has been wearing the same outfit since he came to us. I suspect it starts walking round from the village five minutes before him in the mornings and he catches up with it outside the compound.

I suppose a little water goes a long way in his household. You only really appreciate water, I have learned, when it doesn't come gushing out of your own tap. But I have also learned not to notice these things, the lack of electricity, telephone, tap-water. It's when guests frown at the sanitary arrangements and point out that we have to drive five kilometres for a litre of peanut oil to cook with, or petrol or beer or a tin of coffee, that I have to remind myself that my lifestyle may not seem as wonderful to others as it does to me.

It's certainly better than most of my friends back home seem to imagine. I am NOT living in a mud-hut, I keep writing to them, but they're not convinced. Nothing wrong with mud-huts anyway. Most Gambians who can't afford to build their homes of cement blocks use mud. It is reddish coloured and dries in the wooden moulds to a nice solid consistency that can last for years. Up-river, the houses are built the way most white people imagine – little round huts with pointed roofs made of layers of palm fronds. The nearer you get to the coast, the more the houses develop rectangular lines, grouped in squares round a central yard in which chickens and goats scrabble and babies roll in the dust wearing nothing but their ju-jus – leather thongs round the waist on which little leather packages contain good luck and 'protective substances'. When some of the children smile, you see elaborate traceries of dark blue on the pink of their gums. I was married to Ray for months before I noticed HIS two-tone gums. He revealed, slightly embarrassed, that they were tattooed by one of the village women when he was a small boy. He still remembers the pain. I'm not surprised.

Vanity is rife. The poorest village woman will splash out money on magnificently patterned cottons to make a dress even if she has to go hungry for the rest of the month. No tailor is ever short of business. They sit in their tiny booths with their archaic Singer machines, whirring away at garments layered with frills and peplums, puffed sleeves scalloped and overhung with padded pelmets, contrasting materials stitched in panels and insets with riotous abandon. Simple understatement is not a Gambian fashion trait. If any Gambian woman has a little black dress in her wardrobe you can be sure it's a raggedy thing in which she goes to plant rice or hoe the soil round the occra plants.

Our diet has become more elaborate since we moved from Serrekunda.

My two-ring gas cooker came in our crate from Scotland, so we can scramble eggs and make coffee. The only trouble is, after a long hot day at the beach-bar, we don't really have the energy. We do eat far too many eggs, boiled, scrambled, and omelettes. I tell myself that since we don't eat any meat, my cholesterol count won't shoot through the roof.

We buy the eggs from the Chinese-run hatchery on the outskirts of the village. Needless to say, we don't just pop in, grab the eggs, pay the money and exit. We park the car and a gaggle of cheerful women employees, most of whom are Ray's aunts or second cousins gather round to pass the time of day. They have feathers sticking to their skirts and babies clamped on to their backs like limpets. In long concrete and corrugated iron sheds various levels of poultry noise can be heard. The chickens are very small and white. If you buy one to eat – a lavish extravagance which we seldom allow ourselves – you can take it as it comes, live and squawking, or have it killed and plucked, which is more expensive. To get a tray of eggs we have to wait for someone to go and find the Chinese manager, who takes about fifteen minutes to arrive. He sends someone for the eggs, which takes another ten minutes, then we pay, and finding change adds on yet another five minutes. But the freshness of the eggs is indisputable. They are warm and sticky with feathers and who-knows-what.

The Chinese are everywhere, building roads, new houses for wealthy white settlers, and the stadium in Banjul. Their vehicles, often large Audis and Mercedes, have PRC – People's Republic of China – on the number plates. Their Embassy is off the Fajara Road, just along from the President's house, not far from the British High Commission and the USSR Embassy. But business and commerce, not politics, seems to be their obsession. They sell floor-tiles and American-style jeans and sweatshirts in shops and warehouses all over Banjul and Serrekunda, and their bicycles are the only kind you can buy here.

There are Koreans, Japanese, Swedes and Germans all doing business or providing aid. The largest forestry concern in the country is the German-Gambian Forestry Project, with large forests from here (five minutes from my doorstep) to the distant interior. But the Lebanese are the most ubiquitous of all, running supermarkets, safari companies, import deals and restaurants. They sell cars and cassettes, food and money – for it is they who run the teams of Gambian and Senegalese money-changers strung along the street outside the post office in Banjul, sitting on stools surrounded by heaps of deutschmarks and francs, dollars and sterling notes.

Twenty-five years since Independence, and the Gambians are still colonised. Theirs is the quintessence of a dependent economy. If there is a clinic, road, fisheries project, community programme, hotel complex, Family Planning unit or supermarket that has no foreign input, either governmental or commercial, I have yet to discover it.

But all of this is remote, academic, so far as our day-to-day lives are concerned. One day, maybe we'll have our own chickens and we won't need to buy Chinese eggs. One day maybe we won't need to go to the market or the supermarket for fruit and veg. Maybe. Ray's uncle has just given me half-a-dozen tiny orange trees, which I hope to hide from Musa. Two little boys have arrived with a plastic bag full of coconuts and grapefruit.

The coconut palms are tall and graceful, their fronds delicate as they flutter in the breeze, far different to the stumpy ones in our garden.

Ours have fan-shaped leaves which rustle in the wind like false-teeth rattling in an old man's mouth. It is an uncanny noise, especially at night, forming percussion to the trill of the crickets. Or are they cicada? I wish I knew more about entomology; there's a lot of scope for it here.

The long spines left by these leaves form the criss-cross covering of the trunks, and make strong, savagely sharp-edged posts for local fencing. They also provide Musa with combustible materials for cooking glutinous concoctions of rice when he's not fasting.

Now he's arriving for work, carrying two sticks of hot bread from the village baker. 'Morning, sir!' he barks briskly (after twenty minutes I dare say he'll be asleep somewhere). The Gambians have no genders in their language, so they get confused sometimes with him and her, he and she.

'Salaam Aleikum! Sir!'

'Morning, Musa. Na ka suba sie? How is the morning?' Fine, just fine.

Market Forces

The knack of driving in Serrekunda is in using your horn a lot. Some 80,000 people live here, and most of them seem to be in the streets all the time. Toddlers in tatters, old men squatting at the roadside chanting holy songs, boys rushing about with wheel-barrows piled high with cement, grapefruit, firewood, wobbling sheets of corrugated iron like silver wings. Trios and quartettes of Gambian housewives, strolling and gossiping, babies on their backs, big enamel basins on their heads carrying enormous weights of vegetables and fruits without the merest wobble. The women are straight-backed and graceful.

Sometimes a policeman stands at the main crossroads by the market vaguely flapping his arms and blowing his whistle at the teeming traffic, long buses jam-packed with workers, bush-taxis, their drivers' boys screaming 'Banjul! Banjul! Banjul! Nyetta dalasi!', donkey carts, posh military Nissan Patrols, dilapidated Renault Four taxis with patchwork paintwork and woolly dolls and plastic flowers hanging all over the windows.

Only London's Soho demands more negotiating skills, bravado and bellicose horn-blowing. You zig-zag along the narrow side-streets swerving round vicious potholes and piles of rubbish, churning through sand or mud, depending on the season, trying not to let your wheels spin out of control, missing the two-foot gutters of slimy black water by inches and nudging pedestrians out of the way by sheer klaxon-power. At first, I fondly imagined that if people walking towards you could see your vehicle ploughing steadily towards them, they would, naturally, move aside. 'No, you have to horn them,' said Ray patiently. 'Toot-toot. Toot-toot,' and then they'll slowly amble sideways like crabs to let you past.

Yesterday, we proceeded thus through the teeming lanes behind the market. We usually park next to the auto-repair shop across the road from the market car-park, finding a space between old ladies selling heaps of hot peppers and papayas and huddles of young men in jeans and lurid tee-shirts buying and selling things. I sit in the car, the sun bashing through the windows, sweat streaming down my face, re-reading the Raj Quartet (I've done three; just one to go), while

Ray, ducking and swerving and foraging like an eel, insinuates himself through the clutter of fly-covered produce.

He is better at shopping than I am. He is prepared, as I am not, to spend ten minutes disputing the value of a dead fish or a live chicken or a kilo of tomatoes.

But this time the road was blocked by a yelling, giggling, jumping-up-and-down demo. The bush-taxi drivers, so far as I could make out, had reneged at paying a tariff to use the car-park, while private car-owners slide their vehicles into the gaps without paying anything. They leapt about, vaulting on to the roofs and bonnets, banging car roofs, rocking them vigorously, bawling half-good-natured accusations and supplications at drivers and waving home-made banners. Voluminous and highly indignant African matrons in lavish frocks and head-pieces with handbags and baskets over their arms climbed heavily from cars and were surrounded by chanting strikers. We parked in front of the auto-shop and watched.

The sign over the shop says (sic): 'Sockobservers, new baterys, exosts, pisstons.' Gambian spelling is riotously individualistic. Especially of motor parts. When Ray's Uncle Alieu, the mechanic, wrote us a shopping list for spares for a car he was fixing, it included items like 'saff' (shaft), 'bull-jots' (ball-joints), and 'sillinderhed gaskit'.

A gendarme, one of the strutting, gun-toting paramilitary police cordially regarded with caution by residents and tourists alike, wandered about helplessly trying to recreate order (if such a word could be used to describe the everyday frenetic activity behind the market) then disappeared. I prayed fervently that he hadn't gone for reinforcements. I have strong reservations about the gendarmerie's ability to control anything, let alone an excited crowd, without blood being spilled. At the time of the country's twenty-fifth anniversary celebrations, attended by Princess Anne and President Babangida of Nigeria, one of them fatally shot a German tourist and a Gambian citizen because the safety-catch on his archaic weapon was off while he was pushing back over-enthusiastic onlookers.

We got our shopping anyway and the fracas gave me something to watch to take my mind off the sweat soaking into my shirt.

Ray came back with plastic bags of fish and potatoes and lettuce and stowed them in the boot, then heaved people bodily out of the way, waving his arms about, guiding me out of the mass, backwards, my wheels missing bony black feet and flapping robes by inches, away from the hurly-burly, the shouts and giggles following us all the way to the Post Office.

There was nothing about it on Gambia radio news, so I presume no-one was hurt. Mind you, that's a blinkered assumption. When the bullets were flying on Independence Day, it wasn't mentioned on Radio Gambia till two days later, well down the list after descriptions of the euphoric greetings sent by presidents and potentates from all over the world. This may be a black democracy but it launders its news very carefully before offering it for public consumption.

Shopping, as I've mentioned, takes a long, long time. It would be paramount to bad manners simply to choose a piece of fish and profer the asking price. You examine it, prod it, walk off in disgust, walk back again, enquire after the state of the vendor's health and the well-being of his family and re-negotiate. By the time you go to the ice factory for the expensive block of grubby ice we use to keep the drinks cool in the beach bar, to the Post Office to check our mail box, to the Lebanese supermarket to buy wine and Omo, I am usually in a foul temper. (There are some other soap powder brands here, but the substance is known to everyone by the name 'Omo', whatever it says on the label.)

I occasionally ask Ray if he doesn't wish he'd married a complaisant Gambian wife who wouldn't use bad language and tell him to drive the bloody car himself if he doesn't like my driving. He just grins infuriatingly. He can thole pretty well anything except the fear of competition. If he goes to the loo behind Uncle Dembo's and comes back to find me chatting in a desultory way with another customer about the state of the roads or the price of beer, he becomes very quiet and icily polite towards the third party.

Later he'll ask: 'What did he say to you? Did he make any suggestions? What were you talking about?' Sexual jealousy is a very Muslim characteristic. Or maybe it's a more ancient tribal thing. It's hard to separate the two. Over ninety per cent of Gambians are Muslim, but they also believe quite unequivocally in marabouts and ju-jus, omens and fetishes. If you develop a twitch in one eye, it's because you've spied on your elder and seen the private parts of his body; if something happens to you, anything from a flat tyre to a bad cold, it's probably because someone has put a bad luck spell on you. Every area has its marabout and people will argue vehemently about the relative powers of their marabout versus someone else's. Farbakary in the beach-bar where I first met and fell in love with Ray, was said to spend almost all of his takings on consulting different marabouts seeking a shortcut to prosperity. We tried telling him that if he kept the money he made from the tourists he'd be quite well-off anyway. The logic escaped him.

So far as Ray's macho attitude to marriage is concerned, I can't grumble. If I saw him hobnobbing with an African girl or some nubile Swedish tourist – I'd raise the roof, so it's a fair swop.

Yesterday afternoon, I decided to wash the curtains and sheets. Naturally, at that precise moment, the water went off at the standpipe. I stood there up to my knees in mud, watching with morbid fascination as spasmodic drips plopped sluggishly from the spout.

Musa flip-flopped along carrying the rusty oildrum in which he collects the water he uses to batter my seedlings to death. 'Ndoch? Feeneeshed? Ach!' He grabbed my buckets and disappeared for half-an-hour. When he came back he had filled them with murky fawn liquid from the village well. I suspected that if I washed our dirty linen in it it would come out dirtier than it began.

Murky fawn is also the colour of the dust that covers every surface in the house, no matter how much I attack it with a damp cloth. The local school children, like Musa, think I am fixated. Several dozen of them stand in front of our verandah, watching open-mouthed and nudging each other as I shake rugs, mop floors, and hang out towels they saw me washing just two days ago.

Their interest is friendly, but sometimes I feel like an exhibit, a rare species to be studied for new idiosyncracies. When we took my daughter and baby Cameron to the pretty fishing-beach at Sanyang in South Gambia, we borrowed beach beds from the lone, isolated beach-bar and settled down to eat our picnic, long empty waves of white sand stretching as far as the eye could see, interrupted only by the gaggle of fishing-boats to our left, where the women gutted small sharks and pudgy catfish. Within seconds a group of local children had appeared from nowhere. They brought chunks of tree-trunk and arranged them a few metres from us so that they could sit in silent rows and stare at us. When we moved to a table in the shade to drink our beers, they moved with us and re-positioned their impromptu benches.

In Tanji, another fishing village, where millions of bonga-fish are smoked every month in EEC-funded sheds that smell like kippers, for export to Sierra Leone, Senegal and Ghana, the local children gaze at us with hungry eyes and say 'Give us bread. We are hungry.' Often it's not true. It's just the first in a series of demands demonstrating their knowledge of English. 'Give us sweets. Give us pens. Give us dalasi.' But often it *is* true.

In the market the other day, I saw a young woman hauling herself along the baked, rubbish-strewn earth on her elbows. She had no legs. She smiled radiantly at people's ankles and the hems of their garments. Various charities, notably the Danish Red Cross, supply wheelchairs, but there are never enough. The beggars display a grotesque variety of deformities. Tall old men with sightless eyes will walk through the streets resting their hands on the shoulders of small grandsons, chanting pleas for charity. The boys may spend many hours of every day thus, human guide-dogs, one hand outstretched to receive coins, the other resting on the larger, wrinkled paw that seems glued to their shoulders.

It often seems to me that much of the foreign aid that's chucked into the country never permeates down to the roots of its problems.

There are beggars and badly-equipped schools, hospitals without necessary drugs, villages without decent wells. But there are also government ministers and their relatives in large shiny Mercedes. Enormous sums of money vanish in a series of scandals and sheer incompetences that are seldom aired in the government-controlled press.

Meanwhile the cost of cement soars and dives and soars again. There is a petrol shortage or a diesel shortage every few weeks. Rice prices go up, are yanked down again, then go up even more. You get used to it. What you don't get used to is the army of ants marching across the floor however much you clean it with lethal solutions of bleach and insect-killer. I've just spotted another battalion. They're coming under the French door and there's a black lacy ribbon of them across the living-room floor, into the kitchen and up the wall to the shelf where the sugar is kept.

I attack them with a mop soaked in Domestos. I doubt if the manufacturers ever considered the slaughter of African ants as one of their advertising slogans. And now Musa's jumping up and down outside the window. 'Ndoch! Sir! Mein Gott!' Hooray! He means the water's on, a mere 250 metres way. Buckets, everyone!

Up-Country Matters

Fadda Mike was bending over the innards of his four-year-old Datsun pick-up, thumping the battery connections and muttering, like the White Rabbit, 'I'm late! I'm late!'

Father Michael O'Casey has been in the Gambia for over quarter-of-a-century. He speaks fluent Wollof with a thick Irish brogue and when he comes down to Kombo – the Kombos being the regions south and west of Banjul – he walks into our beach-bar looking vaguely disreputable in old shorts and flip-flops, a Dublin drop-out. Last time he came in for a beer he said: 'Come and see me next time you're in Farafenni.' So we did.

This time he was wearing his white soutane over the flip-flops, waving the hammer like a thurible. It had taken us a long time to find him.

Farafenni, a couple of hundred miles up-river and definitely not a tourist centre, is a broth of a place. To reach it you have to cross the looping arms of the River Gambia by ferry, queueing with Gambians and Senegalese who come to trade and, it is sometimes suggested, enjoy the pleasures of Farafenni at night. Not that it is known for its glamour or beauty; far from it. But it does have a reputation as a gathering point for Senegalese prostitutes who sneak across the nearby border, flitting across the bush at night-time like black butterflies, to ply their trade vigorously among the shanties.

Two little boys took us to the Mission run by Mike and a handful of Sisters. The route involved several false starts along back lanes embedded with decades of rubbish and fringed by rusting remnants of long-dead vehicles. It was dusk. A mauve sky darkened behind the ubiquitous mango trees and the clutter of untamed shrubs and creepers which shield Fadda Mike (this is the way the Gambians say his name) from the squalor beyond, lapping round the shabby, homely bungalow like green water.

'I'm just going to say Mass at Mansa Konko,' he said, as the Datsun suddenly shoogled to life. 'Here's the key; help yourself to the beer and there's some sausages somewhere. Don't touch the fish or I'll have me head in me hands; it belongs to the Sisters. See you later, so long as the ferry's running.' And he was off in a cloud of dust.

It was the first time I'd been up-country. I bought a bush-hat specially. I hoped to look like Meryl Streep on location for *Out of Africa*, but suspect I looked more like Naomi Mitchison. Still, it kept the sun off my head when we rolled back the top of the 2CV; sun which drove downwards like a torch. We missed the sea breeze. And the roads had potholes like the craters of the moon, huge red mouths gaping in the thin tar surface – so thin that the harsh red base bursts through everywhere. An aerial view would show drivers weaving and wiggling all over the road, from side to side and even into the bush in an attempt to avoid the holes. Swerve to avoid one the size of a bus-wheel and you find your spine being jolted violently as you hit one the size of a goldfish pond.

We drove through Dumbuto and Kafuto and scores of other villages which all looked much the same to me, huddles of corrugated iron and grass roofs, palm fencing, dusty mango trees, the old men sitting on the *bantaba*, a low platform of gnarled palm trunks, talking of bygone days, the women at the well, drawing water, gossiping, calling raucous insults to the local boys. We passed patches of rice paddy, clusters of banana palms, carts pulled by donkeys or oxen. The road forging straight ahead like the spine of a feather, the river always out of sight, winding far to right or left, visible only at the ferry crossings which punctuate any journey into the interior.

From the ferries, sometimes hand-pulled, you see the cloudy green water shadowed by never-ending fringes of mangroves sheltering a richness of bird-life and countless nameless things that suck and plop and slurp in the mud. Farafenni, when we reached it, didn't look like a hookers' paradise. The HIV count there is the highest in the country, thanks to its influx of industrious girls. Big carts take the place of motorised taxis, people packed on like sheep at a dalasi a ride.

When Father O'Casey came home we sat on the verandah, swatting mosquitoes and talking into the darkness. Inside, his living-room is a guddle of books and papers and letters piled high on every chair, dominated by a giant clanking refrigerator in one corner, lavishly stocked with beer. 'You'll have a wee something in your coffee,' Mike says, and sloshes some Irish whiskey into the hot water and Nescafe. He invites us to stay the night in his spare room. Ray is aghast at the idea of us sharing a double bed just through a partition wall from a celibate priest, with Jesus staring down at us from one distempered wall.

So we went to Eddy's Hotel, a mere £7.50 a night for the two of us and you get the cockroaches in the bathroom free of charge. The water was off, which was no surprise. An old man brought us a bucket. The floor was covered with greasy lurid Axminster and a picture of a girl with a Sixties beehive hairdo hung at a 45° angle on one wall. Music blared from the disco and we trotted round to sample the nightlife. But there was no-one there, neither bar-man nor customers, just an empty room reverberating to the amplified sounds. It occurred to me that Mike had dispensed the Bush Mills to help me cope with a night at Eddy's.

Next morning we took two more ferries and ended up in Georgetown, described in the guide books as an essential place to visit, a fading relic of the colonial past and capital of the Macarthy Island Division. What Georgetown is, is a school, a prison, depressing ruins of the old slave quarters and a lot of women washing their clothes and their children in the sluggish green-grey water of the riverbank. The school used to be for the sons of village chiefs. It has room for 500 boarders and an excellent reputation. We didn't linger. Another ferry took us to Janjanbure Camp, which is very camp indeed, dinky little African-style chalets with bijou furnishing, window seats and hammock beds.

We fed bananas to the monkeys, a whole colony of them swinging and swaggering around a giant baobab tree. We backed away from a gaggle of hearty English tourists and did out best to avoid swarms of insects with equally healthy appetites. A kora player sang a succession of songs. To me, all kora music sounds the same. They just change the words around now and then. The heat was remarkable. There was no cold drinking water. We paced the tiny chalet floor at 2 am, dripping with sweat, gasping for breath, croaking like Jack McLean before opening time.

Morning coffee sipped as we sat by the tranquil river put us in a better frame of mind. We drove back to the ferry landing-point, ready for the off. We could see it at the other side. The captain was paddling his feet in the waters of the far bank, stretching and chewing on a piece of the twig Africans use to clean their teeth. We shouted and tooted, a throng of would-be travellers, bush-taxis, men and women on foot with giant bundles on their heads. The captain waved back and went on paddling and chewing. Meanwhile, a conference was taking place at the roadside. The *sefo*, or area chief, more important than an alkalo or village headman, had been invited to come and settle a quarrel between two men, one of whom was alleged to have sold the other some stolen goods. The sefo sat, cross-legged and sombre, then rose creakily to his feet and strode up and down, shouting at both men, who hung their heads like small boys.

A donkey and cart joined our queue, then a Land Rover, revving up its engine and snorting its horn, then a woman leading two frisky goats on pieces of string. We all hurled expletives at the captain, which bounced like pebbles across the water to sink unheeded at his feet. The minutes ticked by and the sun rose higher and hotter in the pale empty sky.

At last the captain gave one final mighty stretch, shook himself like a dog and brought the ferry over to us with the air of a patient parent pacifying fretful children. We got to the other bank in the end, muttering to each other about timetables and the bloody-mindedness of up-river Gambians.

Talking of ends, I had wanted to find one high promontory overlooking the river, described in one of the history books I'd browsed through at the School of African and Oriental Studies library in London. It was called Arse Hill, once upon a time. The story is that Bartholemew Stibbs, sent up-river by the Royal African Company in 1723, described how the natives would gather on the hill as ships passed, 'show their behinds, dance and sing and clap their hands.' In later colonial days, as stout-hearted white women began to join their men on their arduous postings to 'the white man's grave', the practice was discouraged to shield the fair sex from shocked embarrassment.

Ray was prim-faced. He said he'd never heard of such a thing, tsk-tsk, certainly not. Wouldn't I like, instead, to go and look at the Wassu stone circles? They are the Stonehenge of the Gambia, but I found them totally resistible. Lumps of stone are lumps of stone, though I know people who are entranced by their mysterious history.

We drove on to Bansang, a market town that straggles between the road and the river, and bought some mangoes. If mangoes were currency, the Gambia would be incredibly wealthy. Every tiny village has its trees, some of them magnificent ancient specimens with trunks as wide as a car. Often the branches form a huge mushroom shape, so that the base of their thickly-plumaged profusion forms a flat green ceiling overhead, obliterating the light of the sun. Every twig bears clusters of fruit, from new small hard green globes the size of ping-pong balls to the large ripe fruit, sometimes the size of rugby balls, the skin clouding from yellow and red to brown. It is an irony that the season of mangoes starts around May – at the end of the tourist season – and finishes around September before the next season starts.

I often get carried away and deliver lectures to anyone who'll listen about the desirability of someone opening a mango canning and bottling plant to preserve the fruit and its generous juices for profit. It grieves me to see, in late summer, piles of rotting orange squashy fruit blackened with flies, wasted because we have all eaten and eaten and eaten mangoes every day and still there are millions too many of them.

When I'm not being boring about bottling factories, I can be boring about Gambian history. Or irritating, according to Ray. I read him a bit from an old book on his country. 'The Jollof (Wollof) race is one of the finest in the whole of Africa, handsome in person, proud in bearing . . . a superior race, intellectually head and shoulders above the negro races of Senegambia.' He smiled in agreement and sat up

straighter in his seat, looking handsome and proud. Then I read on:
'. . . very cleanly, very charitable, hospitable to a degree, courageous in war . . .' He preened himself like a cat. '. . . but more clever in trading, being full of words, and, for the most part, liars and cheats.' He glowered. 'Mariama! This book is full of rubbish!'

Digging In

Ketta the well-digger is down so far that I can't see him in the blackness. I can hear his voice, deep and hollow.

'Mariama! Why don't you come and see!' Not bloody likely.

He dug the first few metres a perfectly circular hole with smooth brown sides punctuated by footholds. It was ninety centimetres in diameter.

Then our friends Matthew and Monica came for coffee. Matthew is a tall rangy Gambian with massive neck-muscles. If you were a wrestling fan in the heyday of Mick McManus and Giant Haystack and Adrian Street, you would know him as Massa Mboula, the terrifying black man in the leopard skin who used to toss opponents out of the ring like empty peanut shells.

He spent forty years in Britain, having sneaked on to a UK-bound ship as a boy, joined the police force, done a bit of boxing, then made his name as a wrestler, a gentle giant with a soft voice and a soft smile and sinews of steel. He married Monica to the horror of her family and all the locals in the small Yorkshire village where she lived. He bought lots of fast cars, drank a lot of whisky, took a lot of punches.

Now he's a teetotal born-again Christian and he and Monica are building a house just behind the village cemetery. His voice is pure Bradford.

'Eeee, Ray. Ninety centimetres is nowt as big as you need,' he said, 'You needs a hundred-and-twenty, man.' We told Ketta. To his credit, he didn't throw his shovel at us.

Once we had assumed that we would be able to take a pipe from the ample supply that feeds the ITC cattle station. We'd pay for the privilege, naturally, and we'd have sparkling running water from the excellent main supply, gushing from our taps and flowing from our cistern.

You should never assume anything. 'It's not possible', said Mr Touray, the depute director. 'If we let you have it, everyone who's building a compound near Bijilo and Ker Seringe will want it.' 'But we'll pay for it,' we whined, 'And we won't tell anyone else,' we coaxed. 'Pleee-eeease!' 'No, it's not possible. Good afternoon.'

The standpipe has been moved even further away from the house than it was before, way over beside the cattle troughs. It was bad enough before. I would step out briskly with my empty buckets, take off my flip-flops and wade into the treacly mud around the tap, trying not to think of what might be wriggling about down there, and fill up. Then I would trudge back slowly, splashing water and feeling my arms growing longer. If I was African, I could carry a bucket on my head. I tried it a few times and ended up soaked to the skin with a stiff neck.

Musa now does the trudging back and forward. He carries on his head a tub the size of a baby's bath. The 'white doctor' as he calls the vet who inspects the herds, grumbles to him that his boss (that's me) uses far too much water from the ITC tap. I haven't at that time met Derek and his charming wife, so I mutter sulkily about it being OK for them. They don't have to wash their hair in half-a-bucketful, then use the soapy remains to clean out the floor-mop, then use that to flush the toilet. I learn to shower in a small jug, as it were, using a sponge. If I hear anyone pouring water down the sink I scream at them to save it for the plants.

Anyway, it was then that we decided we needed to dig a well.

Two wizened old men with venal faces came and said they were the local well-diggers. They asked for so much money we could have built our own pumping station. Matthew told us about Ketta from Majai Kunda, a hamlet near Kololi, so we went to see him. He asked us for about a tenth of the local guys' price.

'Great!' I said, 'Let's hire him.' But Ray looked doubtful. Majai Kunda must be all of three miles away. Ketta was a stranger. Ray and his uncle, the builder, peered at him, circled him suspiciously. 'We don't know him. How do we know he's honest? We must think about this carefully. We should see the alkalo of his village and get him to guarantee him.'

'Stranger', to a Gambian, often translates like the French étranger – a foreigner. Three miles is a long way. 'But he seems like a nice man,' I say. 'And he's cheap.' They shake their heads and sigh and circle again. In the end, Ketta passed muster. He asked us for money to buy equipment. I imagined pulleys, chains, all manner of technology. He came back from the market with one small galvanised bucket and a long strip of tough cotton. He brought his assistant with him.

What happens is, Ketta digs a hole and the assistant empties the sand from the bucket. As the hole gets deeper, Ketta has to climb down further. He fills the bucket, the assistant hauls it up and empties it and lowers it again. They don't come on Mondays and Fridays. 'My marabout told me these were heavy days for work,' Ketta explained reasonably. One day there was a furious argument around my African cooking stove. The assistant was using the stove to boil rice and yams at 10 am for his breakfast. He insisted he couldn't work unless he ate. The thing is, eating here involves about three hours of simmering, stirring, talking, sitting around under a tree and then trying to scrape the last of the burnt rice (regarded as a tidbit) from the round-bottomed African cooking-pot. This looked like slowing down the digging even more than it was slow already.

Ketta barked at the assistant and the assistant barked back. Eventually he left with a torrent of abuse in his ear and Ketta disappeared for three days while he found a replacement. He had estimated that the well, complete with concrete rings round top and bottom, and probably about twenty-five metres deep, would take fifteen days to complete. That was about three weeks ago and he hasn't hit water yet. The hole is surrounded by a high circular mountain-range of sand and gravel. The stuff that comes up in the bucket now is slightly clay-ish.

Ray feels this is a good sign. 'They'll find water in a day or two . . . or maybe three or four,' he says. The nursery school where Ray's mum works is having a well dug too. But they have American charity funding, so they have all kinds of fancy mechanical diggers and hoists and it will cost them £3000 compared to our £150.

There were, while all this digging and delving was going on, a few tense days when Musa's job as watchman was on the line. We found him helping Ketta haul up buckets when his assistant wasn't there. For money. Which was all very well, except that he was supposed to be working for us, hauling up palm roots and 'big potato' plants. The Wollof name for these weeds, which have shiny bright green leaves like young rhododendron, and roots the size of beer barrels, sounds like *mbahanasay*. They spread like dandelions and can only be conquered by digging down about three feet and howking them out.

Already we'd paid a squad of local lads one dalasi per root, but Musa had said he'd be happy to deal with the rest. Now the weeds were re-grouping, growing bigger by the minute, while Musa blacklegged for Ketta. Also, so absorbed was he in his labours, I had no water.

An industrial tribunal was set up under the baobab tree, involving me, Ketta, Musa, Ray, Ray's uncle and several bystanders spoiling for a good fight. All digging stopped as we put forward our submissions, first in modestly muted tones, then in indignant yowls. Someone made attaya. We sipped the hot khaki-coloured liquid and started again. In the end, a fine compromise was reached. Musa will dig up our *mbahanasay*, fetch our water, then work at the well. I feel twinges of guilt ('I'm a racist, capitalist exploiter of the workers,' I mutter to Ray.) I always feel like this during any dealings with local labour. Local labour, in fact, can run rings round me when it comes to driving a bargain. All the same, Ray has to remind me that Musa is far from downtrodden. He spends many hours of each day sitting on our verandah brewing attaya, dropping sugar and fag-ash, and drinking my coffee. And was it not I who bathed and anointed his wife's ankle when she had a septic ulcer, then drove her to the clinic and battled with medical bureaucracy to get her treated while 200 other sick Gambians queued?

Musa's wife, Namjara, came to him from her parents' home in Gunjur just a few weeks ago. She's a tiny thing and their baby, tied to her back, seems almost as big as her, a cuckoo suckled by a sparrow. The sore on her foot has been getting bigger and more revolting every day, mainly because it is wrapped in a filthy rag and topped by a twisted leather ju-ju prescribed by a local medicine man. As I yank her through the crowds of would-be patients at the Medical Research Centre in Fajara, 200 wounds, rashes, fevers, aches and pains are aimed accusingly at me, accompanied by groans and whimpers. I get Namjara treated by dint of shouting at orderlies and lying that she has six sick children at home. 'She has been in agony for weeks', I utter dramatically. This bit is in fact absolutely true.

Anyway, I manage to curb my guilt feelings about Musa. I think to myself that he will be with us for ever, his trail of Lucky Strike packets strewn among the lemon seedlings, his smelly discarded shorts and vests lying like dead animals among the crates of beer, his bananas and pumpkins thriving while my flowers and capsicum seeds shrivel and die. Ketta pays him by the bucketful. It would be nice to think he'd give the extra dalasis to Namjara, but instead he spends them on more Lucky Strike and more attaya. She goes now, once a week, to the clinic in Sukuta to have her wound dressed. She goes on the local donkey cart, a kind of four-legged, two-wheeled taxi.

On these occasions, Musa, with a scowl on his face, looks after their baby, which has, unfortunately, inherited all of his daddy's ungainly sloth, and none of his mum's bright birdlike vitality. 'Pa', as the infant is called after some venerable relative, plods around with vacant eyes and a dangling lip. I suspect lack of ante-natal care has had its effect. Musa is very proud of him, however. 'Say hullo to Mariama,' he gushes in his execrable Senegalese Wollof. Pa swivels his eyes slowly towards me, stares, then starts to sob. He hasn't seen many tubabs.

Perhaps the fact that my nose is twitching like a possum's is what frightens him.

The reason for this is that there's a terrible pong coming from the soakaway. The soakaway is the large concrete 'septic tank' dug into the earth behind the house, surrounded by boulders through which, I understand, waste is meant gradually to degrade. I suspect something has died in it. Looking on the bright side, it almost obscures the niff of dung coming from the cows.

But then the wind changes and all we can smell is the sea and sun-dried grass. We walk to the beach looking for monkeys on the way, with Bawbee bouncing around in front of us, yapping at anything on two or four legs which dares to cross our path. On the sand, vast breakers crash and scatter chunks of foam, which Bawbee chases furiously. I do an old Glasgow Herald crossword, while Ray exchanges gossip with a villager who is hauling in an enormous fish on the end of a piece of nylon string baited with bits of bonga fish. It is called a doctor fish, because it is covered with spines like a porcupine, or like a doctor's hypodermic.

That night, Ray goes to bed early. 'I think I got too much sun,' he says seriously. He certainly has a good tan.

Words and Music

We listen to the radio a lot. Someone once gave Radio Syd a copy of 'Donal', Where's Your Troosers?' and they still play it regularly, alongside Lonnie Donnegan's 'My Old Man's a Dustman'. There's no television station and most folk can't afford newspapers. There's no daily paper anyway. So for job adverts, In Memoriam announcements, school opening dates, plugs for local discos or sports days, you listen to the radio.

'If anyone knows the whereabouts of -------, recently dismissed from the ------- Bank, could they please contact the bank's lawyer,' was one recent broadcast message. 'Anyone who was planning to attend the meeting of Liberian refugees in the Gambia, please note that it has been moved from the YMCA to the Atlantic Hotel' was another.

But mostly, we listen for the African music. Like the other day. I was listening to a sultry mix of sounds from local instruments, with a nice smoochy Western beat to it. 'That's very nice. Who is it?'

'It's Jaliba Kuyeteh. He comes from Brikama.'

'What's he singing about?'

'The owner of the soap and plastic factory in Kanefing.'

'Oh.'

There are lots of songs about the need for people to respect the words of their parents and grandparents, and there's one about 'BB' – the Vice-president's nickname. The recent West African number one hit 'Set', by Senegalese heart-throb Youssu Ndour, translates to 'cleanliness', and is all about the dangers of pollution of the spirit. He has another foot-tapper all about toxic waste. If I was translating the one about our Vice-president into Glaswegian, it would be something on the lines of 'Oh, Vice-president, see you, you are definitely the berries, so you are. I wish everyone could appreciate what a rerr bloke you are, so I do . . . tra la la.'

West African pop heroes, as you can see, don't go much for the kind of lyrics that stir the loins. It behoves them to be nice about their sponsors, political or commercial, who like a wee bit of personal flattery or moral propaganda. Ray can't understand why I go into squawks of laughter every time I hear the soap factory stomp. To me, it's a bit like someone writing a smash hit about the boss of Kwik-Fit tyres.

To be honest, there are quite a few things about me he has to struggle to understand, and it works both ways. The language creates problems. Not the Wollof, that's bad enough, but the kind of English that is common currency here. 'Hand me over that nylon,' he'll say. 'Nylon' is plastic, as in plastic bag. 'Horn him,' he'll instruct me when a teetering cyclist wobbles under his wheels. 'Borrow me one dalasi,' a Gambian will say, meaning 'lend'. 'Stranger' is a visitor. Many words and phrases have elements of prudish colonial times. 'Have you seen what Bawbee has done? He has defecated on the verandah!' Ray will inform me indignantly. Gambians don't pee, they urinate. They don't wear pants or knickers, they wear under-drawers. They often hang up their attire and put on pea-shorts for work.

One doctor friend tells us of the difficulty in getting patients to describe their symptoms. 'I need something for my body,' they'll say. 'Which precise bit of the body is troubling you,' he'll ask patiently. 'Oh, just my body . . .'

My favourite notice is a piece of paper pinned to the wall of Memory Bar on the road to the airport. It says 'Displaying is out of order'. A notice to flashers? A warning to exhibition-holders? No, displaying is Gambian for making too much noise, getting drunk and generally horsing around to the annoyance of other customers.

My second favourite notice is chalked in large letters on the wall next to the basket-maker's stall at Kanefing. It says 'No wetting'. At first I thought it was a mis-spelling of No Waiting, aimed at car-drivers. But it means, of course, what it says: 'Don't piddle here'.

As for Wollof, I try hard to learn it. It's about as subtle as a sledgehammer. 'Get in,' Ray used to say when we were entering a taxi. I used to bridle and ask if he thought he was talking to the dog. He was very hurt. Wollof doesn't have subtleties like 'Would you mind . . .?' or 'Could you possibly see your way . . .?' Nor does it differentiate between the genders, which can be very confusing. 'Go and ask him if he wants to come in and have a beer in the restaurant,' Ray suggests. 'Who?' 'Him. The guy in the yellow bikini.'

Actually, no-one male or female, comes to have a drink or anything else in the restaurant these days. Business is zilch. My former diet of benachin has changed. We've gradually had to shed staff as the season peters out, so the staff rice bowl is no longer called for. It's just us now, sitting disconsolately on our chairs peering along the empty beach, wishing someone would come and order even a plate of chips. We still buy a little fish and prawns at the market, always optimistic that someone will pay to eat them but they never do, so we take them home and I make fish soup and garlic prawns, night after night. Maybe I should try prawn soup and garlic fish . . .

I suppose I should be feeling a bit worried. It's certainly not what a British cafe-owner would regard as economically viable.

Driving to the market, using up petrol, buying sea-food, then ice to keep it fresh, then – if we're really lucky – selling one bottle of Coke all day. But it allows me time to read a lot of books.

It leaves plenty of time to write long, long letters to family and friends. And it also gives me an excuse to listen to Ray's everyday tales of country folk. Like the man from Brufut who had an ugly wife. 'Marrying an ugly wife is supposed to be good luck,' Ray said, eyeing me appraisingly. 'This man, his wife was very, very ugly, but very, very lucky in money. Before, the man's life had been full of disaster and he was very poor. But after he married, he prospered. Everything went well with him and his business. He got tired of being married to a woman so displeasing to look at, so he divorced her and found a pretty girl instead. Suddenly, everything began to go wrong for him. He lost all his business. He went bankrupt.'

'What about the wife?' I ask breathlessly.

'A rich man who owned fishing-boats felt sorry for her and presented her with her own fishing boat. All the money from the catches was hers and she became very comfortable. But she was still ugly.'

There are other stories, about the rich spoiled sons of the Lebanese community who, if they happen to fancy a fling with one of the European air stewardesses who billet at the large hotels, will lavishly bestow champagne on the entire crews. The Lebanese are regarded with a combination of contempt, affection, and envy. Most of them were born here and speak the local languages as their mother-tongue. Many of them live in grand style and have reputations as playboys, womanisers and show-offs.

We sometimes wish we had their Midas touch, as we count out our meagre intake of dalasi and pass yet another empty day on the beach. If it gets too lonely, we pack up and come home early. I make futile stabs at gardening, poking at the brick-hard soil with a trowel and heaving Bawbee off my morning glory plants. None of my onion, pepper, lettuce or sweet-corn seeds has shown the slightest indication of breaking through the crust. I do have a proliferation of basil and tarragon, which I will add to the fish soup.

The bananas seem to be doing OK. And the earth is criss-crossed by tendrils of leaves from what I was given to understand were water-melon, planted by Musa, and have now discovered to be pumpkin. But there's still an awful lot of barren beige earth crackling with dry spiky weeds that tear your hands to ribbons if you try to dislodge them. I yearn for prettiness, but look out on heaps of sand and rubble, where the builders – Ray's uncle and a handful of village men working on piece rates – are finishing our two little African-style huts.

They are hexagonal in shape, the most practical approximation to a roundhouse. They are roofed in thick, tight layers of grass, whose tufts are woven together with cord to form blankets of thatch firmly strapped to the palm-runs that form the rafters. The walls are painted gleaming white and the beds are traditional African ones, simply raised platforms of concrete, on top of which foam mattresses will be placed. They are, I'm assured, orthopoedically excellent.

If I sit on the verandah and half-shut my eyes, I can visualise them skirted by tumbling clusters of red and purple bougainvillaea, surrounded by flowers and trees. But as soon as I open my eyes, the rugged reality reveals itself again. The only thing which grows well even if you trample on it and the dogs widdle on it and the builders drop gravel on it, is a spindly plant called Never Die. It thickens and produces little scarlet flowers. I know this because I've seen it forming chunky hedgerows in the gardens of the British High Commission in Fajara. But ours has a long way to go yet.

Also, on the verandah, we plan our trip to Scotland in the summer. Ray is pointedly blasé about it. 'We'll be going to Angleterre soon,' he mentions casually to friends. Angleterre is Gambian for the UK, much to my annoyance. I try hard to explain to people what Scotland is, but they look bewildered. 'It's in London?' they say blandly. 'Is Finland next to Scotland?' Ray asks me in all seriousness. European geography is as remote to a Gambian as the whereabouts of Mogadishu (capital of Somalia), Gondar (a province of Ethiopia) or the Makgadikgadi Salt Pans of Botswana would be to the average Scottish O-Grade student.

Ray has been in Dakar, so at least he has seen an elevator, traffic lights, trains. Most Gambians haven't. I try describing cash-lines and coffee machines, chain stores and tumble dryers, escalators and subway trains, electric toasters and Hoover vacuum-cleaners, candy-floss and clappie-doos. It's not easy.

We worry about what will happen to our compound while we're away. Everyone thinks I'm crazy because I leave money with Ray's little cousins to make sure they come round and feed the cat every day. Ray's mum says she'll bring rice for Bawbee. Musa is going to occupy one of the huts while we're away. I despair. I envisage the entire one-and-a-half acres knee-deep in his detritus, milk tins and fag packets, abandoned clothing, sugar bags, charcoal cinders.

Ketta promises he will finish digging the well. Our friend Peter from Prestwick promises to pop by from time to time and see that the house is still standing and that Musa hasn't invited his entire family to come and stay. I should be happy about going 'home'. But this is my home. I shut my eyes and dream about bougainvillaea and put Glasgow out of my mind. . . .

The Runaway Hen

'Asalaam aleikum.'

The voice, small and shy as a kitten's, came from behind the wall next to the house. We went out into the dusk to investigate, and a brightly coloured cotton head-tie bobbed up like a flower, and under it the face of the groundnut lady. Big tears dribbled down her flat brown cheeks. The baby on her back grizzled in sympathy, till she hauled him to the front and stuck her teat into his mouth.

I am very fond of the groundnut lady, though I still don't know her name. She would come to our beach-bar every day, trudging along the sand, baby on her back, an enamel basin wrapped in a cloth and balanced firmly on her head, and she would sell us peanuts at fifty bututs a cupful. A vast amount of winnowing and beating and shaking and sifting, then roasting and drying, goes into the production of one basin of peanuts. The groundnut ladies work very hard for their tiny earnings.

I would play with the baby, slip him the occasional small coin, and once I gave her some baby clothes brought out by my daughter. She would give me extra peanuts or a couple of green, sweet little oranges. I had seen her crying before. Life always seemed to have it in for her. Once she came to us weeping because some thieves had broken into her home. She sat on a wobbly wooden bench in the beach-bar, choking back great gulps of sorrow, and described how they had pushed her son aside and taken everything – bedding, clothes, even the family rice basin.

Another time, when we weren't there, one of the staff told her we didn't need any of her peanuts and she went off sobbing and didn't come back for weeks. I met her in the market and told her it wasn't true; her peanuts were the best in the Gambia and if the tourists didn't eat them I certainly would, for I am an addict.

Nowadays, it is Ray's brother who tends the bar most of the time. It's off season, and the customers come at the rate of about two a day, so we reckoned we'd be better off here, watering the pumpkins, and brushing Musa's rubbish from the verandah, and watching Ketta the well-digger tunnelling – it sometimes seems – to the centre of the earth.

It was a surprise, therefore, when she appeared, tear-stained and dishevelled, peering plaintively over the wall. Her village is miles away. She spoke to Ray in Mandinka, her voice a sorrowful sing-song of desolation. She had, she told Ray, brought me a chicken because I was her friend and had given her gifts, and she wanted to repay my kindness. Bear in mind that even a small scrawny Gambian chicken, sold in the marketplace, is worth about thirty-five dalasi (over £2) – more than a day's wages for many people.

'Well, that's wonderful,' I said. 'Why is she crying, though?' 'The chicken escaped and ran away into the bush,' replied Ray solemnly.

She had walked from her village in some 33° centigrade heat, through the bush, clutching the unfortunate – but, as it turned out – resourceful fowl under her arm. On the edge of Bijilo Forest, it gave an almighty squawk and lunged for freedom. She chased it. It flapped its wings and ran, literally, for its life with the groundnut lady in pursuit, baby bouncing up and down on her narrow back.

Ray, not looking very happy about it, went with her to see if they could retrieve the troublesome tribute. They were gone for a long time. They came back dusty, scratched, empty-handed. The bird has flown. If it stays in the forest, it will meet up with snakes or malevolent monkeys, but serves it right!

I told Ray to tell her it didn't matter, really. It was the kindness of the thought that counted and I was very grateful; please don't worry. She looked at me with great tragic eyes and sighed. Life can be a pig sometimes. I gave her a cup of coffee and some baby oil and an old pair of shoes. I discovered that she had several children, mostly in the care of relatives. She didn't seem to have a husband. I told Ray we should run her home in the car. It was a long way to walk and darkness was falling fast. He sighed in exasperation. He cares for me with gentleness and affection, but he couldn't really see why an African girl with a baby on her back couldn't walk home the way she'd come . . . The journey took twenty minutes by car; heaven knows how long it would have taken her on foot. And all the way there, she kept saying: 'Mariama! Oh, Mariama!'

It was a dreich area, far from the scent of the sea, fawn flat landscape broken by the occasional twist of thorn bushes and a few huddles of mud-block houses. We left her outside one sagging mud-house, roofed in corrugated iron and fenced with palm branches that was her home. She was still crying as she waved goodbye.

Chicken is not an everyday meal. You only kill one of your hens when it is a festival or a wedding. The last one we were given was from Ray's mum, to celebrate Khoreti, the end of Ramadan. Ray put it in the kitchen cupboard and it jumped up and down screeching and shat all over the floor. The dog barked furiously (chasing everyone else's chickens is one of Bawbee's favourite pastimes) and the cat tried to shoulder the door in, a mad glint in its eye.

'Well, I'm not killing it,' I pronounced firmly, 'And I'm bloody well not plucking it either.' Chickens, so far as I'm concerned, are naked, immobile objects wrapped in polythene that you buy in a supermarket. He looked at me pityingly. European women can be pretty useless sometimes. He disappeared into the yard and lit a fire to singe off the feathers. He was holding the bird by its feet and carrying a pen-knife. I averted my glance. Local chickens have breasts that make Twiggy look like Samantha Fox. They have spindly thighs. They provide, individually, enough for two people provided the two people are not too hungry. Still, with plenty of rice, occra, peppers and tomatoes, it made a nice meal and a change from fish.

Life goes on lazily, with only the occasional drama. Like at 4 am when Bawbee began to bark dementedly. Ray grudgingly regained consciousness and stumbled about looking for a torch and his underpants. There was a clatter in the hall as he knocked over a broom and collected the cutlass. I stayed in bed. The dog made enough noise to waken the people in Basse, 250 miles away. Ray flashed the torch about, brandished the cutlass and shouted 'Ko ku kalla?' (who is it?) in a rather quavery voice. You can't blame him for being a bit twitchy. Last month, five intruders killed the watchman at our neighbour Saddan's house and broke in. Not that they'd find much.

Saddan, who has a wide winning smile, married a pregnant Englishwoman a few years ago. She wore a white satin dress and a veil over her bulging stomach and they spent the night in the Senegambia Hotel. She provided the money to start building the house, but later Saddan was told that the baby wasn't his, and she went back to England where, rumour has it, she is shacked up with anther Gambian. Saddan is unperturbed. The house has no glass in the windows and the walls and floor are bare concrete, but it's very large and he brings a succession of girlfriends there, since the only furniture is one large bed. It was too heavy for the thieves to carry.

Anyway, Ray finally came back to bed, and the dog settled down. Maybe it was an insomniac monkey or Saddan creeping home to his skeleton house after some romantic assignation.

Other intruders, of the many-legged variety, seem to be taking a pre-summer vacation, maybe gathering their forces for the rains. I haven't seen a cockroach for weeks. All that's left are the small black ants that have made a wee hole at the bottom of the living-room wall. They march in and out importantly, crawling over my feet as I type. If you leave them alone, they just tickle. If you slap at them, they bite.

The only tourists left are a handful of German and French people. I don't know why the British mostly stop coming at the end of April, because the weather through May and June is glorious. If Lamin gets even one customer at the beach-bar, he comes to tell us, it's such an unusual event. The other day though, we strolled along the sand just to see how things were going. We pretended to be tourists, sprawled on the benches sipping beer and staring at the empty beach. A white van came puffing along parallel to the sea and drew up beside us. It said Department of Health and Hygiene on the side. Five people climbed out and advanced across the sand. The two women were wearing elaborate African dress and high-heeled mules. Ray went to speak to them. They wanted to see round the restaurant. Since it's just a concrete base surrounded by woven palm, with a corner containing a table where we prepare the fish and cut up onions, looking round doesn't take long.

I could hear raised voices, mostly Ray's. I decided it would be better for me to stay where I was. There was a lot of arm-waving and expostulating and eventually they stamped off, saying to me as they passed, 'We hope you're enjoying your holiday in the Gambia, madam.' 'Oh, yes, it's lovely,' I said, trying to look like a prosperous tourist instead of an impecunious inkeeper.

'What was all that about?' I asked Ray.

'That woman, that fat one in the stupid dress, she said my kitchen wasn't a real kitchen', he spluttered, fair affronted.

'But it isn't!' I said reasonably.

You can't honestly call a rickety table, some boxes of plates and knives, and a wood fire whose smoke swirls all over the crockery so that we have to wash it ten times a day, and whose flames threaten sometimes to immolate us . . . you can't really call that a proper kitchen.

Ray looked hurt. This is the way Gambians have been feeding the tourists for years; now they want to change everything. The bucket of water, with its clip-on lid, is not satisfactory for holding our cooking water. We must get a water container with a small screw-top cover. Our staff must go to the health department and have their stools and urine checked, then be issued with badges with their photographs! This must change, that must change. A few of the bar-owners, the ones with a wee bit of cash, have built the kind of structures the Tourist Department want, hexagonal buildings made of concrete blocks, with about as much ethnic atmosphere as a skyscraper.

Will we fall into line and do the same? Maybe we can build something that looks pretty and Gambian, but complies with regulations? Or maybe it's all too much trouble and we'll finish building our little huts and try to make enough money to live from renting them out to tourists.

When the sun is shining, it doesn't seem to matter. You get overwhelmed by a kind of comfortable apathy. So long as there are enough dalasis to buy some cigarettes and some bread . . .

We sat on the sand, doodling, doing little drawings of how we might make the beach-bar look, and doing sums of how many bags of cement it would need. It all sounded too expensive so we gave up and went for a swim. Ray plunges headfirst into the breakers, while I tip-toe slowly out trying to keep my balance, and making frantic flapping breast-strokes in the calm troughs between the waves.

As we paddled out again, a happy sight met our eyes. The Health and Hygiene van had stuck in the sand and the passengers were all pushing, including the fat lady in the long dress and high-heeled mules. That'll teach them.

'Do you think we should go and offer to help?' I said. 'Mmmm. Maybe. In a minute,' Ray said, and settled back on a wicker beach-bed and shut his eyes.

Back Home . . .
and Back Home

'Put the cat's rice and fish up on the wall so that the dogs don't steal it. Don't forget to water my coriander. Please be nice to Stanley. Don't kick him if he digs up the bananas!'

Musa looks at me blankly. The idea of dogs and cats as pets with sensitive feelings and specific dietary preferences still hasn't quite got through to him. 'Mariama! Demal! (Go!) Don't worry, be happy. Bring me a present, eh?'

We bumped off over our suddenly precious patch of lumpy baked earth with its thorny weeds and hovering vultures. Ray's mum ran after the car, tears pouring down her face and soaking her orange cotton dress so that she looked like a wilting sunflower. She dragged little Ami behind her. 'Bye-bye, Mariama. Bye-bye. Choke. Sob. Snuffle.'

Back to Scotland to see the family, friends, Neighbours and EastEnders, real shops with a choice of paint-colours and shoe-sizes, numbered buses and nouvelle cuisine. Ray was ecstatic with anticipation. I was crying my heart out. The Gambia is my home. What would I do without the background grumble of the Atlantic nagging the white sand, the taste of ripe mangoes, the smell of woodsmoke and candlewax and the sight of the local kids carrying buckets of water on their heads on the way home from school?

The airport policeman looked as grumpy as I felt. A torrent of malevolent Wollof exploded from his fierce fleshy face on to Ray's head. He thrust his finger at my passport and then at my face. 'What's he on about?' I asked, still thinking about Stanley's wicked sad eyes and the kids chanting after me, 'Mariama, Mariama, why are you going?'

'He says you should have had your resident's permit,' said Ray, stony-faced.

'But it's not my fault,' I wailed, ready to turn around and go back to Bijilo on any old excuse. 'We're trying. We've filled in all the forms, three times. We've . . .' 'Shhhhh!' said Ray. Words were exchanged. We passed, eventually, into the departure lounge. We trotted up the steps of the Gambia Air Shuttle flight for Las Palmas. Tomorrow we'd fly on to London. Everything would be fine. Here we are, off on our hols. Things had to get better, hadn't they? After all, the preparations had been hell. There was the matter of Ray's visa, forms to pore over, photographs to submit, statements of income, intentions, references, absolute guarantees to be given that my husband was only going to Britain to see his mother-in-law and the Art Galleries and some pubs in Partick, then home to Bijilo. Honestly he wasn't a horde of unwelcome black immigrants aching to swarm all over Mrs Thatcher's hallowed soil for ever and ever.

He was interviewed and I was interviewed. In the end, grudgingly, he was given a six months entry permit to the UK. At one point, we'd thought it would be rather jolly to travel via Paris. But that would have needed a French visa. The French consul was on holiday. 'You must go to Dakar,' drawled the girl in the consular office behind the supermarket in Banjul. 'Dakar! Aaargh!' said Ray. According to him, Dakar is a den of knife-waving, murderous, thieving iniquity and he wouldn't go there again without a contingent of SAS to guard him.

British Airways was full. But the new Air Gambia flights were advertised enticingly on Radio Syd. The office was at the top of a disused warehouse, with no sign on the door.

'We have no plane yet,' they informed us smoothly. 'But we will have one soon. Come back next week, or the week after.'

We discovered that Gambia Air Shuttle had a special offer. Fly with them to Las Palmas, one night in a hotel, then on to London in a Spanish plane. You won't need a Spanish visa because you're in transit, they assured us. Wonderful. Here we go, here we go, here we go. We accept a free drink from the hostess and I assure Ray that the plane will not fall apart on take-off. His knuckles are as white as an African's knuckles can be.

But not as white as they became several hours later at Las Palmas passport control. 'Where is your Spanish entry permit?' 'I don't need one. Look, I'm going to London tomorrow morning. See, I have a British entry permit.'

'No good. Need Spanish. Stay here. Don't move.'

Two in the morning found us sprawled on the red vinyl benches in the transit lounge. I was a free agent but Ray was forbidden to step on to Spanish soil. The cleaners looked at us curiously and clattered their buckets loudly. The man in the somnolent snack-bar sneered disbelievingly when we offered him dalasi for a few mouthfuls of hot coffee. He refused Access or Visa. We had no pesetas. We burrowed into the bags, under the bundles of Gambian batik and Youssou Ndour tapes and coconuts until we found the cashew nuts we were planning to give to friends. 'Is the water in the loo safe to drink,' said Ray, who has been drinking village well-water since he was a baby but suspects all things Spanish, possibly with some justification.

We gazed at the neon-lit ceiling and wished we were in Bijilo, on the verandah, with the stars above, the upside-down crescent moon and the dog twitching his nose at the night sounds. By next afternoon we'd be in Heathrow. Ray would see his first travelator, his first cashline, his first underground train. Right now we were displaced persons. We huddled together and I fell asleep, while Ray peered around wakeful, convinced the place was full of bag-snatchers and cashew-nut collectors.

The day after we finally reached London we had to go to a posh lunch at Glasgow City chambers, where I was to pick up a Scottish Press Award plaque and a cheque which would be very useful for luxuries like new buckets and bougainvillaea plants. We bought Ray a suit on the way to the train. He looked astonishingly handsome and dignified, like a black President in civvies. I wore a suit made by Haddy's tailor in Serrekunda, and real shoes which made my feet pinch after so long in flip-flops. Ray shook hands with a number of eminent people and a lot of licentious journalists, and tried to look laid-back and uncaring. 'Has this got pork in it?' he hissed at the starter. There were 300 people there and we felt claustrophobic and longed for a bit of open space, preferably with palm-trees and lizards.

Everyone stared at us surreptitiously to see if we had bones through our noses or bare feet. 'Come to lunch . . . drinks . . . dinner.' So we went to dinner.

The conversation was rich. 'Of course one wife should be enough. But the way a Gambian sees it is, suppose his wife is ill or pregnant and can't cook his food for him and look after his other children and bring the firewood and the water? Then another wife could be very useful.' Ray gazed demurely round the table while I kicked him under the elegant table-cloth.

It was a dinner-party in Bearsden, with a clutch of stalwart feminists, who were in danger of choking over their asparagus spears. Why, they spluttered, couldn't the bloody husband cook his own dinner? And why couldn't he look after his own children? And why was the poor wife expected to bring the wood and water in the first place?

'But that's women's work,' said Ray innocently, knowing just what effect he was having. 'Women carry the water and make the food and plant the rice. It's what they were born for; that and having babies.' Chaos erupted as he sipped gently at his wine. Gambian men enjoy a good wind-up as well as the next man. And he did offer to wash the dishes later.

In the Gambia, they don't have dinner-parties. If you happen to be passing when the communal bowl of benachin is on the floor, you get down on your hunkers and thrust your hand into the rice with everyone else. But Ray is becoming quite blasé about carrot-and-orange soup, chicken chasseur and slabs of chocolate gateaux containing more calories than a week's meals in Bijilo.

Nor, now, does he goggle in amazement as I stick a wee bit of plastic into a slot in the wall and receive a cluster of tenners back. He still leaps off the top of escalators scared they'll swallow his feet, and he still considers the little green man at the traffic lights to be his own personal genie, summoned merely at the pressing of a button.

'How many people live in this compound?' he'll ask our hosts, as we stroll through dining-rooms, and studies, and spare bedrooms, and kitchens full of food-processors and double ovens and microwaves and Marks & Spencer readymade ravioli and risotto. 'Just the two of us,' they'll answer, surprised, and he thinks of his mum and dad and the whole extended family, clustered with the chickens and goats and not a toaster or an electric kettle between them. As for garlic crushers and electric carving knives . . .

So far as MY mum's concerned, she's taken to Ray a treat. In the beginning, when all this started, she'd said: 'He's, er, very BLACK, isn't he?' as though a pale coffee shade would have been less catatonic. Now we're having our second wedding in Martha Street registry office and she cuddles him and toasts him in champagne and we all get very tired and emotional in my wee sister's back garden in Fernhill. Ray's wearing the suit again, and I have a big hat with a chiffon scarf tied round it.

I cry again, just as I did at my first wedding to Ray in the little tin-roofed shack in the village.

That week, after Fernhill, we climbed the Cobbler. As we trudged upwards, a voice wafted up from the shores of Loch Long. 'Haw, Mary! That's that wummin and her man that was in the paper!' Fame at last. I had kind of wondered if people would snigger in the street at our different ages and colour-tones. No need to worry. Bus drivers and barmen and the steward on the Keppel midway between Tighnabruaich and Rothesay all recognised us and smothered us with kindness.

Glasgow Herald readers interrupted their tea and scones or their Soave and soda to come and pat us delicately on the shoulder and say: 'Awfully nice to see you in Glasgow!' Readers of the more rumbustious Daily Record shout 'Haw, missus, was that you in the paper? It wuz, sure it wuz?' In George Square, drunks shake Ray by the hand, tap him for 10p and say: 'By the way, son, the Cameroons was magic, so they wuz.' It is World Cup Year, remember?

One week we stay with farming friends, Margie and Andrew, in Cupar. Come and see the milking, says Andrew, whose farm appears to Ray (and to me) to take up half of east Scotland, lush with rasps and wheat and cauliflowers and self-satisfied animals.

Ray came back looking like someone who has seen a miracle. In the Gambia they milk one scraggy cow at a time, by hand, and get a few measly pints a day. Here he saw 240 being milked mechanically, skooshing out gallons and gallons of milk per udder. His father's 'farm' is an acre of rigid earth with some cassava and occra and maize. Here the cauliflower and peas and corn spread like hundreds of acres of green and gold knitting. He thought of the buckets of water carried from the well to the family plot, drops of moisture to stop everything shrivelling under the searing sun, and he looked sad. Until Andrew persuaded him to try a ' wee malt' and he smiled and went to sleep.

He has become addicted to pakora, soap operas, square sausage. He has been instructed by me not to pee at the side of the road. In the Gambia, there's not a lot of choice, but 'you CAN'T do that here' I squawk in the middle of Glassford Street. It's nice to be here, all the same, even with all these sanitary restrictions.

Nicer to think about going home, though.

We go, at last, after a hundred handshakes and hugs and half-pints of heavy and a quick gallop round London to look at the Queen's house.

In London, we take a trip down the Thames to Kew Gardens and eat in Soho restaurants. Ray conquers his fear of the Underground, which is more than I do. Our airline goes bust. Yes, in our absence, Gambia Air Shuttle has ceased operations. Iberia can take us to Las Palmas, but there will be no connecting flight home.

We panic, argue, make a lot of phone calls. We phone Brendan in Banjul and he and Peter square their shoulders and march into what's left of the Gambia Air Shuttle office and demand that we are flown home. 'You've to go to the Air Ghana desk when you reach Las Palmas,' Brendan tells us, 'They'll have a seat for you. Bring your wellies. It's bloody wet here!' I could hear a noise in the background like Niagara Falls, the Gambian summer rains, making everything green and fertile.

People will be planting feverishly, yams and corn, occra and peanuts. The women's cafos (collectives) will be standing knee-deep in mud in the rice-fields, which will turn into swathes of emerald in the winter months. The forest will be lush and the leaves will be laden with butterflies. Montior lizards will lurch across the muddy paths.

The sea will be calmer, coppery purple in the evening when the sun sinks under its surface. God will dook for it the mornings, as if it was a giant Hallowe'en orange, and restore it to its place in the sky. I can't wait to get back. Good-bye London. I'm going home.

Reunions and Washday Blues

Home again, bang in the middle of the rainy season.

Peter from Prestwick meets us at the airport as we stagger across the tarmac laden with gifts and dirty washing. We had peered down from the skies at a country transformed. What was brown and blasted to brick hardness when we left was now vividly green. Ray pointed from the window of the Air Ghana flight. 'Look, Mariama, look how beautiful it is.' On the ground it was 32°F and rising and the humidity put us into an instant warm sticky bath.

Peter drives with a frown of concentration on his face, like someone crossing a series of minefields, making the Suzuki clamber on to stretches of sopping bush when the road becomes too waterlogged. We splutter through viscous black puddles the size of George Square, steaming like soup under a blowtorch. The path we normally use is completely impassable and we make a snaking, zig-zag detour around Ker Seringe, lunging forward then reversing quickly when we feel our wheels being sucked downwards.

At the compound, the hard yellow earth we left behind us has become squelchy and clothed in green, thick with a dozen different grasses and emerald-green weeds. The bare dead baobab tree is radiantly leafed, its fruits hanging like Chinese lanterns. 'You see! I told you!' shouts Ray in triumph. Before we'd left for Britain the tree was gaunt and bare and I swore it was dead. This annual deliverance from the dead of trees and crops and small animals and insects is one of the miracles of West Africa.

A silver streak shoots across the grass and it is Penny the cat, skinny but glossy and purring like a lawnmower. Bawbee ambles casually towards us then leaps into my arms, grinning vacuously, scratching all the tender sunburn I acquired during our stopover in Las Palmas. 'Aitcha!' we howl in concert. Bawbee is doomed to be told to piss off at regular intervals for the rest of her life. But she is sleek and bonny and smiling toothily under her pale green eyes and I am happy to see her.

No sooner have we dumped our bags on the verandah and brushed some termite trails from around the doorposts than someone pulls a plug in the sky and the world is grey with water.

We give up our attempt to follow Musa and admire the papaya and Salem plum, the peanut plants and avocado seedlings that he has planted in our absence. The rain drums on the roof like a Fula rhythm and small lakes appear in seconds all over the garden. The rain bombards their surfaces so that miniature fountains are splashing everywhere we look. The lane outside is a river. The noise is incredible. Thunder rolls like the Edinburgh Military Tattoo and lightning flashes on and off like the laser effects at a pop concert in Wembley stadium.

In the evening, the rain stops and the wind comes up, clattering through the palm trees which rattle like skeletons. We drink attaya on the verandah. Already Ray's mum has come to welcome us, running through the mud, her cotton skirts sopping brown round the hem, arms outstretched. 'Mariama, Mariama!' she weeps through her smile. Little Ami is with her. She looks up solemnly then shakes hands with a small curtsey. This is how young children greet adults in the Gambia and I find it very touching.

Now the young men of the village come, brothers and half-brothers and cousins, to huddle on the verandah and sip tea and ask: 'How was Europe? How was Angleterre? How is your family? How is the Gambia for you now?' Ray tries to be laid-back and cool about his trip overseas, but finds himself describing castles and motorways, automatic banking and underground trains to a spellbound audience. 'You just put this little card into a hole in the wall, and all this money comes out!' he informs them, and they gasp.

The Gambia has turned into a sponge, alternately blasted to temporary dryness by a scalding sun, then doused in downpours which last for hours, sometimes all night, spurting through the louvre glasses of the windows so that the kitchen floor is awash, our bed is damp, and the water swirls over the verandah and seeps into the walls. Every sock, shoe, sheet and shirt that we left behind is mildewed and stinking with the odour of three months of damp air.

To think that once I cursed the dry powdery dust. Now what I've got instead is fawn scum that lies like silt on window ledges and shelves, and on the floor there are blobs like used engine oil carried from the garden mud on to the smooth red tiles.

On the second day home I throw myself, without enthusiasm, into an orgy of cleaning and washing. A pale green lizard, the colour of Bawbee's eyes, skitters across the bedroom wall when I move a chest of drawers, and long black things, like plastic worms with legs, saunter across the rugs or curl into pretty whorls under the bed. When I read in the evening, by candlelight, things drop on me or bump into me apologetically, squadrons of flies, snowfalls of tiny hair-thin insects, shards of platinum which settle like sun-whitened hairs on my arm then start moving over my wrist, and beetles which are round and black like ladybirds without spots. Squash them and there is an odour like old marzipan.

I wash clothes hour after hour, all the things we brought back with us and all the things we left behind to moulder in the monsoons. The village children hoist water from the well for me, bucketful after bucketful. Yes, the well is really finished; Ketta has kept his word. The water is still beige and cloudy, but it's ours. By the time I manage to get everything hung out, evening is falling, heavy and moist and windless, and I have to take it all in again and drape it over bookcases and chairs and on strings tied to door handles. The house smells like a Glasgow steamie.

There's good old Radio Syd to provide some distraction. Jimpex, the building material company, is pleased to announce a new shipment of pipes and joints 'for plumbing needs'. The Red Cross wants people to write poems about AIDS. The first prize is five hundred dalasis. Maybe I should enter, to try to recoup some of the money we spent in Britain. A Russian language class is being launched, the first in the Gambia. Will the Wollofs and Mandinkas and Fulas rush to learn Russian? It seems unlikely.

The alkalo is dead. He died two days before Tobaski, the celebration of the Prophet's birthday. He was my adopted father, who gave me away (or rather, sold me off) at my wedding in the village, an old rascal who couldn't write, 'signed' his name to legal papers with a thumb-print, but was as sharp-brained as a professor. I feel very sad. I also feel very angry with his son, who – keeping his grief to a minimum – rushed to send me a letter claiming, falsely, that I owed his father 14,000 dalasis for my land but he will settle, generously, for 10,000. I owe the alkalo nothing, so I send the son a message telling him to go and raffle himself and we heard no more about the matter.

As I wash and sweep and mop and eject various insect species, a procession of people come to say welcome back. Aunts and uncles, cousins, nieces and nephews. Nabi and Ibrahim, who tended the beach-bar in our absence. It's closed down now, partly because there's no trade in the summer, partly because they are needed on the land. At this time of year every Gambian, from the smallest child to the oldest grandmother becomes a frantic farmer, wading in the mud to plant peanuts and yams. Out in the fields, groups of women called *compin* in Wollof, sort of cooperative sisterhoods, plant rice, skirts hitched up round their thighs, bent double, their torsos swaying from side to side as they work.

Cousin Hassan, the soldier, comes to bemoañ the fact that he wasn't part of the West African peace-keeping force to Liberia. 'But

Charles Taylor says he'll shoot you all,' I say, remembering how worried we were about him during our absence, as tales of tribal rivalries and vicious feuding filtered through from Monrovia. 'Ha! Let him try!' he swaggers, and launches into talk of military matters, a boy soldier longing to be Clint Eastwood, God help him.

Yesterday Ray went to Banjul to try yet again to get my resident's permit. He was gone till midnight and I sat in the candlelight swatting insects, fretting and fuming and sweating. The bush-taxi wheel had come off on the new highway to Banjul. The driver and two passengers were hurt, or maybe killed, Ray wasn't sure. He and all the other passengers had to go to the police station to make statements. Never sit in the front of an African bush-taxi unless you're wearing a crash helmet. He also just happened to meet some of his friends who wanted to know all about his trip to tubab-land, preferably over some beers, drunk on an empty, nervous stomach. He lurched into the bedroom and collapsed into a deep sleep. I sat up scratching and swatting and dripping with sweat.

Today, though, not a drop of rain. The puddles are drying to a crisp ginger brown like spiced biscuits. Ray has just a teensy bit of a hangover, so we walk to the beach. The path down to the shore is grooved and channelled by the rains, so that we have to jump from side to side of the deep chasms, slithering on the mud. The beach looks clean, washed by the sea and the rain. The sand is ferociously white.

The forest behind it has turned into a lush jungle of trees and shrubs and grasses, where giant speckled butterflies bounce from branch to branch. We sit in a bower of palm leaves, built by Modou the fisherman, and decide that, on balance, this is better than Dunoon.

Weaver birds, butter yellow, cluster round the dog's ricebowl hoping for leavings. Vultures sit on the wall, waiting, perhaps, for me to expire from the heat.

Musa is still as scruffy and silly as ever, but he doesn't seem to have done anything really terrible while we were away, possibly because Peter used to call by to see if everything was still standing. The heap of sand and rubble around the well is peppered with his usual supply of litter, and the hut in which he was sleeping smells pungently, but perhaps that's because he was sharing it with Bawbee. And not just with Bawbee, but with a new arrival on the scene.

Its name is Maradonna, a name chosen by Musa at the height of World Cup fever, as he huddled in his hut listening to the rain above and the excited Radio Senegal commentary on my little Sony. It's a small dog like a fat fawn guinea-pig, with bandy legs and a poor sense of direction. It flops about in all directions at once, banging into things, skidding on the verandah tiles, eating absolutely anything it can lay its tongue on.

It follows both Musa and Bawbee like an adoring page-boy, waddling furiously to keep up. Penny the cat loathes it intensely and keeps batting it on the head with an unsheathed paw, so that it has a permanent open sore which I keep anointing with Dettol and antiseptic cream. It heals, then Penny swats it again. But it will survive. With a name like Maradonna, it must.

Fish-Cakes? No Bother at All!

The other day I invented Gambian fish cakes.
Here's the recipe.
First start the car. The battery is flat again, which isn't surprising, since three of the cells are kaput. Musa and Ray push it back and forward between the well and the baobab tree, while I release the clutch and jerk it into second gear, but nothing happens. They shout 'Now!' and 'Go for it!' in Wollof. Nothing happens. We should buy a new battery, but the smallest cheapest battery costs twice as much as in Britain. We go to one of the battery booths in Serrekunda almost every week, where several young men examine the offending object, shake their heads, tap bits of it with hammers, pour in acid, and quote us £1 for an overnight charge.

On this day, we push it along the thickly-sanded, hillocky track to the 'main' road, a red laterite corrugation which leads down to the beach where the trucks are scooping away building sand at a rate of many tons every day, or up to Sukutu, a neighbouring village. One of the sand-lorries coming up from the foreshore with its ecologically disastrous cargo stops for us, and we jump-start the car. Many people stop to look, as jump-leads are a novelty here.

At last we set off to the fishing village of Tanji to buy the bonga fish.

We're rattling along on our zig-zag course between the bush and the sea; the ball-joints are in a perilous state, and one shock-absorber is catatonic. A group of people standing beside a broken-down bush-taxi leaps in front of us looking for a lift. We explain, since it seems to have escaped their notice, that this is a very small car and we can only squeeze three people in the back. We accept two old ladies and a young man, who claim they are rushing to a funeral in Tanji, and drive off leaving the others shouting and pleading and kicking the bush-taxi in frustration.

There is no bus service to the fishing villages of the south. Tanji, Brufut, Sanyang and Gunjur are served by a scrawny network of ancient bush-taxis. Alternatively there are donkey-carts. Or feet.

We pass Ghanatown, a small enclave entirely populated by Ghanaian immigrants who came for the fishing and stayed. You recognise Ghanatown before you reach it, by the noxious odour which rises from spindly wooden tables spread with hundreds and hundreds of skate and stingrays stretched in the sun to dry. How anyone could live here I can't imagine. There is a small Baptist Church, a white hut with a tin roof.

We stop at Brufut, where we buy lobsters for the beach-bar. They are spiky crayfish of a luxurious blue and turquoise shell-colour, and they lurch about in the boot making scrabbling noises. We buy a couple of beers in Ibrahim's beach-bar. He is a gentle, generous Rasta, who is growing flowers and papaya trees from seed around his place. When the wind blows inwards from the stalls where they sell squid and skate and shark, there is a nasty smell but when the wind is in another direction it is sweet and fresh and pretty.

At last we reach Tanji. We drop off the mourners, who had waited patiently while we haggled for the crayfish and drank our beer. We call in to see Peter who is still wrestling with the problems of unifying a group of villagers whose ethnic and tribal backgrounds are an uncoordinated hodge-podge, into a cohesive construction unit. The community centre is still a rectangle cut into the ground where the concrete will eventually rise. A violent argument over the position of some buttresses is raging, so we make our excuses and leave, for the smoking sheds on the shore.

Bonga fish are like small dark kippers. They taste wonderful, a bit like smoked trout, but they have a multitude of bones for every centimetre of five-times-smoked succulent flesh. If they are smoked the full sequence, they become hard and leathery and they are packed into crates to be exported to the surrounding countries. We haggle over a box of them and pay fifty bututs (about fourpence) per fish. The dog and cat will be sure of breakfast for a couple of weeks, and I have the ingredients for my fish cakes – at least, I have the central ingredient. There's still a long way to go.

Day two. Boil potatoes. We use the gas-ring now, which is less picturesque but a damn sight easier than my African wood cooker (a cylindrical drum with a hole in the middle in which you burn brushwood and palm fronds and coconut shells while smoke blackens your face and makes your eyes water). Potatoes are a problem. Our farming tycoon friend from St Andrews, Andrew, who spent many hours in the beach-bar drinking Gambian-bottled plonk, told us we'd never get good potatoes in the Gambia because the place was riddled with blight. He was something big in the Potato Marketing Board in Scotland, so he must know what he's talking about. Certainly all the potatoes we buy are imported, and pretty pathetic specimens at that. I hack off greenish-black blobs and save as many white bits as I can.

Next, chop a yam into small pieces, wishing I had a mincer, and wishing that yams weren't so tough and stringy. They, from the cassava plant, are, along with rice, the staple diet of the region. They taste like parsnips, but are often left in the ground so long that they grow as tough as old boots. I also chop finely some carrots, onions, occra, leeks, green peppers and tomatoes. The tomatoes and occra come from our own plants which Musa grew under the banana palms. The tomatoes are small and have nasty black bits in the middle, but I carve off the usable pieces. The occra, ladies' fingers, is slimy and sticky and I hate it, but it is almost as prolific as cassava and it would be a waste not to use it. The other vegetables came from Serrekunda market and only took about two hours of sweat, toil and bargaining to purchase, at prices which make Marks & Spencer look cheap.

The real challenge is in flaking the flesh of the bonga fish from the bones. It's even worse that salvaging the reasonable rice from the nasty, dirty Mauritanian rice which the shopkeeper in the village has the cheek to sell at one dalasi a cup. It is always full of nameless foreign bodies, and I should point out that 'a cup' in measuring terms is not a nice big breakfast cup but a small tin receptacle the size of an egg-cup. Ray helps with the fish. There is a sea of bones all round us and the cat is trying to climb up my legs in a frenzy.

About a tablespoon of fish is rescued from each elaborate skeleton of bones and charred black skin. Halfway through, we have to stop, because Ray's mum has arrived with six mangoes, tied up in a piece of frayed batik. I say 'Jerejeff!' (Thank you) several times, forbearing to mention that the cupboard is already heaped high with mangoes brought by local schoolchildren, Ketta the well-digger, Musa's wife, and various grandmothers and aunts. In Scotland, maybe you take a box of shortbread when you visit someone, or a bottle of wine. Here, everyone gives mangoes, mainly because there are so many of the damn things. As I've said before, the Gambia has mangoes like the county of Argyll has fir trees, some of them bigger than the oldest English oak, every twig dripping with fruit, which, in the rainy season, drops to the ground and rots, attracting millions of flies.

We go back to the bonga. An altercation breaks out behind the house, between Bawbee and a herd of cows which are trampling the bananas and trying to eat the fringed green leaves. Three vultures settle on the wall, hoping something will perish. Finally, I mix all the ingredients together with a fork. No, Euphemia, there are no food-processors here. I shape them into patties, dip them in egg (the eggs are brought from the Chinese poultry farm in our village) and fry them in groundnut oil. Ray says they're fantastic and I'm the best cook in Africa. 'Oh, it was nothing!' I say. In local terms, it was nothing. A local woman will spend hours sitting on a low stool pounding a few peanuts in a small wooden bowl with a large wooden pestle the size of a baseball bat to make peanut sauce. She will spend more hours grinding millet to make coos-coos, and that's after she has tramped around the bush searching for firewood and drawn buckets of water from the well in the centre of the village.

There is a naming christening in the village. All the women are pounding furiously to make flour pancakes, globules of pounded maize fried in hot oil. The men are drinking attaya at the bantaba, and playing Crazy Eight. I tend to mention this game a lot, so here are the rules, more or less. It could liven up your Sunday afternoons.

Each player has six cards, and one card from the pack is placed face up to start. For reasons best known to themselves, Gambians play in an anti-clockwise direction. Play a two, and your opponent has to take two cards from the pack. Play a jack, and you jump the next player, who misses a turn. Play a ten, and it reverts the order of play, back to the opponent on your other side (or to you, if there are only two playing). Play an ace, shouting 'Are you strong?' and if your opponent can't play another ace, he has to lift two cards from the pack. Otherwise, you have to try to play cards of the same number or suit (just like Twist) or pick up another card from the pack. An eight has special powers; it can change the suit to whatever you choose. A joker, called Bazooka, with a great flourish, obliges the next player to lift two more cards, and allows you to change the suit to anything you fancy. The idea is to get rid of all your cards. The remaining player or players must count what it is left in his hand (face cards only count as one) and when his score reaches one hundred he's out, and you've won.

So back to the naming christening. The prayers and blessings have taken place in the morning. Now it's loaf-about time for the men, and work-like-mad time for the women. The new mother is sitting on the bed, while her baby is passed round the old ladies of the compound. 'Isn't he an ugly child?' they'll say. Since the babies are almost invariably beautiful little mites of placid temperament and skin like silk this bothers me, till I realise it is unlucky to flatter or praise a child or it will grow up vain and lazy.

'Is it a boy or a girl?' I whisper to Ray. 'I don't know,' shrugs Ray, who doesn't seem to care one way or another. No-one except me takes very much interest in the actual baby or its mum, as everyone is too busy talking, cooking, playing cards. The mother looks wonderful. Many babies die in the Gambia and many mothers die at the birth, but those who survive are tough and strong and beautiful. Long after we've gone home we hear the drums and disco music. And of course, the grandmother of the new arrival gave me a gift – some mangoes! We in turn slipped some money into the hand of the proud father, strutting around like a barnyard cockerel and also to the mother, who is often ignored as though it was the man who'd gone through the whole arduous business of pregnancy and delivery.

Life and death are always close together. The other day, Radio Gambia announced that ten people had died and innumerable livestock succumbed after a rampant outbreak of anthrax. Mindful that we had – very unusually for us – eaten beef from a village cow the previous day, I screeched 'Where? Where s the outbreak?'

'Oh, across on the North Bank somewhere,' said Ray calmly. All the same, I think I'll stick to fish from now on. Maybe I can streamline the fish-cake recipe to hours instead of days?

This morning, the verandah was covered with a fine brown powder from a paper parcel Bawbee had got hold of and chewed to shreds. It was Musa's 'coffee', made from grinding up some kind of local seed-heads. It reminded me of the time in Glasgow, years ago, when people of an ecological bent tried making acorn coffee. I gave Musa some supermarket Nescafe as compensation for his chewed parcel. But maybe I'll get him to show me how to make my own. To gather the seeds and dry them and pound them should only take a few days . . .

Building for Beginners

A few months ago, my shopping list contained items like fish, garlic, paper cups, Bacofoil and blocks of ice for the beach-bar. Hot hours were spent trudging round the market haggling over tomatoes and prawns, then parking the car in the bush behind our pitch and carrying the shopping over the rough terrain, ignoring Lamin's warnings that he saw a snake there the week before.

In the moistness of the night, dirt and dampness would drop down from the palm roof on to the plastic cloth over the tables and benches, ants would penetrate the sugar and sand would blow in from the beach, so the first couple of hours were spent sweeping out, wiping, washing, peeling onions and gathering firewood. The ice, melting fast, would be packed into the rusty old freezer, unconnected to any power supply, and we would pray that it would keep the fish cool long enough to last the day. Gradually, we bought less and less as business trickled away like the melting ice.

Now the beach-bar sits empty. Extra palm branches shield it from the worst of the summer rains; the freezer has become completely red from rust, the lizards are keeping house in the nooks in the walls, the crabs are digging furious holes where once the tourists wiggled their toes in the sand. It is off-season, hot and clammy but as unprofitable as a cold wet February in Rothesay. Will we open up again when the season starts? We don't think so.

The Tourist Office are bustling about trying to tart up the Gambia's beach-side image. They would prefer to reduce, dramatically, the number of beach-bars and they would like those that remain to be built as permanent structures of concrete. They've even designed a master-plan, showing a hard hexagonal outline in concrete blocks, with proper storage rooms and kitchen, and ladies' and gents' toilets! Remember that there is no water supply reaching anywhere near the beach. Our lads tramp five hundred yards along the beach and fetch buckets of water on their heads, from the standpipe next to the defunct casino. We built a palm screen round a small sandy area with a toilet roll hanging on a bit of string and a bucket of water and a towel. This was for the privacy of lady customers, who couldn't, like their menfolk, go into the bush when nature called.

But to build proper toilets with lavatories and wash-basins would be expensive – and pointless without a water supply. If we scrape up every dalasi we have and build what they'd like us to build, how many years would it take us to make our money back? Would we want to start selling beefburgers and chips, surrounded by concrete? We sit once more scribbling sums on bits of paper, adding up the cost of all that masonry, plus new tables and chairs and kitchen equipment, and in the end we decide to abandon ship. It is an emotional moment for Ray. He started this place three years ago. Before that he'd worked for the German-Gambian Forestry Company (he speaks fluent German) and hated having a boss. Having his own place, even if it was just a little shack with a wood fire and rickety tables and stools, was something special for him. He made many friends from Germany, Britain and Scandinavia. They would come back to visit his place when I was there and he'd introduce me and we'd cook lobsters or barracuda for them. If we close down, they'll come back next season and find an empty patch of sand. I worried. If I voted for closing down – which I know is the practical, pragmatic solution – would he blame me for changing his life?

But he's pretty pragmatic himself. 'If we forget the beach-bar, we can concentrate on our huts. And I can write to all my old customers and maybe they'll come and see us and stay in our huts.' So we took the plunge, and decided to build Hut Three, to join the two little round huts we built before the rains. Our plan is to entice travellers, rather than tourists, who will appreciate a real African-style holiday far from the bingo and Black and White Minstrel Shows (yes, honestly, I've seen them with my own eyes!) of the hotels.

Last time we just let Uncle-the-Builder, as I call him, get on with it. A skinny, sweet-faced, devout Muslim, who interrupted his work five times a day to say his prayers and brought me grapefruit and coconuts from his prolific garden at the entrance to the village. A pillar of the community – but he ripped us off in spectacular fashion.

'I am making no profit on this at all,' he used to say sorrowfully, as we handed him large bundles of dirty green ten-dalasi notes for his latest requisition of gravel or sand or paint. 'I only do it for such a low price because Relwan is like a son to me.' Then would follow a heart-rending catalogue of cement prices and increases in the cost of a lorryload of sand. My heart would bleed. But, even so, when I considered his bottom-line estimate for this third hut, which was to be built rectangular in contrast to the two circular ones, it seemed unco high to me. Little seeds of doubt and suspicion entered my canny Scots mind.

'Ah, Mariama,' he would say, 'if only it was you who had to go and find all the materials. Then you would know how hard it was for me.' His palms were folded devoutly in his lap and his head was bowed humbly in the sight of Allah. He sat up suddenly when I rose to the challenge. 'OK,' I said boldly, 'I hate to see you suffering all these problems. From now on, we'll buy the materials, and we'll pay you a fee for construction and overseeing the project.' He smiled weakly. 'Oh . . . er, yes, yes, very good. It will be a big weight off my mind.' But he didn't look very pleased.

That is how I came to do a swift practical crash course in quantity surveying, estimating, building methods and purchasing. First I drew a plan of exactly the size and shape the hut was to be. Then I sat down and scribbled on bits of paper while Ray looked suitably impressed, if somewhat bewildered. I think my highest moment was dredging old Pythagoras from the dim recesses of my memory to help me work out the length of the corrugate for the sloping gabled roof. 'If the square of the height of the roof, plus half the width equals the length of the corrugated iron sheeting, squared, in other words, the hypotenuse, then the corrugate needs to be eight feet long,' I muttered. Ray looked completely baffled, and went off to argue with a truck-driver about the price of a load of sand.

The fact that Peter has been overseeing the building of the Tanji Community Project was a godsend. As a hardnosed Scot, he was able to tell us exactly how much cement it took to make how many blocks, and how many barrowloads of sand and gravel to mix with each bag for the right consistency. He told us how many blocks to the metre, how many steel rods to buy.

He added many other technical niceties that allowed me to look tough and knowledgeable in the face of the most imaginative pleadings of the people selling the materials. For they, of course, saw a tubab coming, a female tubab at that, and asked for prices as high as the sky. I, in turn, told them I knew exactly what the regular price was, so don't mess with me, mate. It was about that time that we found it was quite possible to buy a load of sand for two-hundred dalasi, or even one-hundred-and-fifty. How very odd, we reflected, that our worshipful uncle had charged us seven-hundred-and-fifty for the last load he purchased on our behalf!

So now my shopping list is different. It includes things like bags of cement, palm-runs (palm trunks split down the middle into long, strong sinewy, narrow timbers) for rafters, timbers for door-frames, louvre glasses for windows, paint, nails, hinges, hacksaw blades. A trip to the cement-suppliers goes thus: first you check out three other suppliers, so that you have an approximate idea of the correct price. The cost of cement has shot up so much recently that there have been questions in Parliament about hoarding and artificial price-fixing.

Then negotiate with the owner of a dilapidated Land Rover who will deliver for us. A clutch of these chaps hang about with their vehicles outside Jimpex, the building store at Kanefing. Each has at least three or four companions, who leap upon anyone leaving the store offering to deliver his goods, fighting off the competition with many shouts and grabbings of the hapless customers' arms. We chose Dawda and the opposition retreated to watch for another quarry. Next we stand in the blazing sun and the appalling sticky humidity of the rainy season, sweat trickling down our faces and arms, watching the cement being loaded. The loaders' skins and tattered clothes are all a uniform pale musty grey, caked with cement, so that they look like moving pottery figures. They load fifty bags, carrying them on their heads, the dust falling on them and adding to their ghostly appearance. I suggest putting down the tailgate of the Land Rover to make access easier. 'If we do that, it will fall off,' they tell me patiently.

Clouds of cement fill the air and my nostrils and throat. An old man hobbles out and waves for me to go into the office and pay. Several young men are there, all talking at the tops of their voices so that every time we start counting the money, we lose the place and have to start again. We share our dusty bad temper between us, cursing the boys. He screeches Aitcha! at them, and I show off my minimal Wollof by remarking that they sound like 'gannar' (chickens). He is impressed. We start counting again.

Some sheets of hardboard, a hardwood door and miscellaneous bits and pieces are balanced precariously on top of the fifty bags and we set of, me in front, in the 2CV, the Land Rover behind, clanking and shuddering in a terrifying manner, its lower regions threatening to drag in the mud. A tropical cloudburst turns the air into a never-ending waterfall and we inch forward through puddles like lakes.

The police, who set up checkpoints, I sometimes think, wherever they feel like it and whenever they feel bored or broke, decide to stop the Land Rover. Locals say there is a system in their approach – ten dalasi to ignore signals that don't work, fifteen for no brake-lights, twenty-five for no brakes. 'Have you stolen these goods?' they bark menacingly at the driver. We park in a trench of Flanders mud and run back, drenched, to produce receipts and glare indignantly at the sodden coppers. Looking disappointed, they wave us on.

The 2CV gets bogged down in a particularly unpleasant puddle and the delivery team leaps out, throws off its flip-flops and pushes me out, grinning broadly, probably thinking in Wollof: 'Bloody woman driver.' Their own vehicle gets even more bogged down in the glutinous gunge outside our gate and I smirk, while trying to look sympathetic. When free, it lurches into the compound leaving deep furrows in what we laughingly call our driveway, which is the section of ground in which Musa hasn't managed to plant bananas or peanuts.

Previously, before we became steely-eyed, flint-hearted building experts, we would see bags of cement coming and going. We had no idea how many were being used, what the cost or how many managed to grow legs and walk. Now we dispense the stuff one bag at a time and I walk about with a notebook, looking suspicious and tut-tutting a lot, and making observations about shuttering and lintels. It lacks a little of the charm of serving shrimps and beer on the beach, and there are times when you want to wrap a piece of steel rod round the neck of some trader and drop a bag of cement on his head from a great height. But it has a certain fascination. And we reckon we've cut Uncle-the-Builder's estimate by seventy per cent.

There are ways to get away from it all. Last night Peter brought a bottle of Rose d'Anjou and we went to the beach to fish by moonlight, taking the bottle and three glasses. I caught a shiny-nose (so called because its snout glows in the dark). Ray caught a catfish. A pirogue was silhouetted against the skyline, and lightning flashes illuminated the forest behind us. 'Do you miss the beach-bar?' I asked Ray. 'What beach-bar?' he replied.

Not That I'm One to Gossip, But . . .

Poor Doodoo was looking very depressed. He is forty, with a grizzled beard and a small pot-belly. His backside sticks out like a shelf when he walks, which he usually does with a buoyant swagger. He is one of our close friends, a man given to philosophical discussion and reminiscence.

We were therefore sad to see him shuffle glumly into Uncle Dembo's and slump over a beer with a heavy sigh. 'My wife hasn't written to me since July,' he revealed. 'Why she is ignoring me I cannot understand.' And he slumped even further down into his chair.

The tale of Doodoo and his German wife Renata deserves telling. She is German and used to come regularly to the Gambia. She even bought shares in various plots of land and on one pretty spot behind Bijilo she set Doodoo to building a house and planting a garden. Their marriage was in the village, a Muslim ceremony. There was one small unconventional detail; Doodoo already had a Gambian wife and numerous children. But apparently Renata knew this and accepted it.

Last time she was here though, she was, said Doodoo, in a contentious frame of mind. The neat rows of vegetables planted by Doodoo in their garden didn't impress her. She accused him of using the money she sent him to finance his first wife and family. 'I want to meet this woman,' she demanded. Ironically, when she did, the two of them got on like a house on fire. For the rest of her visit, all was sweetness and light. Doodoo showed her how hard he'd worked, pulling up water from the well and moistening the steel-hard ground round the plants, and she said she loved him and would come back soon.

'But she hasn't written to me. She hasn't left any phone messages. A man cannot understand such behaviour,' Doodoo moped. He has begun to lose weight. The buoyant bum now seems to trail mournfully behind him. The perky pot-belly is disappearing. We try to bolster him up with jokes and words of encouragement, but nothing helps.

In the case of Yeti, an Austrian who fell in love with a Gambian, things happened the other way round. They married and she invested in his beach-bar. Things began to go downhill very quickly. Yeti wold be there, making sure the place was clean, serving cups of coffee to homesick Europeans, reading a book and gazing thoughtfully out to sea. The husband rarely showed up. 'She looks very sad,' I whispered to Ray one day. 'Her husband has just taken another wife,' he explained.

Soon afterwards, Yeti told us she was going home. She would walk along the beach every day, a dumpy, dejected figure, her small dog scampering at her heels. 'I am hoping someone will send me some money so that I can buy a ticket, and also get a box made for the dog. I wouldn't go home without my dog.'

Joanna, a blonde barmaid from Worcester, pined over Kebba, a safari-truck driver. He told her he loved her. In the middle of their romance he asked her for some money to help pay the costs of a naming christening, which he said was for his brother's child. It was only afterwards that she learned that the baby was his, and he'd married its mother – as is the custom – the day before the christening. Joanna brooded and wept, and Kebba kept sending her little love notes, saying he still fancied her but his family had forced him into the local marriage. That just made her cry more.

Brendan, our Irish friend, has had a run of bad luck which has nothing to do with his love-life, but puts a new complexion on the phrase 'the luck of the Irish.'

First, he went to Soma and Mansa Konka, up-river, to visit friends. They all gathered in a sinister Soma pub, where the locals glowered at them like characters from Cold Comfort Farm. Only when they'd left and gone many miles down the road, did they discover that Brendan's pocket-book, containing money, driving-licence, passport and other essentials, was missing from his pocket.

When they managed to find a police station, things got a bit out of hand. The police here don't do things by halves. They swooped on the pub and arrested everyone in it. Brendan had an uneasy feeling that their methods of questioning would be less than gentle, but he never got his pocket-book back.

He was just getting over that, when he had to make a trip to Basse, the big trading town right at the other end of the Gambia. It's a sweltering place full of wharves and warehouses and traders from Senegal, Mali and Mauritania. Senegalese cattle rustlers sneak over the border at night and steal Gambian cows; they are, say the locals, armed with guns and cutlasses. Brendan survived a couple of days there then, thankfully, headed home, only to have the long-suffering engine of his jeep finally groan, splutter and shudder to a grinding halt. It wasn't just feeling poorly; it had died, and nothing was going to restore it to life except a major transplant.

The jeep had to be hoisted all the way back to Bakau behind a breakdown truck, at enormous expense. Meanwhile, Brendan borrowed a Renault and someone tried to steal it, in the process of which they broke the ignition lock. The Renault went to the garage. When it was time to collect it, the watchman wouldn't let him have the car because his boss had gone home. He borrowed Peter's jeep and locked himself out of it. He keeps telling himself, and us, that nothing else can possibly go wrong, but it probably will.

Running a car here is hard. Only the most robust vehicle can stand up to the tortuous ridged and rutted tracks through the bush, which are, nevertheless, better by far than the ostensibly tarmacadamed roads which have a million hidden bumps and potholes. In summer, a car left to sit in one place for long suffers from the climate; its tyres get soaked in the torrential rains then blasted by 40°C of heat from the sun, which can ruin them for ever. Spare parts are hard to get and expensive.

Gambian mechanics try hard, but sometimes they have their off-days. Peter's Suzuki had a series of problems which graduated upwards from a new gasket through to a new engine.

We would meet him sometimes in Serrekunda, queueing for a bush taxi or trudging along the road in the rain, shoulders hunched, muttering '**** this for a game of soldiers'. Meanwhile, we have our own – comparatively minor – problems. Like Momodou the carpenter.

Momodou works as a beach attendant-cum-lifeguard at the nearby watersports club. Or rather, doesn't work, as he and his colleagues have been on strike for several months for better pay and conditions. But the management seems not to have noticed. Possibly the fact that the chaps who owned the watersports gear – sailboards and speedboats and suchlike – walked off in a huff leaving a noticeable void in the services the club could offer, made Momodou's absence seem of minor importance.

Since he was a carpenter by trade (this is what he told us at the time; in fact we discovered later that it is his brother who is a carpenter and Momodou just hoped some of his skills had magically transferred themselves to him) we thought it would be a kindness to offer him some work. Today he got into a bad mood about something, handed in the saw and plane (which belong to us) and stomped off the site.

Then the builder insisted that he needed to sub-contract a vital part of the construction of our hut to a man whose genuine job description is 'the steel-rod bender'. He is the man who comes in with his blowtorch and heats and bends the steel rods used for strengthening the concrete.

When these arguments with the great Gambian workforce get too much for me, I try to find solace in gardening. I dig and hoe and rake and gently press seeds into place – seeds of pumpkin, sweetcorn, carrots, onions, marigolds and geraniums. Every morning I rush out hoping to see the sweet green shoots curling eagerly upwards. All I see are large black millipedes slinking away, licking their lips.

The occra alone thrives. But since Peter described 'sooppa', the soup the village women make from occra, as having 'the consistency of snotters', I've gone right off ladies' fingers, thank you.

Musa, of the ham-like hands and boat-like feet, has no such problems. His corn and yams and peanuts proliferate all over the compound. We sack him on an average once a month. He is filthy, foolish, fretful, forever wheedling cigarettes and dalasi from our friends while doing innumerable outside jobs on the side. If he goes to the village to buy us some candles he takes a couple of hours, and spreads colourful tales about his employers as he goes. I suspect he has told them he works for a rich tubab. This rankles, as I try to battle with a rice diet, a constant overdraft and a feeling that a financial chasm is yawning a few centimetres in front of my feet. Whatever the reason, a constant stream of visitors arrives on the verandah, to greet us, ask after our health and our families, and request us to 'dash them' fifty dalasi to go to a naming christening, or ten dalasi to go to a disco, or 300 dalasi for a child's school fees, or two dalasi to buy four loose cigarettes, or 150 for a sack of rice.

Fortunately, they don't take offence when we say No, but just smile and shrug and go off to try someone else.

I mentioned the rice diet. It's true I now make better benachin than Ray's mum (or so he tells me, but I don't suppose he'd say it to her). But I tried something different last night. If you ask Ray what he liked most about Scotland when we were there on holiday, he won't tell you the Burrell Collection or Frasers or the Citizens or even the underground trains. He'll tell you 'Pakora!' His mouth waters nostalgically for the Ashoka and the Shish Mahal. So, using a recipe from the excellent Shish-Mahal recipe book, thoughtfully sent out to me by my son, and spices bought in the Indian supermarket in Bakau, I made my first-ever pakora. It tasted not at all bad. Even Musa has pronounced it OK, but then I think Musa would eat anything he was offered.

The only other bit of gossip is that Bawbee is in heat.

She is being wooed virtually simultaneously by four bright-eyed curly-tailed tenacious Gambian dogs. The noise of their romantic unions keeps us awake at night. Bawbee plays hard-to-get, snarling and chasing them away from the gate by day. This is obviously for our benefit.

At night, she sneaks out and takes her pick, and in the morning she is slumped sleepily on the verandah with a stupid grin on her face. I rather like the fact that, in canine terms at least, one female can receive the ardent attentions of four males. This is the exact opposite of the human state of affairs in this merrily Muslim country, as Renata, Yeti and Joanna would testify through their tears.

Take One Small Chicken

'There is a man in this village. If you have a sprained ankle, or even a broken leg, he will fix it. First, he will take one chicken and break its leg.'

We all gaped at Ray in disapproval. Poor wee chicken.

'Then he will cause the chicken to get up and walk, and when the chicken walks, the patient will walk also, all his pain gone.' Ray sat back smugly, waiting for us to be impressed at his version of the Gambian-style NHS. We looked a bit upset about the chicken so he told us that, if it was just a sprain, you could go and find a mother of twins. You ask her to stand on your bad ankle and shoogle about a bit, and you'll be as right as ninepence in no time at all.

Unfortunately for Ray, his audience was less than spellbound as he recounted, in all seriousness, these interesting and economical forms of treatment. We were sitting on the end of Tendaba jetty at midnight, with Peter and Brendan and two vivacious Irish girls they'd met in Serrekunda and brought along for the drive. I don't know what Selina and Barbara thought of the journey, over roads like the surface of the moon, only with more craters. But since they were both medical graduates, it was obvious what they thought of the Gambian approach to medicine.

'Yes, to be sure,' said Barbara sweetly. 'We could get one hospital bed for the patient, and one for the chicken.' I should mention that a fair amount of beer, Bacardi and night air having been consumed, we had been lulled into lazy conviviality by the slap of the bottle-green water on the jetty, while turtles drifted under the surface and African music floated from the fishing village nearby. The conversation had become zanier and zanier and Ray had been getting ribbed more and more.

'Tell me, then,' said Peter, a typical contentious Scot, 'why do Gambian men always hold their – er, the front of their trousers – while they dance? While the women hitch their skirts up and waggle their bums? Is it some old sexual tradition?' Ray opened his eyes wide and shook his head innocently. 'I have never seen this. I don't know what you mean.'

Oooo! Wash his mouth out with soapy water! In fact, anyone who's been in the Gambia and watched the locals dancing to the pulsating rhythms of drums and other seductive instruments knows that it is wonderfully, uninhibitedly erotic, full of thrusting pelvises and hips, a hundred times more lusty than anything Presley or Jagger ever did on stage.

As for Gambian healing methods . . . I mentioned them to our friend from Farafenni, Father Mike, who came to Bijilo to show off the new Nissan pick-up the Bishop has finally bought him to replace the rattle-trap he had before. 'Mother-of-twins, eh?' he reflected. 'Ach, sure, it's no different from what happens in Ireland, where the seventh daughter of a seventh daughter has special powers.'

We haven't sprained or broken anything yet, so I haven't been able to check out the local therapies. But I wouldn't rush to pooh-pooh anything. When I burned my arm, the villagers told me I should put raw egg on it, which probably wouldn't have been any less effective than the cream they gave me at the clinic. For colds, eat calves foot cooked with enough chilli pepper to blow your head off. Also used for colds, sore lips, earache and chest infections is the ubiquitous mentholatum, which, literally, grows on trees – or at least is made from the eucalyptus trees with their slender willow-like leaves, which grow everywhere in the Gambia.

When Ray got an abscess in his ear, however, more conventional steps had to be taken. There is virtually only one type of antibiotic available in the Gambia, and it is used for everything. We bought it, and some ear-drops, from a chemist in Bakau, and I sloshed a lot of Dettol around, and he was fine in a couple of days. At least he didn't insist on rushing to the hospital, which is what many Gambians seem to do for very trivial complaints. They're only really satisfied if they get an injection, and it seems to me that the staff in the local clinics are needle-happy, zapping huge doses of penicillin for the merest pain or cough. One woman who was doing some washing for me complained of pains around her shoulders and back. My diagnosis was that it was either the onset of menstruation or she'd pulled up too many heavy buckets of water.

But she went to the clinic in Sukuta and came back with various pills, and a certificate that said she was being treated for 'fever and dizziness'. She was as cool as a cucumber and as steady as a rock. I don't think Gambians are necessarily very good at explaining their symptoms.

Boils and abscesses are very common. My first few months here saw me peppered with small boils on the back of the neck and the legs. You see kids with shaved heads and their scalps a mass of sores.

But they seem to clear up as fast as they come. Respiratory infections are endemic, and many babies have a constant wheezy cough. They never complain, but the adults only need to have a wee cold or a sore back and they think they're dying.

My own particular medical moans concern mosquito bites and insomnia. The two are not unrelated. If we go for a stroll round the compound in the evening, or, even worse, fishing on the beach after dark, I come back with my ankles and feet a mass of bites. These and the heat and the humidity conspire, night after night to rob me of my sleep. I get up and light a candle and read and write letters and drink warm milk and count sheep and splash myself with cool water to get rid of the perspiration, but it doesn't help. The cattle at the ITC make things worse by emitting eldritch sounds in the small hours. Some locals go out hunting with fearsome-looking home-made guns which let off a sound like Mons Meg. Bawbee barks at every passing creature, on two legs or four. I've decided I just have to learn to live with hardly any sleep; what else can I do?

The ills of the populace are catered for by a growing number of community health schemes, including a commendable network of rural birth attendants and health visitors who go out to small remote villages. The ills of the nation are, however, less easily cured. Seldom a day goes by without a policeman stopping us, hoping to chivvy us into giving him some dalasi to forget some minuscule, or even imaginary, defect in the car. Since my lights, brakes, brake-lights and trafficators are all in perfect working order, I now use attack as the best means of defence.

The cops wave us on, I think, rather than listen to a torrent of righteous indignation in Wollof from Ray and in English from me. The iniquity of the system is that there are countless trucks and bush-taxis on the roads with no indicators, no brake-lights and, often, no brakes. These continue to endanger the lives of pedestrians and passengers because in many cases a small bribe from the driver to the police every so often keeps them mobile.

Rumbles of corruption in government and civil service were heard all summer. The Minister of Tourism resigned hastily after some particularly colourful accusations were made against him in the brave little opposition newspapers Forayaa and Nation, which are typewritten sheets of cheap A4 paper roneoed and stapled together. Most people can't afford to buy newspapers, so one copy may be passed round the whole village, and these 'unofficial' papers are the only alternative source of information the public has. The 'official' newspapers and Radio Gambia are carefully vetted.

Actually if all the ministers who were accused of malpractice were to resign there'd be no government left. Forayaa, the Nation, and the Gambia's only news magazine, Topic, fulminate bravely about price-fixing, hoarding, inefficiency and dishonesty among businesses and bureaucrats. The sad truth is that many Gambians are unable to read them because their educational standard is so low; thumbprints are still a common form of signature on official documents. But it doesn't matter. The Gambians know what's going on – by word of mouth news magically spreads from village to village, street to street, and you can hear vigorous discussion of current affairs at any street corner.

If something sometimes seems to smell in the state of the Gambia, something also pongs in our bathroom. Or maybe it's coming through the window from the 'soakaway' behind the house. I wander about sniffing and twitching my nose like a guinea-pig, squirting bleach and disinfectant into every porcelain orifice. We now have our imposing four-metre high water-tower installed, topped by a thousand-litre water tank. All we need is for the generator and the water-pump to arrive in a crate from the UK and we should be able to turn on taps and flush the loo instead of pouring endless pails of water down it. Hallelujah!

The firm who made the water-tower are also making gates for us, large, ugly, but, we hope, strong concoctions of corrugated iron and angle iron. Their premises are in Bakau, and, as usual, we haggled with them for about three-quarters of an hour before a price, which I still thought was extortionate, was reached. Come back on Tuesday to collect your stuff, they told us. So we did. The power had been off so they hadn't been able to weld. Come back on Thursday, they said. So we did. The boy has been sick, they told us, come back on Saturday. This is normal in the Gambia, not just with tradesmen but with lawyers and public officials.

The Immigration Department take a similar approach. Come back tomorrow, they say every time we go there to try to get my resident's permit. You get used to it.

Maybe such irritations are harder to thole in the heat and humidity that's prevalent right now. Peter comes to visit us some evenings and sits on the sofa with a glower on his face. '****ing weather,' he grumbles, wiping sweat from his brow with his hankie. We play Crazy Eight by candlelight. I find a few hands of this vicious card game soothes my tetchy, sweaty spirit amazingly effectively. You have to throw yourself into it with histrionic gusto. 'Are you strong?' you shout smugly when you throw down an ace. 'Jump you!' you snap when you offer a Jack. 'Hah! Take two,' you roar, always slapping your cards down with great force. The best one is the joker. 'BOOM!' you screech, as you wham it on to the table, and your partner crumples in defeat.

Peter is still overseeing the building of Tanji Community Centre, although I don't know if that's the correct way to describe it. Usually when we pop down to visit him he's up to his waist in a deep trench in the earth, wielding a shovel, while the Mandinkas on his workforce stand or sit or lie, watching him, and offering advice. When they do work, huge arguments break out over the positioning of a cornerstone or who should be pushing the wheel-barrow. Peter has an individual approach to personnel management. He settles down on a wooden box or a concrete block, gazes at the scene of hand-waving, foot-stamping, jumping up and down and roaring at the tops of many voices. His face is expressionless.

Sometimes he shuts his eyes. The waves of sound wash over him. People break away from the melee and come to him in supplication, pleading for justice on their side. 'No, no. Listen to us!' bawls the opposing group. Peter just gazes at them, grimly. Frustrated by lack of an appreciative audience, they simmer down, shrug, pick up their spades and resume work.

This is possibly the only way to stay sane. Entering a Gambian argument is like throwing yourself into a pool of crocodiles. You know you can't win by arguing with them, so it's better to stay on the safety of the bank.

Anyway, when the fight's over, no-one sulks for long. In the heat of the sun, smiling's easier than scowling.

Water, Water,
Give Us Water

Ketta the well-digger has dug in his heels.

'No, I'm sorry. I cannot dig for you today. I have to go and find a sheep.' His rope – actually a kind of webbing, which doesn't tear the hands like rope – remains rolled up in his galvanised metal bucket, and his shovel leans obstinately against the wall.

'I didn't know you'd lost a sheep, Ketta,' I reply through gritted teeth.

'No, no. I have to kill a sheep for the celebration.'

'What celebration, Ketta?' I don't feel like celebrating. I feel like having another metre dug down our well so that, one day, we can actually pull up some clear water.

'The naming christening for the baby. My wife delivered yesterday.'

So, can he come on Friday? No, no. You remember his marabout told him Fridays and Mondays were heavy days for work. In the end, with the air of one bestowing largesse, he agrees to come next Tuesday. Perhaps.

The well was, in principle, finished months ago. It was possible then to pull up buckets of delicately fawn-coloured liquid with which to flush the loo and wash the verandah. But now that our generator is working, growling away in its little white hut every evening, a whole new world SHOULD be opening up for us. I toddle around with a silly grin on my face, switching on lights. After a year of candles and kerosene lamps, this is ecstasy! I bask in belches of cold air from our large pale green floor-standing fan, which looks a little like a demented Dalek. We can plug in the radio instead of buying batteries which last a couple of days and cost a fortune here.

But the real advance would be to get the water pump working. If switching on a light is luxury, think of the sheer hedonism of being able turn on a tap or pull the plug in the loo!

But first we had to summon Ketta back. And not just Ketta; there are suddenly swarms of men all over the place. Ketta the plumber has peered down the hole, examined the pump, and ordained that the well must be dug several metres deeper so that clear water can be sucked up the long grey plastic pipe, into the pale blue glass fibre tank which sits on the top of its tower like a lurid ice-cream cone, and thence into the arteries of our primitive plumbing system. Ketta the well-digger came, dug a little, then announced his need to find a sheep.

Meanwhile, Ketta the electrician has wired up the generator not just to our house but to the tourist huts and the 'bantaba' area under the baobab tree. Strings of red and black wires loop from tree to tree and tumble down the plastic conduit tubing to the water-pump, twenty-five metres deep and going deeper all the time. I feel we are tunnelling to the centre of the earth. Or we would be if Ketta didn't have to go sheep-hunting. All these Kettas are confusing. To add to my bewilderment, the electrician's son is called Modou and his nephew is called Musa; they are his apprentices. Our watchman is called Musa and the carpenter and the builder who are working on a small store-room for us are both called Modou, as is Ray's second youngest brother. It's a bit like being in a Welsh village with Jones the Fish, Jones the Post and Jones the Baker.

On an average day I make benachin rice for twelve. My saucepans aren't really big enough for such large-scale catering and the rice bubbles up and drips all over the cooker. I mutter about Scottish wives giving their men 'pieces' to take to work with them. Why can't Gambian wives do the same?

Violent arguments break out regularly. The compound was beginning to look quite pretty, with its little thatched huts and the palm-roofed bar-and-breakfast area under the baobab. Even the weeds had their charm, some with great pink bell-like flowers, or clusters of yellow seed-heads. Now there are trenches all over the place for water pipes and electric cables, and there are huddles of Kettas and Musas and Modous making attaya and spilling crumpled paper and sugar and cigarette packets everywhere they go.

'Mariama! It's going to be soon! In twenty minutes we will have water!' Ray shouted one day. Two weeks ago. I waited, hand poised trembling on the kitchen tap. An hour went by, then two, then three. We sacked the plumber and found another one. He came for a day, then disappeared for a week. 'I was tired,' he explained on his eventual return. Now that Ketta the well-digger has gone off to buy, slaughter and eat his ceremonial sheep, the plumber says he can do nothing till he returns, so he's gone home too.

We have lately established ourselves as definitely upper-crust, by buying our own wheel-barrow. There are only about three of them – 'puss-puss', they're called – in the village and their owners were loath to lend them out. One, indeed, began charging ten dalasis a day for his. We went to the National Trading Company and bought a shiny green metal one. It cost over £30 but we felt it was a sound investment. If we ever get really hard-up we can take our barrow to the market and earn money hurling it around laden with logs, cement, rice and fruit, charging by the kilometre.

After someone tried to charge us one hundred dalasi for the use of a hacksaw to cut through a piece of steel rod, we bought our own; not to mention a hammer, a plane and a glass-cutter. We are the envy of the neighbourhood. As for the jump-leads we keep in the back of the car, people come for miles to watch them in use. It is possible that we are among the very few jump-lead owners in the entire country.

They come also to watch me painting doors and benches and sandpapering window-frames. 'Psssst! Look! A tubab working. A lady tubab!' Ray stopped me from pushing the wheel-barrow loaded with concrete blocks. 'Stop acting like a man!' he said severely. 'Wait for Musa to do it!' He himself went back to the arduous physical manly labour of cutting a bleach bottle in half to make a funnel for pouring petrol into the generator. To be fair, he has done a fair amount of barrow-pushing himself lately, using the mountains of gravelly sand and clay dug from the well to make little paths to the huts. There is enough dirt from the well to make a highway to Mansa Konko, I sometimes think.

Ray and Musa took turns at piling it into the barrow, dumping it where the paths are to be, then spreading it out with a rake, then I walked back and forwards, back and forwards, stamping my feet to try to flatten it down. The mountainous yellow heaps by the well never seem to get any smaller though.

Sometimes, we need to get away from it all. So the other day we went to another naming christening in the village. I took a bundle of tiny baby dresses for the new arrival.

All the women were clustered in one room, dressed up to the nines, surrounding the new mother. I say 'new', but although she looks about 22, this is her sixth baby. I must say she looks extremely well and happy. The infant mortality rate in the Gambia is about twelve times higher than in Glasgow, and many mothers die in childbirth, but the tots and mums who survive must be made of tough stuff, because as I've said before they always look beautiful. More women arrived and pounded maize for coos porridge, to be served with sweetened sour milk. Peppery rice was simmered in huge cauldrons. In the morning, the Imam conducted the religious part of the proceedings and a goat was killed. In the afternoon, the women cook and gossip, and the men lie around in broken armchairs or balance on wobbly stools, under the mango tree in the centre of the village, and play cards and Scrabble and listen to Gregory Isaacs and

Peter Tosh on the cassette player they borrowed from us, powered from an old car battery.

I was secretly pleased when the two Scottish friends we took with us got soundly trounced at Scrabble by the village champions. Gambians are not too hot at spelling but they have a cunning remembrance of words like *zygal* and *quark* and *em*, and these were not the first over-confident tubabs to find themselves floundering against skilled local players.

Two female griots turned up. Griots are, traditionally, kind of singing town-criers, who grace important occasions and chant tributes to the participants, recounting virtues and family background and flattering any important guests. Before they did anything, they demanded some dalasi from everyone.

Looking round and spotting white visitors, they shrewdly began chanting in Wollof 'May the friendship between the black people and the white people always be strong; may there always be good feeling between them.' Ray translated for our guests and they looked modestly pleased and produced a few more dalasi which disappeared instantly into the voluminous cotton-covered bosoms of the griots. We waited for them to move on to some traditional folk-tale or community history, but instead they disappeared into the kitchen and began blethering with the other women. The kitchen is a wood fire surrounded by a wall of mud-bricks baked black by years of smoke. Heaps of yams and onions lie in a corner and children come running with bundles of firewood. The custom is for one woman in the family to provide the raw materials and do the cooking for the whole group for a week, then another woman takes over and so on. That's for normal family meals. But in this case, everyone chips in with contributions of food or cash and endless advice for the mother on how to rear her child. The granny will croon delightedly, 'Look what a horrible nose he has! What a funny-shaped chin!' This is all meant well, you'll recall, the mother doesn't leap up and flounce from the room as she might do if she was a white girl.

The baby dresses which were my contribution were part of a bin-bag full which came out in our last shipment from Britain. They were squeezed in the crate beside the generator, water pump, garden chairs, boxes of coffee, Dream Topping, Bisto and Knorr stock cubes, a bicycle, supplies of hair conditioner, typing paper and towels. The woman customs officer who inspected the crate prodded everything suspiciously with her plump fingers. 'What is this?' she said, pulling a Baby-Gro from the plastic bag. 'It's clothing for the people in my village,' I informed her crisply, but she looked dubious, obviously suspecting drugs or guns. I have now bestowed infant clothing on our friend the basket-maker in Kanefing, the peanut lady (the one, you recall, who walked four miles to visit me the day the chicken escaped), innumerable relatives of Ray's, Ketta the well-digger and many others.

If we go up-river, we stop at tiny hamlets far from the popular tourist track, and dish out rompers and smocks and miniature shorts and trousers. I feel a bit like Princess Anne, as toddlers cling to my hands and skirts and mothers snatch gratefully at the clothes.

I had one embarrassing moment here in the compound yesterday. Ray's mum was round feeding the dogs on the left-over rice and I was trying to explain that Bawbee was pregnant. I pointed to the dog and made swelling motions around my stomach, muttering 'Dom', which means baby. 'Ah, Mariama! A baby! For you!' 'No, no, no!' I had to screech back. She was very disappointed. My Wollof remains minimal, which is why I keep getting caught in communications snarl-ups like this. And even if it was flawless, I'd still have problems. When I try to have a fight with Ketta the well-digger, I discover that he's Mandago. The electrician is Jola. The watchman is Senegalese and Senegalese Wollof and Gambian Wollof bear the same relationship as English spoken in the heart of Fife to English spoken in Cornwall.

Language can be a problem. Our friend Big Maggie from Wolverhampton, an ample, lovable lady who reminds me of Victoria Woods, the very clever writer-performer, was thrilled the other day at what she heard as a compliment. 'Listen, Ray. That nice boy thinks I'm a tender lassie,' she gurgled happily. Ray didn't have the heart to reveal that the boy was actually asking her for ten dalasi. He, in turn, was positively appalled when I told him that one of my cats in Glasgow was called Chou-chou. Apparently that's the Wollof word for a . . . well, you know. A willie.

On Frogs
and Frauds

One day the store cupboard will be another outside toilet for the use of tourists who stay in our little huts. At the moment it's just a small concrete space piled high with bags of cement, door-posts and tools. I went there this morning to try to restore order from the chaos, and exposed a colony of frogs. They blinked and stretched and eyed me indignantly, grannies and grandpas, mums and dads and hordes of tiny babies. Presumably they do their tadpole bit in the vast viscous puddles in the garden and the lane during the rainy season. I apologised and they all climbed back on top of each other behind a piece of hardboard and went back to sleep.

One independent-minded frog insists on sleeping on the verandah. I don't know why. I rescue him regularly from Penny the cat. He's chosen a daft place to squat, if you ask me. You'd think he'd know by now that I move the box of nails and tools and bits of wire every morning to brush and mop the tiles. But he always looks surprised and embarrassed when I expose his little browny-green body to the sunlight.

Our resident gecko lives behind an old framed Tron Theatre Club poster in the living-room, darting out occasionally to streak round the wall and insinuate himself behind another poster for an exhibition of modern art held in Berlin during its year as City of Culture. This gecko is into culture. The theory is that he and the many and varied species of spiders who are shacked up behind shoe-boxes, coffee-tins, books and gas canisters will eat the flies and other insects in return for our hospitality. Being Gambian creatures, and therefore of a fairly leisurely turn of mind, they seem to sleep most of the time. In the evening small black beetles fall from nowhere on to my shoulders and grasshoppers leap into my hair, which I admit sometimes must look like a dishevelled piece of undergrowth.

A swarm of locusts flew over the Gambia a few weeks ago and the Ministry of Agriculture quivered apprehensively, but they moved on, maybe to Mali or Mauritania. A swarm of African bees, much nastier by far than plump, honeyed British bees, staged an airborne takeover of a junction in Banjul and the Public Works Department moved in to deal with them.

They broadcast an anxious message to all residents to stay indoors and lock their livestock and chickens out of sight while they sprayed the area. I understand these are the same bees which now terrorise parts of America and once inspired a ghoulish horror movie.

I spotted a slender black snake wending its way into some weeds in the garden and told myself not to panic. Then, on a visit to Tendaba, I found a book of West African snakes and identified it as something uncannily resembling a burrowing viper, extremely toxic. I'm still trying not to panic. Just so long as it keeps burrowing.

There was a loud scuttling noise on the verandah the other night. When I went out with the torch, I saw several black beetles the size of mice, which had somehow crash-landed on their backs, and were wiggling their little legs frantically, trying to right themselves. The dogs yelped and charged at them, then backed off as the insects clattered about like little mechanical toy cars.

Long languorous hours are spent with tweezers and cigarette lighter, removing and burning ticks from Maradonna's furry hide, and, worst of all, from inside its ears. The ticks proliferate because of the ITC cattle herd nearby. Some of the cows are a mass of disgusting pinky-black blobs, the swollen blood-filled bodies clinging to their skin with feet like pincers. And poor Maradonna is a victim too. 'Kerosene!' cried Musa the watchman authoritatively, and poured half-a-pint into the dog's lugs. It certainly discouraged the ticks. I suspect it also cancelled out whatever minute brain-power Maradonna might have had; he is an extremely stupid dog but lovable, in a lumpish sort of way.

Now Bawbee has produced four pups in the narrow uncomfortable foot-wide gap between the garden wall and the small hut I use as an office. They were there the day before yesterday, and Musa came running to tell me, a beaming smile on his baw face. 'Babeees! Bawbee's babeees!' he shouted proudly. She allows me to take her breakfast in bed and murmur congratulatory sounds over her little family, but she growls ferociously at anyone else who goes near.

Three of the new arrivals are typical Gambian mutts, white with large tan blotches. One is all brown and I wonder if it will have Bawbee's pale green eyes, though I doubt it. I think Bawbee is a one-off. I would like her to have had a cosy corner with a blanket for her confinement but she refuses to move from the harsh, stony fissure she has chosen.

For a few days, we had a small ginger kitten with blue eyes. It was called Rusty, after my beloved pet who now lives happily in an adopted home in the south side of Glasgow. Poor little Rusty. It was

Brendan who brought it to us and we all sat making cooing noises and tickling it under the chin till we suddenly realised it was louping with fleas. I put it outside to sleep on the verandah on an old towel, and it skipped around quite happily. Then one morning I found it dead. Musa's theory is that Maradonna, in an over-enthusiastic burst of playfulness, had picked it up in its big, sloppy mouth and killed it. There is no malice in Maradonna, but a great deal of clumsy idiocy. And also a lot of fleas. Where do you buy flea powder in the Gambia, I keep asking people, and get blank looks. I send desperate messages to friends. Never mind sending me shortbread or calendars with scenes of Scottish lochs. Just send me flea powder.

And give me patience to deal with some of the people I meet. One world-weary tourist in the Kombo Beach Hotel told me in a sophisticated drawl: 'Oh, I wouldn't come back here. It doesn't feel like Africa, you know?' 'What feels like Africa?' I asked naively. 'Oh, Kenya, my dear. All these large animals.'

Silly cow. Who wants to live in a giant safari park? I have enough diversion dealing with frogs and lizards and beetles. You can keep your giraffes and elephants and lions, thank you very much. Who needs them, when you can be driving along a popular tourist road and have to brake because a large monitor lizard, up to three feet long is waddling ponderously from one side to the other? They appear in the most unlikely places, their big heavy tails trailing behind them. And there are rabbits, big as baby kangaroos, hopping around the bush where a pair of birds as big as turkeys, black with red ruffs, are roosting, the remarkable ground hornbill.

And there are squirrels and civets and mongooses and antelopes and hyenas. I haven't actually seen any hyenas in the wild, but the Gambians are convinced that they lurk in the bush at night, ready to pounce on wayfarers. They are to a Gambian youngster what the bogeyman is to kids in a Glasgow back close. Stories about them abound. When the frogs set up their clamorous nightly concert, Ray says they're sending word to the hyenas that someone is passing by, so that the hyenas can come and attack. Useless for me to say that I always thought hyenas were scavengers who ate flesh that other beasts had killed. What do I know? I'm just a tubab.

I heard the other day that a Brit working for one of the hotels had accused me of doing a dis-service to the tourist industry by writing about my encounters with primitive plumbing, bent coppers and creepy-crawlies. I hope that's not true. The hotels for the typical tourist are excellent. They have air-conditioning, flush toilets, electric lights and European menus. You might as well say that someone writing about living in a croft in the Outer Hebrides was going to damage the reputation of Glasgow's Holiday Inn. Anyway, our tourists, though they are only a tiny handful in number, seem to like the place. People like Callum and Betty from Pollokshaws, an artist-cum-jazz-musician and a fashion designer, sturdy souls who enjoy the great outdoors and aren't into package holidays. They were actually booked into a hotel midway between Serrekunda and Banjul, with pretty bedrooms and a nice pool. But they fled and came to stay in our huts. 'It's the bloody hotel disco!' growled Callum. 'It's driving us crazy!'

Like me, they enjoy frogs in the loo and monitor lizards on the road. They think it feels like Africa, and not a lion in sight!

As for the frogs, and the locusts, not to mention the boils on the back of my neck, they have a Biblical ring to them. Our own little personal plagues. But I prefer them to the bronchitis or cold sores I'd be having in Glasgow.

And we're not THAT primitive. For the first few months, when we lived in Serrekunda, any shopping we did was from the little local shops, tiny hole-in-the-wall places which open till all hours and sell tomato paste, black mints, candles and canned milk. Or in the market, where you can buy bay-leaves by the kilo and all manner of local produce. It was only later that I discovered the Lebanese supermarket. And now a very swishy new one has opened in Kairaba Avenue, which is the Park Avenue of the Gambia, site of the American Embassy, the Human Rights office and lots of relatively posh housing. The new supermarket has air conditioning and a delicatessen counter, kitchen gadgets and an ice-cream machine. But I don't plan to go there very often. When I chatted to the English manager, a pompous, scowling chap, he said to me as he bustled around directing the staff, 'Whatever you do, never trust a Gambian.' I maintained a rictal smile and cooed, between clenched teeth 'Well, actually I'm married to one, and I trust him implicitly.' That put his gas at a peep.

I don't know how long he'll last here. The trouble is, every second tubab who comes here on holiday envisages vast fortunes to be made by importing shoes, lorries, out-of-date tinned food and tins of paint. Or opening a bar, or a nightclub. Frequently, they get ripped off by their Gambian partners. But then, quite a few of them, in my opinion, only started their businesses here because they thought they'd find cheap labour and make a quick buck.

Let me tell you about Alieu the seller of wood-carvings. A German husband and wife bought some of his deep purply-black elephants and rich brown tribal masks and said to him: 'These are beautiful. Where did you get them?' 'Oh, er, I carve them myself,' he lied, merely trying to add a bit of ethnic authenticity to the bargain. In fact, almost all the wood-carvings are made at Brikama market. The hucksters will buy a batch of them and take them to the beach area or a market stall and sit rubbing and polishing them to a fine sheen, pretending they're all their own work.

'We could make a fortune selling these in Germany!' said Fritz and his frau.

So they took Alieu back to Germany with them, rented a workshop and handed him a chisel and some sandpaper. The poor devil, who barely knew one end of a chisel from another, was paralysed with embarrassment. He was sent home in disgrace. People still giggle when he passes, and he hardly goes out of his compound, for the shame of it all.

We took Big Maggie from Wolverhampton to Brufut beach, where she began snapping photographs of the Ghanaian women cleaning the ladyfish and barracuda. 'One dalasi for the baby,' flashed one pert young mother as she scraped the scales from the silvery sides of a giant skate. Maggie looked alarmed. 'She means a dalasi to take his picture,' I explained. And why not? With an average income of £33 a month, the locals have to make their money any way they can.

Flushed With Success

Oh, I'm so excited. It's here at last! I suppose we should have a bottle of champagne to crack, but we made do with a couple of Julbrew beers. Yes, you've guessed it.

A gentle push down, a satisfying woosh and a throaty gurgle. The first time you pull your own plug on your own loo in the Gambia is a pretty significant moment. As you know, the whole introductory process has been affected by what you might call industrial constipation, what with errant plumbers, disappearing well-diggers, air bubbles and, last of all, Musa's disinclination to go down the well and check out the joints in the pipe.

I freely admit that you wouldn't get ME down there for a million pounds, but we felt Musa might be daft enough to have a go. Private incantations of magic words and the eating of certain magical herbs didn't bolster up his courage enough, so he tried ceremonial urination behind the tomatoes, but that didn't work either. We watched all this from a discreet distance, saw him staring wide-eyed at the well and shaking his head. 'We can't go looking for Ketta again!' I nagged at Ray. 'Maybe you could go down?' Ray looked at me in shock. 'Me? Down there? Only an idiot would go down there! Musa, come here!' The two of them conferred, something changed hands, and Musa, whistling, clambered down the well, feet finding the little holes Ketta gouged in the sides all the way down, hands clutching solidly on the rope. 'What did you give him?' I whispered. 'A magic talisman?'

'Ten dalasi,' said Ray, and swaggered over to the well to shout encouraging words into the shadows below.

The tank contains one thousand litres of water, which sounds like an awful lot. But it isn't. When we have guests in our huts, all washing and peeing and flushing and showering, it disappears remarkably fast. When the generator is on at night (one gallon of petrol providing about four hours of power) we pump water frantically, and I have the feeling both items of equipment will very quickly suffer from terminal exhaustion. The answer is, of course, solar power. I've been drooling over the swanky array of panels at the small German motel along the track from us. The motel is run as a kind of cooperative venture, by fifteen earnest young Germans.

It's a very earnest sort of place, in fact, with holidays for young women who want to study local rice-growing projects and family planning clinics, serious workshops on drumming and dancing and archaeological and historical tours. All good worthy stuff, but no-one ever looks as though it was a fun holiday. Maybe if there were fifteen of us we could manage power from the sun. As it is we'll make do, as always, with candles, hurricane lamps and these occasional bursts of growling energy from the generator.

If it gets exhausted sometimes, I know how it feels. My own bursts of activity are pretty impressive, swilling out the outside lavvies (guests for the use of) at dawn, before they all trudge out with their soap-bags and towels. Sweeping the frogs (about fifteen of them at the last count) from the little breakfast hut. Then setting out bread and fruit and jam and dealing with those who need strong coffee and those who prefer weak tea and those who slurp a whole tin of milk (about thirty pence a can) on their cornflakes.

Then there's washing sheets and towels and cleaning out the cold boxes and counting the beers and soft drinks and driving five miles to fetch the ice . . . Ray pedals vigorously to the village to buy bread at seven in the morning. He wrings out sheets for me and fusses over our erratic light and water supplies and makes me endless cups of coffee and tholes my grumping and niggling with commendable patience and affection. We keep saying tomorrow we'll go fishing or lie in the sun, but it never happens, because there's always so much to do. Still, there are compensations. We get some very interesting characters here.

I already mentioned Betty and Callum, the Glasgow Herald readers who found our place more laid-back than their hotel. She flops in the sun with her book and he – being an artist by trade – sketches our brothers and sisters from the village and designs possible logos for our embryo holiday company. He is a dab-hand at the drums, only since we haven't got any he improvises on old metal fuel cans. It's one in the eye for our Gambian friends who thought that only Africans could beat out a tune on a tom-tom.

There were the intrepid explorer types, who arrived replete with rucksacks, cases, boxes full of gas lamps and cookers. They produced packets of Knorr soup and dehydrated chilli con carne, water bottles and stout walking shoes. They ignored our offers of hospitality and sat in their hut by their own gas-light, brewing up things in camping-pans. I understand that he slept with his money-belt on, and he wore his rucksack when he went to the loo. It was all very rugged and self-reliant, until he came quaking and begging me to remove a large spider from the ceiling.

The Gambia's foremost bird-watcher, Mass Cham, spent a night with us. I saw him sitting dreamily staring into the dawn before breakfast, and was impressed when he later came with a list of the nineteen different species of birds he'd spotted in forty reflective minutes. A long-tailed parakeet, a Senegalese yellow-bellied parrot, a red-beaked hornbill and a double-spurred francolin, to name but a few. The forest and fields nearby are gloriously rampant with birds of all kinds, and Mass says we're in one of the best bird-watching areas in a country beloved by ornithologists.

The really big news, however, is that we've bought a Land Rover. It has left us without a butut in the bank, but it's a fine big diesel-fuelled, double-cabined, ten-passenger gilt-edged investment. At least that's what we keep telling ourselves, as we circle it warily and try not to think about the cost of spares and maintenance. Only time will tell. In between pouring bleach down the loos and serving up Wollof rice in multiples of six and eight, I concoct little posters with my felt pens. 'The South Gambia Sojourn – rural and fishing villages; see the bonga fish being smoked, the crayfish being landed; relax on idyllic sandy beaches; all at unbeatable prices.' It's all a bit vulgar, with ham-handed little drawings of palm-trees and highlights round the prices, but it's the best I can do on our budget.

Ray does his tour-guide bit, desperately trying to remember the English names for the various species of fowl and fruit and crops that they pass on their excursions. 'Just make them up,' I advised wickedly when I acted as his co-guide one day. 'That, of course,' I murmured, 'is a greater yam-eating yatter-bird.'

The passengers looked fascinated and scribbled things down on their sandwich menus. One day I'll get caught out by someone who actually knows the difference between a hornbill and a heron. Our passengers come back here with us for a tea or coffee or a slice of melon. This gives me a captive audience to show off our huts to. Two couples have promised to book with us for next year.

I'd like to tell you we were making a fortune, but the contrary is true. Most of our live-in customers have been the non-paying kind, like my son and his three friends, who lolled about all over the place guzzling our beer and spreading sweetie papers around and reading Stephen King and James Herbert. Most of the passengers in the Land Rover too have been friends. There is the blessed Brian, who is a regular visitor to the Gambia, exporting trucks and car batteries and stuff here. He brings us such treasures as an accelerator cable for the Land Rover, a starter for the 2CV and, last time, fan belts, and, at last, some flea powder for the dogs. That's what I call friendship. And there's the lovely Lesley from Callander, who arrived with a late

Christmas pudding, some shortbread and a pink bath-mat for the bathroom (not that we have a bath, but it does add a much-needed touch of comfort).

Since all our friends are nice people, they ply us with money for fuel and buy us drinks, but I still have the feeling I'm not really cut out to be a hard-headed business tycoon, since I'd rather trundle across the bush with Brian and Lesley than with real customers garnered from the hotel area. As it is, all the tourist taxi-drivers hate us because our prices are so low. So we have to run the gauntlet of fierce looks and resentful grumblings. Also, the only place to find customers is the bars, so we tend to spend our takings in advance on beers and kebabs. I have a suspicion that safari tours may not be on our agenda for very long. Yesterday we had to borrow money so that we could pay El – otherwise known as Momodou – who drives for us. This was mainly because we bankrupted ourselves by holding a jolly party under the baobab tree for twenty-five people.

This involved splurging out almost all the money we've made so far on half-a-stone of prawns, a gigantic tuna fish, crates of beer and bottles of wine, melons and bananas and papaya. But it was worth it just for the people who came.

There was Big Fred the Ned, all gold medallions and teeth, a kind of Arthur Daley character. He was with his 'little bit on the side', who got extremely tired and emotional and threatened to throw up in the Land Rover. There was Terry Palmer, author of an excellent guide book to the Gambia, and his sweet, gentle wife Joan. She allowed herself a large gin and sat back to watch the antics of the others. Peter from Prestwick was there, being very thrawn and cynical and Scottish in the midst of so many English people. He danced with his girlfriend Caroline, who always looks exasperatingly cool and poised and elegant even though, as a development worker, she lives in a mud-hut in a remote fishing village.

Joe, the Sierra Leonean artist, was there with tales to tell of working on an underground newspaper in Freetown and having to flee the country before he got arrested. Nowadays he paints deliciously delicate little land-, sea- and village-scapes, all pastel and pale, and gets frustrated when potential buyers ask for 'bright African colours'. The colours of Africa are in fact the soft pinkish-brick red of the laterite roads, the pale fawn of the sand and the dust and the mud-huts and the silvery-grey of the sky. It is the birds and the vivid dresses of the women that give it its reputation of being brightly-coloured, I think.

Hassan our soldier cousin was there, regaling anyone who'd listen with tales of firing mechanisms and bush marches. Hassan has large gaps in his front teeth and a high-pitched voice like a saw being rubbed over metal, but he loves being a soldier and poses for my camera in his jungle-green uniform looking tough. Musa the watchman is there, naturally, grinning at everyone and scrounging cigarettes.

Fred the Ned and his bit on the side moved onto the gin and when that ran out they demanded whisky. Musa's little wife and large placid baby gazed at the sight of white people making fools of themselves. We danced to Youssa Ndour and Ba Ba Maal and Dire Straits and endless reggae. Bob Marley makes all the Gambians go emotional. He is a bigger hero here than even in his homeland, and on the anniversary of his death the radio plays his music all day and discos of the Wailers are held all over the country. 'Ah, Bob. Bob was a wonderful man,' murmurs Ray, slightly sentimental after copious quantities of beer, as he tends the fire under the tuna fish, sweat pouring down his face and soot on his nice yellow shorts.

I rebel and put on Beethoven, which goes down like a lead brick. Caroline changes it for Barry White and she and Peter dance in slow motion gazing into each other's eyes. Somewhere along the way, the generator runs out of petrol, and we light candles, which keep flickering out. The water pump packs up again and next morning I have to pour gallons of water drawn up in buckets from the well, down the loos where twenty-five people have felt the effects of all that gin and beer. The joys of being a hostess.

The dogs wander about chewing fish-heads and fighting over surplus prawns and the cat nips in between them and steals the shellfish while they're squabbling. Earlier, Fred and friends had announced that they didn't actually like garlic prawns (how could anyone not like garlic prawns?) and I'd rushed into the house to whip up some omelettes, pretending it was 'no bother, no bother at all'.

In the morning also we had to take another hard look at our lighting and plumbing arrangements. Will Ketta have to come back and dig yet more dirt from the bottom of the well? Will a thousand-litre water-tank service the needs of all our guests in the future? Will I spend the rest of my life swilling out toilets for other people? Will we ever have another party? Er, yes, I think we're having another one next weekend. This is the Gambia. Or 'Fie Gambia-La' as we say here.

South of The Border

'Please, take me to Senegal,' said our new friend Terry Palmer, who is updating his excellent guide-book on the Gambia.

Terry is a paunchy, pleasant, incredibly energetic chap who bustles about the world girded with notebooks and recorders and cameras, leaping on and off buses and in and out of hotels, government offices and supermarkets, recording prices, times, terms and tourist attractions.

We knew we weren't in for a leisurely jaunt. Not with Terry calling the shots. On the other hand, his wife Joan is a dreamy gentle soul who is happy to gaze at the sky, count the leaves on the trees and watch the fat blonde flowers falling from the baobab tree like candle-wax.

There are two ways to go to Senegal. Up the way or down the way. North takes you to Dakar. Ray says he wouldn't go to Dakar again for all the Julbrew in the factory. Last time, he was chaperoning a group of randy German tourists, who wanted to sample the seedier side of Senegalese nightlife. They were menaced up a dark alley by evil-looking guys with knives which, if you ask me, serves them jolly well right.

Anyway, south is best, into Casamance, which is the lush rural part of the country which surrounds our little 200-mile long, 20-mile wide midget of a country. Off and on, there has been trouble simmering in Casamance in recent years, as the local 'liberation' group sought independence. My sympathies lay with them in a way. Casamance is the rich part of Senegal in terms of agriculture, and it feeds the north, rather in the way that Catalonia is the productive food-basket of Spain or in the way that Scottish oil, hydro-electric power and whisky get soaked up by the rest of the UK. Anyway, the army were mostly on red alert, fearing revolution at any minute, or so they said. But President Diouf has quietened things down now, signed an amnesty and, as far as I can make out, peace reigns among the cashew trees and rice-fields.

As for the Gambia, it has been called the hot dog in the Senegal sandwich.

It has also been referred to as the arrow pointing at the heart of

Senegal. After the attempted Gambian coup led by Kukoi in 1981, it was Senegalese troops who were called in to help restore order. President Jawara's wife had been held hostage, with his children, rebels were shooting paratroopers from the sky, shops and factories and the radio station were looted and there was blood on the streets. There is a feeling here that Senegal rather thought that after that debacle the proposed Senegambia Confederation would really be a takeover with little Gambia taking a subsidiary, obedient role. Negotiations rumbled on for years then puttered to a stop in 1990. There are close links between the two countries, which were once part of the great West African Empire that existed before the Europeans came and started chopping the land up between them. The Wollof race spreads across both countries and most families have relatives across the border. Nevertheless, they don't actually LIKE each other too much. Or at least, they view each other rather as the Scots view the English and vice versa.

If anything naughty happens here, like a pocket being picked, a burglary, a whore hustling, or a thief running off with a pair of jeans from a market stall, it's always a Senegalese who's responsible. At least, that's what a Gambian will tell you, gazing virtuously into your eyes and swearing that Gambians never steal or cheat or become hookers. When the negotiations for confederation collapsed, the tetchy relationship became volatile. And a stream of Liberian and other refugees coming across the Gambian border via Senegal made border guards on both sides even fussier and more bloody-minded than usual.

On the whole, though, they don't mind tubabs. They hope they will spend money in Casamance, and since the Senegalese franc is worth a small fraction of a penny, they need all the foreign currency they can get.

To get there, you just head up the road past the airport and turn right. At the border, you have to change some money into CFA, pronounced 'sefa' and hang around looking respectful and respectable while the guards peer at your passports and bristle with guns and suspicious looks. Kids surround the Land Rover asking for *l'argent, les biros, les bon-bons.* You suddenly feel the change in the atmosphere. French, instead of English. Everyone who isn't speaking Wollof or Jola is speaking French, and the kids wear tee-shirts and jeans to school instead of the demure uniforms they wear in the Gambia. There are green-painted louvre shutters and shops labelled *alimentation* or *boulangerie.*

Rodger Rabbit is driving. He's one of our amiable motor-dealing friends, cute as a monkey and common as muck, and he floors the fierce-looking patrols with remarks like 'Watcher, mate?' and 'Ow's it goin' then, me old son?' As we bounce along between the rice plantations and mahogany forests, Terry is writing everything down assiduously in his notebook, and keeps asking questions about the price of gasoline and the hotel tarrifs in Kafountine. Right outside a military barracks, he suddenly barks at Rodger to stop so that he can look at a map. It is not the done thing to stop outside military barracks in this country and two rifle-toting sentries advance on us threateningly in case we are freedom-fighters cunningly disguised. Ray speaks to them soothingly in Wollof and they wave us on grimly. The road becomes a pleasant meander through cashew woods and coconut trees and green paddies, and suddenly Ray screeches at Rodger (poor patient Rodger) to stop again. 'Back up, back up!' he yells, and we look around fearfully in case we're being ambushed. 'No, no! Look! There! There are some . . . er, some . . . these things, you know.' Sometimes he has difficulty remembering the English word; it drives us all mad with frustration. We are agog. Then we see a family of baboons, sitting on a low tree-branch scratching and staring back at us. 'These things!' bawls Ray triumphantly, and our cameras click furiously.

It took five rocky hours to get to Cap Skiring, past many sudden stops by uneasy soldiers in jungle gear and red berets. Cap Skiring is all Club Med and heavily walled and thickly shrubbed gardens round the hotels. Rich tourists ensconced in little luxury enclaves with guards on the gates. We finally found a piece of public beach, very rugged and pretty, but were immediately set upon by hustlers who made the Gambians look positively shy and retiring in comparison.

We drove back late at night, with a bitter wind skiting through the open back of the Land Rover. I was colder than I'd ever been in Scotland, and my bones ached with every bump. We were accosted by customs men in ragged shirts and dilapidated trousers asking for 'overtime' payment. Ray told them to take a running jump, in Wollof, and we drove off without being arrested, though shadowy soldiers kept bouncing out of the bush in front of us trying to look like Burt Reynolds. Terry, who'd managed to get himself a seat inside the Land Rover cabin, looked very smug and kept scribbling in his notebook. I had goose-pimples as big as groundnuts and my hair was blown into a Brillo-pad beehive.

Back home, I am still trying very hard to become an official bona fide resident of the Gambia, but it ain't easy. The theory is that you get your passport stamped three times with a visitors' monthly pass till you establish ninety days residency, then you get your permit. That's the theory. I've been here over a year right now, and I'm still an alien. When I protested mildly to the Chief of Immigration, after several consecutive days and weeks of sitting in queues in his waiting room and being told to come back tomorrow, he gave me a lecture with ominous overtones.

'We don't have computers like you people in Britain,' he reminded me. 'All the processing has to be written by hand then passed to the Ministry of Justice for approval then returned to us. This room is full of applications; yours isn't the only one. If you complain, it could go the worse for you,' he glowered. Indeed, his office was piled high with dusty folders, some of which looked as though they might have been there since the White Man's Burden was still being shouldered in puttees and pink gins. I forebore to say that if his minions stopped blethering at their desks and learned to write joined-up letters a bit faster things might move along more briskly.

Downstairs in the Aliens Office, part of the Immigration Police, a winsome German wench was leaning provocatively over a desk cooing at a copper in the hope that he'd hurry through her permit. An abject Frenchman was pleading with another one to find the key to unlock the drawer where he knew his passport had been gathering dust for several weeks.

A Gambian was steering a Chinese friend through the convoluted process of having his passport stamped. The Chinese spoke not one word of anything but his own language, but kept pointing to his passport and making stamping gestures, looking at the forms he was offered with blank disbelief.

In the end, we left this scene of Kafka-esque quaintness and fled to the Oasis Bar to eat kebabs, absolutely the best kebabs in the country. The establishment also upholds the fine old Gambian tradition of having festering toilets but cheap beer and cheerful murals.

Talking of toilets (and we often do, since nice ones are rare, and treasured by collectors. You pass on details to friends if you discover a new one that has toilet rolls or running water, or even a bucket of water if the loo's not flushing) . . . talking of toilets, our state of euphoria over being able to flush our own has swiftly evaporated. After two spasmodic weeks, the water pump died on us and it's back to buckets again. Fortunately, any visitors who stay in our huts seem to regard this as ever so colourful and ethnic. Some of the lustier ones actually insist on pulling up their own water, which is fine by me.

Musa the watchman went into a terrible huff the other night, stomping among the bananas and muttering like a sweetie-wife. It was my fault. He'd apparently been asking me for ages to buy him a new bucket but my Wollof's so wobbly I hadn't grasped his gist. The receptacle in question is made from inner tube, black rubber hand-sewn, looking rather like a pig's bladder, or what I would imagine a pig's bladder to look like if I wanted to imagine a pig's bladder at all . . . They begin to leak very quickly, specially with the heavy use they get in our compound. I made a point of buying him the de-luxe fifteen dalasi one rather than the ordinary twelve dalasi model, and he has simmered down a bit now, especially since I began giving him lemon-curd on his bread.

My hut-dwellers consume so much jam and marmalade that I'm planning to make my own. Kind friends and Glasgow Herald readers in Scotland sent me recipes for marmalade, which took so long to get here in the post that the citrus fruit season has passed. But I'll do it next season. And maybe mango chutney.

In return for the marmalade recipes, I sent my recipe for what the locals call my tubab benachin, which you might like to have a bash at.

In a large pan, simmer till soft a couple of chopped onions, as much chopped crushed garlic as you think your breath and your loved-ones can stand, some diced yams (you can substitute carrot or turnip) some chunks of clean white cabbage, in a generous cupful of oil (we use groundnut or palm oil, but any kind will do). Add two or three cupfuls of washed rice and stir frantically so that the rice becomes impregnated with the oil, cooking as long as you can without water before it starts sticking to the pot. Stir in a large teaspoon of black pepper, one of salt, and one of chilli pepper (less if you have a fragile palate), a couple of crushed Maggi cubes (that's what we use here; you can use Oxo or Knorr beef or vegetable cubes) and top it up with water. Oh, sorry, forgot – a dollop of tomato puree or some tinned tomatoes adds to the colour and flavour. Simmer, stirring every now and then, and topping up with water if necessary, till the rice is well-cooked and the liquid is all absorbed. Add a couple of bay leaves along the way; vital for the right aroma.

It's very nice as a hot side-dish or a cold rice salad, but the Gambians serve it with fish, mutton or chicken (when they can afford it) which has also been fried with onion, garlic and chilli. We often just add a tin of sardines and some sliced hard boiled egg. If it does stick to the pan a bit, then you've achieved the real Gambian flavour! They eat the burnt bits next morning for breakfast! I don't expect you to cook it in a cauldron over a wood fire the way they do. Nor to add lumps of sea-snail, as they do. Though, don't let me put you off, if you can lay your hands on some sea-snail . . .

You Can Take a White Horse Anywhere

'The mayor of Banjul wishes it to be known that a white sheep has entered his compound. Would the owner please come and collect it as soon as possible?' A lunchtime announcement on Radio Syd.

Well, here is an announcement from me. There is a white horse tethered in the garden behind the baobab tree, and we seem to have four dogs now, and there is a dead rabbit in a cardboard box on the verandah. I feel vaguely concerned about all this livestock, but I am so busy with my usual loo-swilling operations and serving breakfast to Swiss yuppies and washing dishes and mopping floors, that my attention keeps wandering.

The horse and the rabbit are here because of Modou, Ray's handsome, naughty, swaggering 16-year-old brother, who is an animal-lover. The horse actually belongs to another Modou, a stately chap who sells us water-melons from time to time, but he is anxious to sell us the poor patient beast and is using young Modou as a kind of sales rep. He rides it showily along the lane and into the compound, doing little twirls which I feel are a bit much for his mount, which is not in the first flush of youth. The idea is that we will be impressed and offer a large sum of money to purchase the animal. Sometimes Modou, who I suspect goes to the movies in Serrekunda and watches cowboy films, spins a rope lariat as he rides, and makes the kind of 'Aieee!' noises he feels appropriate to the occasion. I think he is on commission.

He has in the past brought me lame birds. Yesterday morning he brought me this terrified baby rabbit, which would have been much better off where he found it, in the woods with its mammy. Boys from the village often go rabbiting with packs of excited yapping dogs, and occasionally try to sell us their catch, alive or dead, but I have always managed to resist. As for the baby rabbit, I fed it diluted tinned milk from an eye-dropper and it scuttled around the house looking wild-eyed but potentially healthy until this morning, when I found it stiff and cold under our bed. I suspect that it saw the cat and had a heart attack.

The frogs have almost all died. Caroline is overjoyed about this, since she kept finding them in her knicker-bag and make-up box in the compound in Tanji where she is based. I'm told that I will now probably smell strange odours coming from hidden spots in cupboards and under the sink where the frogs have gone to die. I go around sniffing like a hound.

I actually miss the little creatures. The tourists were usually quite charmed to see them hopping around in the breakfast room and goggling at them from shady spots under the chairs on the verandah.

Our Swiss tourists are great. Young, trendy in a laid-back sort of way, with designer Rasta tee-shirts and straw coolie hats bought in Bakau market. We kidnapped them at the airport. We got fed-up waiting for holidaymakers to come to us, so we went up to Yundum and watched for backpackers coming off the Friday afternoon flight. A posse of taxi-drivers ran after us and cursed us for 'stealing' their passengers as we drove away, assuring the bemused Swiss that they'd be sure to like our huts and even if they didn't they'd saved themselves a hundred dalasi in taxi-fares.

Regina, the slender beautiful blonde German-Swiss, and her boyfriend Jan had met up with Jacques, the tubby, scruffy French-Swiss and his girlfriend Marie on the plane. They all said they'd try us for a night, but on the second morning they said they loved the place and would stay for their whole holiday. Regina sells factory units in the USSR and is convinced the notorious Swiss security police have a secret file on her; Jan is an interior designer who used to be a fashion designer; Jacques is a typewriter mechanic and Marie is a photographer.

We're quite excited because they're our first real paying guests, and we're falling over ourselves to make sure everything goes well. They seem to like our cooking. I make them Wollof rice, and Ray barbecues barracuda over the fire in the garden under the moonlight. I cut up all his onions and garlic and potatoes, and lay out the chilli and salt and pepper and bay leaves, and I lay the table and cut the bread and make the tomato salads, and everyone says: 'Ray, what a wonderful meal! You're a terrific cook.' After a few days I discovered that Jan doesn't eat any vegetables whatsoever, and Regina doesn't eat any fish or meat whatsoever. So I only charge them for one meal between two. He eats the fish and she mops up the tomato salad, and they seem quite happy with the arrangement.

We keep having parties, in spite of ourselves. They start off as buffet suppers for our paying guests, but other people turn up. 'Get me a couple of boys with drums and a couple of girls who can waggle their bums,' I asked Ray the other day, having confidently written 'African drums and dancing' on the menu. Half of Bijilo turned up. Toddlers, teenagers, mothers with babies on their backs and several imposing large mammas with vast bosoms.

The mammas organised the younger folk into a remarkably efficient carnival of dancing and drumming which rivalled the stuff in the hotels. I forgot to mention that it was New Year's Eve. We had lobster and prawns for our Swiss people, and some phoney champagne and loud music on the cassette-player when the drummers stopped for breath. At half-an-hour before midnight, Brian and his wife turned up with nine friends from their hotel. 'I know you Scots like a bit of company at Hogmanay,' he said cheerfully. We dashed around trying to find enough glasses, and opening bottles of wine. The eleven English people were already pleasantly tipsy and led the Gambian contingent round the compound in an elaborate conga, while the white horse chewed thoughtfully on my banana plants and the Swiss looked on in amazement.

Brian's friend Rodger and his wife produced bags full of streamers and paper hats and whistles and the kids went crazy, tooting and giggling and waving their streamers and shouting 'Happy New Year!' at the tops of their voices. Peter sat in a corner mumbling about English people not being able to hold their liquor and Caroline and Ray and I wandered about finishing off everyone's champagne (someone had brought some real bubbly by this time). Next morning, I crawled around in a bad temper picking fronds of streamer from every inch of the compound. I found coloured crepe and empty plastic cups in the bananas and papayas and fish-heads and prawn shells in the areas we pretend are flower-beds. We walked slowly down to the beach and washed away our hangovers with buffeting salty waves.

The activity that absorbs the Swiss most of all is not bird-watching or bicycling or swimming, though they've tried all of these. It's removing ticks from the coats and ears of our dogs. There are now two puppies, and Regina gently pours oil into their ears then removes the ticks with tweezers and the boys burn them with their cigarette lighters.

Two of the puppies were run over by El in the Land Rover. He was distraught and I wouldn't speak to him, but went around snuffling and glaring at him reproachfully until he begged me to forgive him. Fifi and Stanley survive and now eat rice, bread, barracuda heads and anything else they can lay their teeth on. The reason for a silly name like Fifi is that Joe the Sierra Leonean artist is going to adopt him and he insists on the name. He is a big butch wall-eyed lump (the pup, not Joe) who terrorises Maradonna and walks like a Japanese wrestler.

Stanley, on the other hand, is the whingeing, weak-looking runt of the litter, but is developing a sulky self-confidence and even faces up to Fifi when it's a matter of disputed ownership of a chicken-bone or a fish-head.

One of our parties was put into some disarray because Musa and Ray disappeared into the shadows behind the house with torches and cutlasses. The barracuda seemed likely to char to a cinder and people were looking hungry. 'What are you DOING?' I hissed at Ray when I tracked him down next to the 'soakaway'. 'We are chasing a snake,' he said, 'a very big one.' 'It can't have been THAT big,' I girned. Then he showed me the track it had left, a long SSSS as wide as a tyre track. They didn't catch it. I didn't tell the guests about it either; might have spoiled their appetites.

Otherwise, the only snake I've seen recently was a skinny little yellow and black one at Abuka Nature Reserve. It's a wonderful place. The forests swayed around us like silver-green curtains and branches held hands overhead, linked by creepers and weighed down here and there by families of monkeys.

The Ladies and Gents are called Janes and Tarzans, which is a bit naff, but at least they are real African latrines, sort of holes in a raised hillock, which you have to climb up on and squat over while holding the woven-grass door shut with your foot. A couple of crocodiles stare back at you when you clamber on to the observation platform over the lake and there are all sorts of interesting birds whose names I forget or never knew. Normally I'm too busy fulfilling my real role in life (cludgie-cleaner, sweeper and rice-maker) to visit tourist attractions like Abuko, so it was quite a treat for me to go there, while Ray looked slightly bored, having taken tourists there more times than he can count. I think the crocodiles and monkeys recognise him now.

The reason we went this time was to show it off to my son and his three friends, who visited us for three weeks. They enjoyed the wild life reserve but their real highlight was going to Brikama wood-carvers' market. In fact they went a bit berserk, haggling wildly for wooden elephants, hippos, salad bowls, statuettes and masks. I kept telling the stall-holders that my son was a poor student with no money, but my credibility suffered when he started buying with the abandon of a compulsive gambler in a casino. When he ran out of cash, he bartered his Walkman, his girlfriend's watch and, eventually his shoes.

He returned to Bijilo barefoot but boasting about his bargaining techniques. It didn't seem fair to tell him that his Walkman was worth more than the whole collection of wooden artefacts put together. 'Gran can have an elephant, and we'll give a hippo to Andrea's mum . . .' he began. Then looked thoughtful: 'Maybe we could open a stall at the Barras?' he ruminated.

As we waved them off at Yundum Airport (the day we kidnapped the Swiss), they were all staggering under the weight of half-a-forest's worth of trophies. The carvings are nice but their manufacture, by hand, while absorbing to watch and undeniably skilful, uses up vast quantities of redwood and does nothing at all for Gambia's serious deforestation problem.

Bawbee has decided that she has nurtured her puppies – those of them that are left – quite long enough. I think she was secretly relieved when two of them disappeared under the wheels of the Land Rover. She spends a lot of time running away from their greedy sucking little mouths. She has decided there's more to life than motherhood. When we drive along the perilous sandy track (one false move and you're up to your door-handles and stuck fast) to Uncle Dembo's for a beer, we often look down to find her sitting beside us, or lying under a table, puffing and panting but with the smug look of a parent who's out on the town for the evening without the kids.

Stanley emitted a piercing howl the other day and it took us a long time to find him, lurching around among the pepper plants with an empty cat-food tin jammed over his head.

Fortunately he wasn't around at Uncle Dembo's the night the rat caused havoc. It was a special lobster barbecue to celebrate the festival season. Bakary and the boys from the kebab stall chased the rat, which had popped its head up between some cardboard boxes, round and round the tables and between the barbecue grill and the buffet bar, but it ran off grinning. Gambians often call rats mice, just as they call large prawns shrimps. I wonder sometimes if the Gambian word for small – tuti – is related to the Scottish word, toty? And you'll be amused to know that the Wollof word for sexual intercourse is nuke – pronounced nookie!

Best Foot Forward

In the summer of 1981, while President Jawara was wearing his dignified robes at the wedding of Prince Charles and Lady Diana Spencer, there was an attempted coup in the Gambia. It didn't mean much to me then. I was at the Royal Wedding, reporting on the sentimental splendour of it all for the Glasgow Evening Times, and someone pointed out all the Commonwealth Heads of State to me, including slim, bespectacled Sir Dawda Jawara.

The poor man didn't have much time to revel in it all because a call came through to say that his country was being taken over by rebels and his wife and children had been taken hostage. The British SAS and Senegalese troops were called in to help restore order, but not before an estimated 800 people were dead. As I have recalled before, car dealers and shops were looted, the national radio station was taken over and despoiled. Ray was splashing about in the water with his sisters on the beach at Bijilo when the Senegalese landed troops here in the bay, shouting at all the local youngsters to run and hide. There were dead bodies everywhere and the smell of dead flesh. Ray found a rifle beside a dead soldier and ran with it to the Alkalo.

The Bijilo Bar and Restaurant, built around a pleasant courtyard surrounded by trees where once top West African bands had performed, was looted. It is across the road from Ray's uncle the builder's house and it lies there empty still. The Lebanese who owns it would like to sell it for a lot of money but so far hasn't had any buyers.

Now, the thing is, no-one has ever taken the words Bijilo Bar and Restaurant from the map in the tourist brochures. The other day, while Ray was away guiding our Swiss PGs around the nature reserve, a taxi pulled into our compound with two middle-aged French people in the back seat. They got out and said 'Bonjour!' and stared at me expectantly. We smiled lamely at one another. Then the driver, a large jolly Gambian in traditional robes jumped out and slammed his door and said: 'I've brought you some tubabs!' It dawned on me slowly that they had come for lunch. 'Isn't this the Bijilo Bar and Restaurant?' asked the driver reasonably.

We had a few eggs and some day-old bread in the house. When

you don't have a regular power supply, you don't have a fridge, so you don't buy fish and prawns unless you know for sure someone's going to be there to eat them.

But I pulled myself together, smiled urbanely and said: 'Bienvenu! Asseyez-vous! Vous voulez boire du vin?' with what I hoped was the expression of a time-served innkeeper. *Malheureusement,* I told them, our policy of providing ocean-fresh produce at all times required that *il faut* order in advance for sea-food, but how would they fancy a nice Gambian omelette *du pays* (in other words full of any bits of left-over potato, peppers, onions and tomatoes I could lay my hands on)? *'Ah, oui, c'est bon* etc,' they said, and got wellied into a bottle of supermarket screw-top wine with a satisfying 150% mark-up (about which I feel no qualms of guilt since I drank the same stuff in the Cantonese restaurant in Bakau at a 350% mark-up!)

They seemed to enjoy their meal and the taxi-driver promised he'd bring me more customers in the future. Yesterday a young Gambian tourist-follower came at dusk to tell me he had informed his 'friend' who was staying at the Kololi Beach Club that we had a restaurant and she would like to come with him for lunch next day. Yes, yes, I said, no problem. Our little group of rickety tables and stools under the baobab isn't my idea of a real restaurant but I'm quite prepared to improvise if it'll bring in a few dalasi. Not that it was easy. For one thing, since I stepped into a large hole in the dark, wrenching my ankle agonisingly, I have been hobbling about slowly and saying 'Ouch!' with every step. For another thing, Ray is off with the Swiss to Georgetown and won't be back till very late tonight.

For yet another thing, Musa and I have had a parting of the ways and we were between watchmen, as it were. I know regular readers of the Herald column have come to know and love Musa, a cross between a Flowerpot Man, a condemned scarecrow and an old sweetie-wife. I have a certain affection for him too, the kind you have for an intransigent puppy that keeps chewing the furniture and eating the soap. As a matter of fact that's just what our puppies do at the moment, but even they don't drive me as crazy as Musa does. Matters came to a head when I had to haul water out of the well to replenish the outside loo, with my back aching and my ankle throbbing, until Musa wandered in to work at 10.30 am and promptly fell asleep in the wheel-barrow.

We suggested ever so gently that he might just possibly see his way to doing a bit of weeding and checking that there was water in the PGs' buckets and so forth, and he went into a sulk and said he wanted more money. This from a man who often eats garlic prawns and pakora with us, wheedles innumerable cigarettes, dalasis, tee-shirts, sweets, and even radios and watches from our guests; a man who provides endless photo-opportunities as he lies snoring in the puss-puss (barrow) wearing my straw-hat over his face to keep the sun out of his open mouth!

Ray told him with what I thought was commendable patience to go home to his compound to think things over. His discontent arose from the fact that he was talking to the watchmen at the ITC cattle-station, who earn twenty-five dalasi per month more than he does. Useless to explain that they don't get meals (let alone pakora) laid on, nor do they get gifts and tips from tolerant tourists. Or that they are employed by a large well-funded organisation, whereas we are permanently on the edge of bankruptcy. I don't know if he's still considering but in any case, as of today, he still hasn't come back and I am here alone with the dogs, feeling sorry for myself.

At eight o'clock this morning I was hauling the seventh bucket of water twenty-five metres up the well's black interior when the whole caboodle broke loose. The rope had frayed through and the bucket plummeted to the bottom with a dull echoing plop. I couldn't even stamp my foot, it was throbbing so much. Fortunately, Jouf suddenly arrived.

Jouf was the watchman at the guest-house in the village when I came back to the Gambia last June and told Ray that, yes, I would marry him. The guest-house is a shabby two-roomed shack with an execrable toilet at the other side of the yard, torn curtains and a lumpy straw mattress, but it has certain tender romantic memories, and Jouf was always smiling and swift on his feet, and wouldn't dream of letting me fetch my own water. He had always maintained that we should have given him the watchman's job here, so when he heard through the grapevine that Musa was gone, he nipped into the job on the double. He has now watered all the poor thirsty bananas that have been crying out for moisture for weeks, and he has filled all the buckets and he hasn't dropped a single cigarette-end or put a single muddy footprint on the verandah.

And I now had time to think about my lunch-guests. I laid a tray for two people, improvised a menu that said: Special Sunday Lunch, and wheedled Peter and Caroline, who were staying in the huts and had slept peacefully through my travails with the bucket and the well and had finally surfaced about 11 am, to go to Bakau market and buy me some fish and fruit and bread. My clutch foot was completely hors de combat, I explained pathetically.

At 1.10 pm, the Gambian hustler arrived with not one but FIVE Swedish friends. 'Don't panic!' I muttered to myself, as I waddled at a snail's pace to the baobab tree and took their order. 'No, zanking-you, ve dent waownt any feesh,' they said heavily, just as Peter and Caroline throttled in the gate carrying the last four grey mullet they had had in the market. 'No problem,' I smiled brightly through clenched teeth. 'No problem whatsoever. Perhaps a Gambian country omelette?'

They had that, and went off happy. As I was crawling back and forth to the tree (Peter and Caroline having gone to play tennis) carrying bread and cutlery and plates and trying to whisper Ouch! instead of yelling it out loud, I told myself that maybe next time they have a coup they'll loot this place too, then I can have a quiet Sunday to myself. On a technical note: it is 150 tortured steps to the tables under the tree. There and back once to take the order and give them their drinks, once with the cutlery, bread and salad, twice with the omelettes (sorry, but I can only carry three plates at a time; I'm a novice at this game, and the ground's too rough for a trolley even if we had one), and twice to take their money and clear everything away, adds up to just over a mile. And me wi' a bad leg, as Billy Connolly would say.

Peter and Caroline came back after their game of tennis. 'Everything all right?' they asked solicitously. They gaze into each other's eyes a lot just now, as Peter is going home tomorrow. Tremulous tears hover on their eyelids. It's been made worse by the fact that he was supposed to go home three days ago, and they did all their fond good-byes already. Then his flight was put back three days so we're having to go through it all again. 'If you want an omelette, you can make it yourselves,' I snarled and went to soak my foot in a basin of hot water.

Later I went to check the loos again. I never dreamed that people's bladders and bowels would come to play such an important part in my life. Sometimes I fall asleep counting toilet-rolls and towels. Right now I find Maradonna munching a piece of cow-dung outside the loo door, and Fifi inside eating the pink soap. Fifi grows bigger and bouncier by the minute, smooth and white with tan patches and a tail like a catherine-wheel. I bawl at him in thunderous tones and he drops the soap and comes to wiggle round my feet and munch my toes, his tail wagging frantically. I can't kick him; it would hurt my ankle too much.

Every time I open the front door of the house, one or both of the pups bolts inside and jumps into the rubbish box, scattering peelings and egg-shells all over the floor. At night, they sleep on the verandah, fitfully, yelping and squeaking and occasionally waking up to chew lumps from the foam mattress on the small folding bed where Musa used to kip down if we went out at night.

Bawbee takes nothing whatsoever to do with them, and I don't blame her. It occurs to me that the reason I'm feeling too gloomy and irritable for words is that this is the first time Ray and I have been separated for more than a few hours since we got married. I should be able to settle down with a book, a cushion under my ankle, and enjoy the solitude now that Peter and Caroline have left, the pups seem to have settled down under the baobab, sniffing about for scraps of bread left by the Swedes, and Jouf is singing quietly to himself as he waters the plants. But I limp about tidying things that don't need tidied, until I hear the rumble of the Land Rover and see the headlights in the darkness.

'Hullo!' carol the Swiss. 'Did you have a nice rest while we were away?' I control my reply and kiss my husband. 'Did you enjoy your trip?' I ask them. 'It was wonderful. Georgetown was so interesting; we wanted to stay one more night, but your husband wouldn't let us. He said he had to come home to you or he would go crazy.'

Ray looked embarrassed. But it was good to have him back. 'DID you have a nice rest?' he asked mildly. 'As for me, I'm exhausted; it's very tiring, acting as a guide . . .' He looked surprised when I burst into tears.

Just Another Seaside Landlady

A crayfish has just jabbed my elbow with one of its long waving antennae. It and some of its chums are lurching about feebly in the sink next to which I am typing this paragraph. They are a gorgeous shade of purply-blue with diaphanous speckles of jade green, and they are what the Gambians refer to as lobsters.

My knees are squeezed in between the Le Creuset cooking pots which were given to me by the nice people at Frasers' Buchanan Street store in Glasgow as a wedding present when I left Glasgow. I have no shelves or cupboards, so they are hanging on hooks along the edge of the limited wooden workspace (made from part of the crate in which my books and plates came from Scotland) on which my typewriter now rests. If I move the carriage too hard, it knocks the salt over, and there is an aroma of garlic beginning to seep into the pages of paper.

The reason I am perched thus on a wobbly stool in the kitchen is that the pine table, which is also my desk, is on the verandah, loaded with bread and jam and German elbows. The small hut which was our breakfast room is currently occupied by my daughter Carol and my grandson Cameron, who arrived out of the blue last week and are kipped down at nights on a blow-up mattress. The fax telling me she was coming, which we picked up by chance at the local branch of the Gambia Telecommunications Service (a remarkably fine organisation, I have to say) made me weep and giggle so much I couldn't concentrate on my cooking and cleaning. We went to the airport and I clung to the ugly wire fence like a refugee, with tears streaming down my face, until I saw her holding Cameron aloft over the heads of the tired, hot tourists queueing for their luggage.

Right now, Cameron, aged 19 months, blond and beatific in appearance, is being wheeled round the compound in the puss-puss by Elimman, looking smug and growing more golden-brown by the minute.

The Germans whose elbows are on my table are five in number, two sleepy-eyed middle-aged hippies from Bremen and three flashing-eyed young Bavarians who make the merest request for plum jam sound like a military command. They now breakfast and dine on the verandah, which means I can't say anything rude about them while I'm cooking, or they might hear me. We ourselves eat our rice in what's left of my dishes on our knees, sitting on the remaining chairs.

My old, precious plates, which hung on the wall when I was married before, left with me when my first marriage broke up, and stood prettily on shelves in my flat in Glasgow, are now co-opted into use to carry salads and bread and melon slices. We are into our second month of real business and most of our towels and pillow-cases are doing duty for other people, along with our mirrors, soap dishes and candle-holders.

I have mixed feelings about constantly dealing with the public. Werner and Marianne are fine. They just amble gently from their hut-door to the baobab, stopping off to grab some beers from the cool-box then flopping down for hours on end, watching the weeds growing. Werner drinks copious quantities of beer, so the profits are good, and Marianne frequently brushes out their hut herself and makes the bed.

Ulie, Monika and Anton are quite another kettle of *njinn* (that's Wollof for fish). Anton is a lanky Ichabod Crane figure, who looks like a sort of distended Dustin Hoffman, swallows palm wine by the bottleful and is, by profession, a taxi driver in Munich. He wears a beret and a supercilious expression, but he's usually OK in a weird sort of way. Ulie is a bristling, sulky youth who, unbelievably, used to be a social worker. He dislikes Ray intensely; that has been obvious since day one, and is entirely reciprocal. I think the idea of a black African as co-boss rather than the sweeper-up, is hard for him to accept. I scurry between them smiling till my teeth hurt, trying to keep international relations amiable, and telling Ray to keep his head down and think of the money they owe us.

Monika has long dark pigtails which she wears wound round her head like Heidi, and she is frequently, elegantly, unwell. She reclines on the bed tastefully draped in a piece of batik, pillows under her pigtails, sipping camomile tea and maintaining that she can't possibly eat whatever's on the menu for the evening meal. Her appetite may of course be inhibited by the amount of cheese, butter and jam she has consumed at breakfast, but nevertheless Ulie appears at the door at regular intervals, eyes flashing. 'Monika vould like ein small omelette, yah, mit no salt and just a little onion.' 'Monika wishes you to put the generator off, NOW. Ze noise is giving her ein headache.'

To be fair, things have gone rather awry for Monika since she went to a wedding celebration in Sukuta. She was dancing uninhibitedly to the tom-toms, surrounded by local lads with lustful eyes, when one of them surreptitiously snipped off a large tuft from the end of one of her pigtails. El, the Land Rover driver, and Ray, who is heartily sick of the sight and sound of them, assured Monika that whichever boy had taken her hair was obviously going to take it to a marabout, who would put a spell on it. This spell would swiftly make Monika lose all interest in Ulie and fall in love with the secret suitor. It was then that she took to her bed with a vengeance, and Ulie sulked and eyed every passing Gambian with brooding suspicion.

Whether because of the marabout or just because Ulie's such a prat, they bickered for days after that, but not enough to make Monika go searching for a Gambian Lothario, unfortunately. In between bouts of bed-rest, Monika would stride off to the beach, giving me a chance to try to clean their room. Our huts are very small, and she seemed to have a tremendous amount of luggage, all of it strewn on the floor and all over the bed, mixed with banana skins, peanut shells, crumpled tissue paper, soggy biscuits and discarded knickers. When I was a little girl I never wanted to be a chambermaid when I grew up, and now I know I was right.

My daughter helps; she actually did hotel management at college once, so she gives a certain air of professionalism to the job. She has her own problems. Cameron, in spite of a healthy appetite for bananas and coconut and chicken domada, still wanted to breast-feed. 'What do Gambian mothers do?' she moaned to El one day. 'Oh, they go to the Imam and he says some words and there is no more problem,' said El enigmatically, 'but I don't think it would work for you because you aren't a Muslim.'

Fortunately, after a week of being wheeled in the wheelbarrow, splashed in the pool at the Senegambia Hotel, following Musa around like a puppy and visiting the local day nursery, Cameron became so absorbed in other things that he has completely abandoned Carol's boobs and makes, instead, for the supply of beer we keep for the guests.

At the day centre, his sturdy little white figure caused total chaos for a morning, as all the kids crowded round to have a look at the little tubab boy, feeling his golden hair and touching his pink-gold skin. He was a celebrity. Carol ended up distracting them by leading off a garbled game of Ring-a-ring-a-roses, while the teachers thankfully went off for a sit-down and a natter.

Bijilo Day Centre is funded by an American organisation, so it has cute little hexagonal rooms with pictures of jolly black toddlers cleaning their teeth, alphabet pictures and little seats and tables. But in the vicinity of many primary schools it's not at all uncommon to see kids walking to school with their home-made benches on their heads, because the school itself hasn't any furniture. Our own local primary, considered one of the best in the area, has sandy cement floors, a shortage of seats, no glass in the windows, and corrugated iron doors.

All the same, iron discipline is is enforced in most schools –
sometimes so stringently that it amazes me that the African
Commission for Human Rights (which is, after all, based in this
country) doesn't intervene. There are tales of pubescent girls being
held down over tables and beaten with sticks or straps for forgetting
their homework or being inattentive. One way or another, Gambian
schoolchildren are very well-behaved, positively docile, in the
classroom. Outside they can be engaging and lovable, or, like Scottish
kids and kids the world over, they can be a pain in the neck.

I now feel less than charitable when every small child I meet
yells, 'Tubab, gimme pen; gimme mints; gimme dalasi!' So I treat
them the way I'd treat a cheeky wean in my own city of Glasgow. I
give them a real telling off and they nod abjectly, promise not to do it
again, then go off and do exactly the same thing to someone else! My
reasoning is that if they need pens, it's for class-work, but if they're
out begging for pens, they're not in class . . . if you see what I mean!
Things aren't helped by the fact that many of the pens and books
donated by generous tourists are subsequently taken home by the
teachers for their own families, or sold for hard cash.

I'm not really a hard-hearted Hannah, honestly! The small
beggar-boys in the towns, with their pleading eyes and skinny limbs
and empty tomato-cans and tattered clothes are a different matter
entirely.

As for the old men in wheelchairs, or crawling along the earth
with missing legs and arms, they break my heart. I carry a supply of
coins with me because I know that I will have to pass through a group
of them outside very shop I enter. Some have been born deformed
because of inadequate pre-natal care of their mothers, some have had
leprosy, some have been injured, but they all depend entirely on
charity to survive.

I get guilt complexes all the time, as I prepare ample meals for
ample Germans and take orders for 'three more beers and some wine,
please, Mariama.'

The call has just come through from our Bavarians. 'Ve would
like tonight to eat much yams and some steak.' I stamp my foot and
bang a spoon on the small space between the typewriter and the
cooker. 'Tell them,' I say to Ray, 'that the cook has already sweated
over chicken, egg-plant, courgettes and white cabbage appetisingly
blended with finely chopped onion and garlic, butter and black
pepper, and that's what they're bloody well going to eat.'

I suppose I should take it as a compliment that the whole
flaming lot of them refuse to go and eat in any of the cafés and
restaurants in the tourist area and insist on eating here every night.
Day after day, my afternoons are filled with the production of plain
omelettes, filled omelettes, sandwiches and coffee. My evenings are a

fluster of garlic prawns and peppery meat balls, a guddle of curried chicken and rice and pasta and salads. 'Your cooking is ze best,' murmurs Marianne, who, like me, sometimes seems to wish the Bavarians would bustle off and leave us all in peace.

'I did not sleep last night. I was menstruating. When I am menstruating, I always have to sit outside and gaze at the moon and the stars,' Monika informed me this morning, selecting more medication from a bag like Boots the Chemist.

Meanwhile, the Land Rover trippers have included rugged combinations of Angus farmers, comely lady lawyers, a young man who used to cook the food for the Bergerac TV programme, and Mandy, who used to be a holiday rep in Majorca. Other more personal visitors come and go. Joan, wife of Sir Alwyn Williams, former Chancellor of Glasgow University, poured me large vodkas and tonic on her patio at the Novotel Kombo Beach, and came to lunch.

It was a ladies' lunch, with Caroline from Tanji, Lizzie (my friend from Scottish Television) and Saptieu, the delightful editor of the Gambian Women's Group magazine Awa. Ray winced and retreated under the baobab to where we keep the cool-box with the beers.

It was while bathing near the limpid water slapping a particular string of black rocks near Tanji that Lady Williams got bitten by a stone-fish. Sir Alwyn, a paleantologist by trade, was here to crawl about these rocks searching out the breeding grounds of an apparently fascinating creature whose family has been on earth for 600 million years. Joan describes it as being an almost invisible lop-sided limpet. Her bite was so painful she had to be carried to the car, then, on arriving back at her hotel, carried ignominiously through the gardens, piggy-back style to her room. She laughed uproariously at the memory of it.

Talking of things that bite, I wondered the other evening why El was driving the Land Rover at an even more erratic course than usual (given that the only way to deal with our pot-holed roads is to follow a track like an electrocardiogram, zig-zagging furiously). 'He was running over that big black snake that was crossing to the nursery school,' explained Ray casually. Oh.

Call Me Madame

'And how is our Madame Relwan today?' asked the watchman at the Senegambia Hotel. It made me feel rather grand. The manager of the Kololi Tavern is an elegant and indomitable German lady who, I suspect, intimidates even her Gambian bosses, and she is known submissively to her staff as Madame Lou. She watches for unemptied waste-buckets, uncleaned ashtrays and unchanged towels with eyes like a hovering vulture. Her technique has improved the Tavern tremendously. Maybe I'm becoming a bit like her. Madame Relwan? Mmmm.

Ray's real name is Relwan, but the name-game is very complicated here. Some of his documents say Lerwan, because Gambian tongues get confused between the two consonants. His mum calls him Lerwan. Many people also call him Ceesay, because he once adopted that as a middle name, in tribute to a certain Banjul Police Commander whom he'd admired. This gets shortened to 'S', pronounced 'Ess'. His young brother Lamin is more usually called Pa Faal (pronounced Paffal), after a highly respected member of the family. Babies are often called Pa-something after an elder, and the name sticks.

El the Land Rover driver is really Momodou, but nicknamed Lamin, shortened to El. My little sister-in-law, Janqui, is actually Mariama, but another sister is also Mariama . . . as for Elimman, our wee brother, his real name is Ebrima, and he is also called Alhaji, after an elder who went to Mecca. Are you still with me?

When Ray calls: 'Oh, look! There's Lamin!' I have to wonder which of the scores of thousands of Lamins it might be, since this is the name given to all first-born sons of Mandinka families, not to mention many sons of Wollof, Jola and other tribal groupings. It makes John and Jim sound deliciously out-of-the-ordinary.

As for me, I'm Mariama, never mind the name on the front of this book which is only used by a few British friends here, and in letters from home. 'Mariama! Mariama!' the name is carolled from the lane as the children pass on their way to school, or to the standpipes as they fill plastic bottles with water and carry them on their heads during the morning break. The name is bellowed by friendly wine-tappers and the old women of the village, or crooned at me by beautiful young mothers with their babies on their backs. I like it.

When Ray (Relwan, Lerwan, Ceesay, Ess) says it, it's either a long melodious sound like a love-potion or a bark like a hyena. 'Mariama! Where is my that knife?' (Gambians use the possessive and definite articles in tandem). We both lose things a lot. The other day, just as he was due to go and pick up nine tourists and take them on a trip to south Senegal, he lost the only key to the Land Rover. 'You must have put it somewhere!' he roared. Then: 'Cameron must have taken it!' My grandson chewed thoughtfully on a banana and ignored this slur on his good name. 'Lamin must have lifted it!'

In the end, of course, the key was found on the bookshelf, under his calculator, where he had put it. But this was only after I had dropped my preparations for the Germans' breakfast, leapt into the 2CV and driven to Sukuta to find a mechanic who could start the motor without the key. As we bucked over hillocks and dipped into sandy troughs, I grumbled and nagged: 'Any self-respecting 15-year-old Glasgow delinquent could start the bloody thing with a piece of wire!' By the time we got to Sukuta we had blamed each other for everything but the start of the Gulf War.

Our tourists, happily, didn't complain about the delay in their coffee, bread, honey and water-melon. Neither did the Land Rover passengers complain when Ray turned up three-quarters of an hour late. And that night he brought them back for a lobster barbecue. Big Sara from the village did her usual number with a hand-picked squad of young drummers and dancers, and everyone danced in the firelight till midnight.

Last night, the Germans drank all the whisky and moved onto the gin. My daughter was with them till 3.30 am, on the pretext of improving her German. She looked slightly pale this morning, but I didn't have the heart to ask her the German for 'I have a hangover'. Now that Ulie and Monika are due to leave, and have paid their bill in full (after checking my arithmetic carefully with a pocket calculator) I feel more kindly disposed to them. Ulie's eyes still flash, and Monika still over-acts, but they are almost weeping at the idea of leaving us! They plan to come back soon. Three days ago, the very thought would have filled me with horror, but this evening I find myself saying: 'How nice, we'd love to have you back.' These days, it's Anton that Ray is cross with. Anton remarked on our lack of proper ablutions and the fact that, he said, there was dog-shit in the area behind Hut A.

I personally marked out every metre and couldn't see anything that looked like a dog-turd but, even if there was, the poor beasts have to go somewhere. Tourists, I grumbled to myself, shouldn't be wandering about in that area, which is adjacent to the generator house, anyway. As for our loos and showers, bearing in mind the prices we charge, I think they're pretty good. We may have a problem with our pump, but they ALWAYS have buckets of water, clean bowls and cisterns, towels and soap – which is more than can be said for some restaurants and hotels. I did my Madame Relwan bit and smiled crisply at Anton, making some witty sally calculated to cool tempers. Ray, on the other hand, looked very upset and suggested that if Anton didn't like it, he could go elsewhere. So then Anton looked upset. 'It was a joke,' he said. But Gambians, particularly Wollofs, are very sensitive souls.

In Glasgow, Ray had looked stunned when he heard husbands calling to their wives 'Come on, ratbag!' Or girlfriends saying: 'Look at the silly eejit, he's as ****ed as a newt!' Merry sarcasm and good-natured verbal abuse are lost on a Wollof. They can brood and sulk for days on end, and have to be coaxed out of it by abject apologies, flattering and appeals to their Muslim charity and benevolence of spirit. To be fair, they also forgive things that would cause three-hundred years of clan warfare in Scotland. Bakary from Uncle Dembo's told us: 'Oh, dear, this is terrible. My wife's sister has been beaten by her husband and she is now in hospital with a fractured skull. She might die.' I asked about the husband, the brute who put her there. 'Oh, the doctor says we should call the police, but he is just a boy. We will ask the girl to forgive him, and he is very, very sorry and promises never to do such a thing again.' Huh! As a matter of interest, she was released from hospital and she did forgive him.

A man went to buy a car on behalf of his best friend, who had given him several thousand dalasi (call it £350, a lot of lolly here) for the transaction. The man never reached the car, but spent the money on – so we heard – drink, women and presents for himself. His friend raged and wept. But he forgave him. I am now quite used to Ray blowing his top at his brothers or some acquaintance from Bijilo and yelling: 'I will never speak to him again! He will never put a foot in this compound again!' Then, a few days later, he'll offer a grudging 'N'anga def?' (How are you), and the day after that, the fall-out might never have happened.

Anyway, I smoothed things over, and Anton is still here. Ebou the builder is making a concrete tower behind the visitors' loo. Ray, stung by Anton's criticisms of our lavatories, is creating a kind of Heath Robinson arrangement, whereby an oil drum will be heaved on top of this tower and filled with water every day. A pipe will supply the water to the two cisterns. This will entail Ray and Musa clambering up and down a wobbly ladder handing buckets of water to each other which have been pulled from the well, and pouring them into the oil drum, but it means flushing will once more be possible and Anton will make no more snide remarks, and Ray will not go into any more huffs.

I bet the alkalo in a certain neighbouring village has no problems with HIS loo. HE probably has a jacuzzi. I say this because the venal old opium-smoker has lately acquired solar power in his mud-brick, tin-roofed compound up-wind of the fishing harbour. There has been a certain amount of speculation as to where he got the dosh for such sophisticated equipment.

Sefos are chiefs of whole areas, while alkalos are village chiefs. Usually it's the alkalos who must put their signature (or more often their thumb-print) on official documents regarding land-purchasing or leasing. They were, I think, at one time expected by the colonial powers to use money gained from the sale of land for the benefit of the community. They were trustees for the whole village. Nowadays, it appears that some of them sell every scrap of land that's undeveloped, and pocket the cash. There are even tales of land being sold several times to the same person, or of people buying land in good faith, only to be told that it is government-controlled and they have no title to it.

People who do manage to buy land seldom build anything on it for years. For a Gambian, land spells security. Our own patch is about an acre-and-a-half, and I have finally persuaded Musa to amble down to the ITC cattle area and come back with some barrowloads of manure for the bananas and other plants which are supposed to fill up the gaps behind the huts. Let's hope Anton doesn't complain about cow-dung in the garden.

Yesterday we took Cameron to Abuko. I've mentioned the nature reserve several times. It entrances me. It was five o'clock and the big colobus monkeys with furry golden-yellow sleeves and cravats were strolling down for their evening refreshment at the lake, babies clinging to bellies, tails held high.

Two antelopes spurted through the lacy green curtains of the forest like wraiths; now you see them, now you don't. Cameron did something inevitable in his nappy and the old park ranger led us to a water-pump and solicitously sluiced cool clear water over Cameron's hindquarters. Bodily functions are regarded with healthy lack of embarrassment here. As there are no public toilets, chaps pee discreetly at the edges of the roads (notably outside Serrekunda market where the aroma is vicious). Signs here and there say No Wetting, or It is Forbidden to Urinate, but I suppose a man's gotta do what a man's gotta do.

Earlier we went to Brufut to buy crayfish. Elimman came with us and we taught him to sing Old Macdonald Had a Farm. Ibrahim, our Rasta friend with the beach-bar, went to haggle for the crayfish for me, but even he could only get them for about £10 a kilo. Considering the thirty-minute drive along roads like scar tissue, and waiting for the fishermen to bring in their creels, and then haggling over prices, the whole performance would be an extortionate nuisance. But Brufut is bonny, and the fishing-boats are painted blue and red and yellow and flanked by mounds of creamy-coloured sea-snails, sail-shaped giant skates and huge turtles. The sale of turtle shells is illegal, but it would be fanciful to pretend that there isn't a lively market in passing them off to tourists, who presumably wrap them in their beach-towels and smuggle them through Customs to hang them on their walls in Frankfurt and Finchley.

One of the nice things about Abuko is the educational aspect. There is a large, low, cool room perched high above the lake, where series of pictures and charts display the havoc that mankind is wreaking on its environment. The wildlife there – apart from a few robust lions and hyenas – exists in a satisfyingly natural habitat, and the Reserve also provides a veterinary service where local people can take their sick pets, have them neutered or, if necessary, painlessly put down. Not enough people make use of the service. There are packs of stray dogs everywhere, and poor skinny dogs sleep in the middle of the roads at night, gazing at the drivers who swerve to avoid them with lacklustre eyes.

I've put off telling the next bit for many pages, because I cry when I think of it. Bawbee is dead. You'll remember her habit of loping across the bush to meet up with us when we went for a drink at Uncle Dembo's, or shopping at the supermarket?

One cold, windy night we took the Land Rover along with some of our guests. I settled them down at Uncle Dembo's while I went to the telephone box waiting for a call from Carol in Scotland. This was a few weeks before she arrived unexpectedly at Yundum airport and she was worried sick about the Gulf Crisis, then at its menacing worst. I had received frightened, panicky letters from her. 'What if the Israelis respond? What if it develops into a nuclear confrontation? What if . . .?' I noticed Bawbee panting up to our table, grinning guiltily, green eyes ghostly in the moonlight, and patted her absent-mindedly before going to the phone. The call, when it came, just upset me more than ever. 'Maybe I'll take Cameron somewhere safe . . . the Pacific . . . somewhere far away from the centre of the conflict . . .' Then the fifty-pences ran out at her end, and I was left wondering when I'd ever see her again.

We had to push the Land Rover to start it, the weather was so cold that I was shivering violently (this DOES happen here, believe it or not, even when the days are hot as a vindaloo), and we were all feeling grouchy. We drove off without Bawbee. We came back five minutes later but she was gone, and we thought she must have made her own way back to the compound. I spent a grim fitful night, worrying about Carol, worrying about Bawbee, and at dawn we drove back to Uncle Dembo's and found her brown body lying, as though asleep, at the side of the taxi rank. 'Don't look! Don't look!'

Ray cried. The magical green eyes were finally closed. I still imagine that I see her, under the baobab or on look-out duty at the gate. Do dogs have ghosts? She was our first pup, right from the time we began to build our lives here. She shared our love for each other. Silly to feel like this about a dog, but I can't help it.

On Drink, Dustbins and Improvisation

The exhaust pipe of the 2CV was ready to crumble to pieces again, so we took it to the blacksmith at London Corner in Serrekunda so that he could patch it up once more. His yard is a higgledy-piggledy mess of bits of cars, wrought-iron gates, the shells of lorries and the rusting corpses of innumerable mysterious objects.

You have to get the nomenclature right. His is a welding repair-shop. A garage is what they call the bush-taxi stances, like the hectic sprawl behind the market, where the legless beggars crawl between the women selling bread and tomatoes, and cars and mini-vans ply for trade, their boys yelling 'Banjul! Banjul! Bakau! Bakau!' and hauling passengers in as fast as they can at two or three dalasi a time. Young men selling bales of striped cotton, calabashes full of mangoes, imported cotton shirts and kola nuts thrust their wares through the open windows, running after moving vehicles if necessary to complete a transaction.

Workshops are therefore not called garages; neither are petrol stations. And petrol stations don't provide air for your tyres, water for your radiator or charges for your battery. Often, they don't even provide petrol, now that I come to think of it. You go to a tyre-shop for air, for which you pay up to five dalasi per wheel (about 35p). One day I was sitting in the Land Rover waiting for the Senegalese tyre-man to finish checking our tyres when there was a violent explosion. He'd been chatting to someone while filling the rear nearside tyre and it just blew up!

In the workshops the various tradesmen, wearing incredibly filthy torn clothes, each do their own thing. The welder welds, the mechanic mends, the electrician fixes your lights and each gets paid separately. Each has his sons or nephews with him, aged maybe six or seven or eight, who hand him his spanners or hold the sizzling blowtorch while he goes off for a cigarette. These tiny apprentices must learn a lot even if they never go to school. Chickens run about between the clutter of cars being repaired. In the corner is a furniture business where a man is sawing and planing and varnishing elaborate chairs. In another corner the women are making a huge pot of rice. There are no pits or ramps or tuning equipment, but they do a pretty good job. If they need a grease-gun they have to go and find the one man in the area who owns one, and pay him ten dalasi to use it, not counting the grease. Once, the mechanic couldn't find the size of spanner he needed so he took a bush-taxi to Old Jeshwan, borrowed one, and was back within half-an-hour to continue the job.

The beggar-boys come in there too. I get furious even thinking about these wild-eyed little urchins, who go to Muslim teachers who are supposed to teach them the Koran and look after their moral development. In fact, like so many Fagans, they send them out every morning dressed in rags, hungry and hollow-eyed, to dangle their large tomato-paste tins in front of likely-looking donors. The coins they collect are for Allah, but I think the teachers pocket most of it. The little boys will – if you insist – recite chunks of the Koran, like parrots, totally unaware of the message of the words. If you give a dalasi to one, you suddenly find yourself surrounded by ten or twenty all clutching your arms like spiders. It is sometimes frightening, always pathetic, and distresses me a lot.

Anyway, back to London Corner. The welder said it would take maybe forty minutes to tack our exhaust together, so we went for a stroll. This is our old stomping ground. We lived along the lane, past the piggery, in the compound that crooked, thieving lovable Olla ran for his brother. I don't know why the area is called London Corner. For a start it isn't a corner, and it sure doesn't look like London. We felt sloppy and nostalgic remembering the days when we lived on bread and sardines because Olla had nicked the wiring and piping for the kitchens that were supposed to be built behind the rented rooms in the compound.

We went for a drink in the City Edge pub, a real Gambian pub where I am almost the only tubab ever seen and no-one stares, and working men come into gossip and sip Guinness or Vimto. The barmaid is called Mariama too, and nods a greeting, even though she hasn't seen us for a year. There's a high battered unvarnished counter and some spindly shelves carrying dusty bottles. Some benches teeter outside under the corrugated iron awning, and there is an atmosphere of unflurried competent service, even if you have to drink beer from the bottle and stub your cigarettes out on the concrete floor.

I drank White of Whites wine, an imported Spanish wine which is bottled in Banjul in bottles the same as the ones the Guinness comes in, complete with screw-top. It is very drinkable – a robust little rot-gut – and only costs six-and-a-half dalasi a bottle (about 45p). Johnny Walker Black Label is 42p a shot and there are cobwebby bottles of

Moet at half the supermarket price. We buy the Gambian-bottled wine, red and white, in bulk for our tourists. We used to sell the red in the beach-bar. One group of Germans became addicted to it, and Ray had to keep rushing into town for more crates as they thumped the table and called 'Wein!'

They got very merry on it, and came every day for hours at a time. The women, large and hearty, got frisky and began flirting with the beach-boys, like large white sharks pouncing on blue-black mackerel. Then they would reel along the sand back to their hotel, shouting, 'Tomorrow! You get more wine and we come again tomorrow!'

Now, at our huts, I think I treat my tourists pretty well. I ply them with free jugs of coffee (which is bloody expensive here) and I sell them whisky and gin at half the price of the nice earnest German motel in Kerr Seringe, with its solar power and callisthenics. Most of our guests drink beer, some of them faster than we can supply it. It would be nice to buy by the gross, but we never seem to have the capital. Today's dalasi are tomorrow's cement, or fish or watchman's wages, and now Ray's mum wants me to buy her a new mattress because she has a sore back. I have a sore back too, but I suppose mothers-in-law must be humoured. If I oblige her, it will have to be with an African mattress, a large bag of canvas sacking stuffed with straw, which is very serviceable provided you get good-quality stuffing from which most of the insects have been excised. It gets lumpy after a while, but then you empty out the straw, cut some new stuff and fill it again.

Ray's mum has never asked me for anything before, except a photo of my own mum, which is stuck to the wall in her house, so I can't complain. And I feel guilty because I have been just a mite extravagant on my own behalf for a change. Caroline and I went to the market to buy fabric. The fabric is the best thing in the Gambia (apart from the sun, the sea, the monkeys and the birds). Not just the local batiks, stiff cottons tie-dyed in luscious natural dyes, but the imported cottons and silks and soft cotton-jersey which sell at about £1 a metre. Gambian tailors can copy anything, from faded magazine pictures to an old pair of trousers, down to the last pleat and tuck and the final buttonhole. It usually takes a couple of days to get even the most elaborate outfit made up. This time Muna the tailor took longer because he was frantically stitching, often through the night, at a host of blue school dresses for children to wear in a parade in front of the President. He was frustrated by the fact that the GUC kept cutting off his power just when he was in the middle of a waistband or a zip. His machine is electric, which is very sophisticated for a local tailor, but less practical than the old treadles and hand-machines you see in most shops.

Lesley, our friend from Callander, is finding old machines for Tanji. The women in Caroline's project there are ecstatic when a sewing-machine arrives. They are building up a series of workshops, from soap-making to carpentry, and with their venerable Singers they'll make bedspreads and wraparound skirts to sell to tourists, and baby clothes for their own families. I feel rather proud of the fact that, through me, Caroline met Lesley, who then introduced a series of goodhearted Scots to the Tanji Project. There's a publican and a local newspaper editor in the east of Scotland, a couple who run a newsagent's and gift shop at the motorway service station at Gretna, and a couple who live in Gatwick. It's Douglas from Gatwick who works in airport handling, who smooths the way for crates of sewing-machines, children's bikes, medical supplies and books to come from Scottish donors to the Gambia for the people of Tanji.

Muna eventually produced a pair of dashingly tailored shorts for me, a skirt and blouse and some baggy shorts for the beach. I felt as thrilled as though I'd just had a shopping spree in Harrods. My other extravagance is plants. Gradually I'm building up a collection: tiny strands of bougainvillaea, hibiscus, Christmas roses, coleus, eucalyptus saplings. I buy them from an enterprising young man who's started a 'garden centre' on the Badala Highway on the road to Bakau. He makes concrete decorative tubs for the plants too. He has a well in the middle of his patch, and he mixes up the concrete then puts it into 'moulds' which are actually just smooth basin-shaped holes dug out of the hard earth.

I have so far planted about fifty things, but they look puny beside the weeds and scrub, especially as Musa who, against my better judgement, is working for us once more, is so busy fawning over the tourists, scrounging money, cigarettes, tee-shirts and Cokes from them, that he has no time for anything as mundane as watering plants.

I always pay Namjara, Musa's tiny but tough wife, surreptitiously, when he's nowhere around, otherwise he swoops on her and demands money for cigarettes. They end up yelling blue murder at one another, and their snotty-nosed son howls and dribbles, and it's just not worth all the aggro. Musa has the technique of wheedling honed to perfection. 'I am a very poor man. These people they do not pay me much money. It is a very hard life,' he'll sigh, when he can manage to haul himself out of the wheelbarrow long enough to stand up and plead his case. He does a roaring trade in our empty wine, whisky and gin bottles (emptied not by us but by the tourists, I hasten to add), which he sells to shops.

Containers of any description are prized. The large empty tomato paste tins are used not just by the beggar-boys, but for the dogs' rice which Ray's mum brings round every afternoon, for mixing paint and boiling water. The bottles with a spout and a plunger in which a certain brand of window-cleaning liquid is sold in the supermarkets are highly prized when they can be found in tubab dustbins – they are used for spraying plants, greasing axles and all manner of things. Our empty bottles can be sold to Mauritanian shopkeepers or Gambian market-stall owners, who use them to hold groundnut and palm oil, kerosene and water. Plastic bags are carefully filched from our rubbish and washed for carrying fish, peanut paste, flour, rice, cassavas.

Tin cans are hammered flat and used to make cups and pots. I used to sneer at the scrap vehicles I saw scattered along the roadside or lying in the bush, but Ray pointed out that every bit is gradually taken to patch up some other car; whole roofs are burned off, doors are appropriated, wings, axles, wheels. It is not uncommon to see mongrel cars made up of a rich assortment of pieces from different sources, or cars swaying along lop-sidedly on tyres two different widths. Make-do-and-mend is a way of life.

Lots of elderly men have managed to acquire umbrellas, usually big black city-gent brollies, with spokes missing, which they carry solemnly on high to shield them from the sun. But when it's the rainy season, most people use the large spreading-fingered leaves of the 'fan' palm-tree to keep the rain off their heads. Children's toys are unknown, unless a kindly brother or uncle makes a simple wooden doll for a favourite child, but the kids themselves attach tin-cans to sticks and push them around the way spoiled European brats push their expensive wheeled playthings.

Women who are lucky enough to find a discarded tubab brassiere or nylon camisole-topped underskirt wear them proudly, often without anything on top (though always lots of fabric wrapped around from the waist down, as – as I've told you before – it's the lower regions which are the erogenous zones). Wily tourists barter such items for batiks and wooden craftwork.

Every rusty nail, scrap of wire, off-cut of wood or vinyl discovered on an ex-pat's building plot is snatched and hidden away by the locals. For all of these items are difficult and expensive to buy.

Labour is cheap. When we had a wickedly smashed front wing fixed by our blacksmith friend at London Corner, it cost about £8 for a job that would have cost hundreds of pounds sterling in Scotland. But materials are often amazingly expensive. Raw white timber planking, which usually warps because it hasn't been seasoned properly, is about 80p a metre, and a kilo of nails is well over £1 – a lot when you remember the average Gambian wage is around £33 a month. A jar of decent jam is almost £2.00. The fact that so many things must be imported is one of the reasons for steep prices. But avocados, which grow profusely on trees all over the place, were costing 42p EACH in a shop I called at yesterday. I long for the day when our own avocados, bananas, papaya and aubergines will flourish among the flowers and weeds.

Meanwhile, I entertain Musa by filling our rubbish-hole (where I burn everything after he's had time to do his midgie-raker routine) with interesting things like empty cat-food tins, shampoo bottles and dead torch batteries. I don't know what he does with the discarded letters from my bank-manager, but he's more than welcome to them!

Going Dutch . . .
And a Little Bit
of Irish

Roel and Helma and three-year-old Ian rolled up one day in an eighteen-year-old red ex-British Army Land Rover ambulance. Richard, a doctor at the Royal Victoria Hospital, had found them driving slowly round the market area in Bakau and brought them along here. 'They need a place to park,' he said. Now they more or less live here, though I suppose one day they'll have to go back to the Hague.

They drove down from Holland, through Europe, into Africa – Algeria, Morocco, Mauritania, Burkina, Faso, Benin, Togo, Ghana and Senegal, living in the back of the ambulance, which is cunningly fitted out with little cupboards under Ian's bunk and a deep storage area under Helma and Roel's space on the floor. It's not everyone who can say: 'When we were arrested in Ougadougou . . .' or 'We almost bought a beautiful armchair in Togo . . .' but they can. Roel is a rangy, rascally ex-lorry driver, with devastating blue eyes, a cross between Rod Stewart, Richard Harris and Gerard Depardieu. He drinks beer in impressively large quantities and is learning to play African drums. Helma is a slender, tranquil but tough, fabric designer. She reminds me of the mum in Swiss Family Robinson. Her boxes and bags contain sewing things, spices and herbs, a knife sharpener, prickly heat powder, egg-whisks, Dutch storybooks, everything a family needs for a year in Africa.

Roel lounges in a deck-chair reading, drinking or sleeping. He is an engaging, infuriating male chauvinist pig. Helma washes or sews or paints pictures with Ian. Ian is a holy terror, lithe and strong and white-blond, who runs around naked screaming 'Musa! Musa!' and terrorising the dogs. He speaks Dutch, French, English and various West African dialects in confused smatterings. Helma and I rub soap into sheets beside the well, squatting on low wooden stools, and she tells me of the batiks in Ghana, the time Ian nearly died of fever, the bicycles in Benin.

This week we have an English girl in Hut B and an earnest, ecologically aware couple of bird-watchers in Hut C. These two get up at dawn and stride along the forest path spotting obscure feathered species, which they note down earnestly in their little pads. When you have a conversation with them, their eyes are always gazing into the distance, in case something flies down and settles on a branch. Last week we had a couple who were reading the auto-biographies of Norman Tebbitt and Edwina Currie, which I thought was highly suspicious. He was older than her, grey-haired and dignified and said he owned an estate agency. We speculated that he was really a runaway vicar or a high-ranking civil servant.

We reckoned she was his secretary and he'd told his wife he was going to a conference or a religious retreat. Not that there was a lot of visible passion. Mostly they just studied the lives of the Tories and sipped tea in the garden.

Our very favourite people of the moment, apart from Helma and Roel, are a Belgian couple, Za-za and Szimmie. They're on honeymoon and touchingly in love. Za-za owns a prosperous little supermarket in Bruges, where Szimmie makes the quiches and salads in the delicatessen department. He is short and fat and ugly and splendidly dead-pan when he utters hilarious one-liners. She is dark and sweet and adores him. They are staying at a very posh hotel, but they hate its pompous sophistication and sneak away at every opportunity to drink beer from the bottle and eat Ray's baked fish and play with the cats and dogs. Za-za looks like Mel Smith and thinks Ray is a marvellous guy, which is true. They insist we visit them in Belgium whenever we go to Europe, and they have given Ray a peaked cap emblazoned with the name of their shop.

I don't recall ever meeting so many interesting people when I was a journalist. 'Who did you interview?' Ray asks me sometimes, and I have to struggle to remember the shadowy figures. David 'Dr Death' Owen . . . Cliff Richard . . . Jeffrey Archer . . . John Smith . . . Lord Linlithgow . . . Kenny Everett . . . Max Bygraves . . . Ian Botham . . . lots of footballers and actors and MPs. But none of them seem as funny and interesting and entertaining as Helma and Roel and Za-za and Szimmie.

Last night we went to a St Patrick's night party. Ironically, it was held in the restaurant of a pair of true-blue Brits with Union Jacks on their walls, because they'd offered the organisers a cheap menu. But some of the Irish guests felt ill-at-ease and the discussion ranged vigorously over various aspects of English oppression and colonial imperialism. Ray was one of the only two black people there. The other was Rauchie, a nice Fula girl who is the girlfriend of an English water engineer. Donal the priest, who is far too attractive to be obliged to be celibate, was leading off the dancing of Irish jigs, assisted by our little carrotty-haired friend, Brendan, who takes these things ever so seriously. He was annoyed because the British hosts had put all their pals and regular customers in the good seats near the centre, and shoved the Irish Society lot into the seats near the door. The English types sang Roll Out the Barrel and Waltzing Matilda.

They sang it loud enough to blot out the jig music, but the dancers jumped and twirled on pugnaciously. 'Don't worry at all,' said one sonsy Irish colleen. 'The English always start very loud, but they fade early.' She was right. By ten o'clock they were all sweating and sagging over their green-dyed beer and the Irish were up on their feet singing the kind of songs that make you weep for your mother and your history and the smell of a peat fire.

One of them is Peter, an archivist at Banjul Museum, who is searching out and writing down a collection of Gambian folk tales and songs which have been handed down through families and recounted by the griots but never written on paper before. Sometimes, he admits wickedly, the stories lack a good punchline, so he embellishes them just a little, but with sympathy and affection. The water engineer moaned about how he really wanted to stay on and instigate a village hygiene programme, but he can't get the funding so he has to go home and look for another job. I wonder if he'll take Rauchie with him? There was a midwife running a village birthing programme for mothers in tiny inaccessible hamlets up-river. There was a financial wizard who advises the President on fiscal matters. And lots of other folk called Sean and Siobhan and Patrick. Peter swore he had his shamrock delivered by courier.

I heard afterwards that there had been a fight outside between two of the English guests. The Irish all went to each other's houses and played sentimental songs and drank Guinness and whiskey till the sky grew light and the cocks crowed. I believe on St Andrew's Night some hotels have functions at which dark-skinned people appear in kilts and sporrans, but I haven't sampled that. I know that the nice Wollof who works in the National Trading Company store where we buy our hardboard and paint is a keen member of a Scottish country dancing group.

Last week we went back to Casamance. There is a hotel there, in Abène, ten kilometres from Kafountine, which is my idea of paradise. It has smooth emerald lawns and mountains of bougainvillaea and hibiscus, and you can play bowls in a grove shaded by tall palms and eucalpytus, or just stroll through the lush gardens, down the white terrace steps to the beach. It's miles from anywhere and no-one tries to sell you water-melon or invite you to their compound because there just isn't anyone there at all.

In fact, when we were there, there were no tourists either, or if so, they were well hidden. The owner is French and has four hotels, each managed by one of his sons. The rooms are beautiful with fluffy pink towels and pink soap and extra pillows, the gardens are trimmed and watered constantly, and the restaurant serves succulent French food. According to the staff, each son has his own aeroplane. I don't know if that's true, but certainly Michel, the son who runs this place, has a plane, which he lands on a small isolated strip adjacent to the hotel.

We brought some tourists here once, just for a drink. They looked around and said: 'Hmmm. It's very nice of course, but what do you DO here? Do they have entertainment in the bar in the evenings? Isn't there a swimming-pool? A disco?' Tourists can be very exasperating people. We really meant to go and stay in a *campement* in Kafountine where the accommodation is three quid a night. We made the fortunate mistake of calling in at the Kalissai Hotel first. When we reached the *campement*, with its little grey huts and army blankets and mosquitoes, the water was off because the well had run dry and we sat on the bed snarling at each other until we both said at the same time: 'Let's go back to Kalissai!'

It cost us all the money we were going to use for cement and timber and corrugated iron for our new huts, but we felt it was worth it. A couple of days later the English tourists and the bird-watchers and Za-za and Szimmie all said they'd like to go in the Land Rover for a day-trip to Casamance, so that paid for the building materials. We don't have cash flow, so much as a cash trickle, but we get along.

For weeks on end there has been either no petrol or no diesel in the Gambia. People have been queueing at petrol stations for hours on end, or wandering about with jerry-cans trying to buy fuel on the black market, at grossly inflated prices. Lorries and cars and taxis are strung along the road where they've run out of gas. Hotels have been periodically cutting off their electricity to conserve supplies of diesel for their generators. The GUC (Gambia Utilities Corporation) has been lopping off power supplies for days on end because they don't have fuel for their power station. We scrounged some gasoline from Michel, the aeroplane-owning hotel manager, as Senegal doesn't seem to have the same supply problems as the Gambia.

Last night we sat in Uncle Dembo's in the dark, because he had even run out of candles. People kept striking matches so that they could see how much beer they had left. As for us, we did in fact buy three jerry cans from Roel some time ago, intending to fill them and stockpile for emergencies, but the trouble is, as soon as we buy it we use it. We also bought Roel's very swanky de luxe portable integrated stereo component system (what I would call a radio cassette player) and their five-year guaranteed heavy-duty no-maintenance battery.

I say bought, but what we do is a kind of barter system. So many nights' use of their pitch equals one jerry can, with extra points for the well-water and the use of the toilets. A certain number of suppers of barbecued fish, garlic prawns or kefta and a far greater number of bottles of beer to slake Roel's immense thirst equals one de luxe portable integrated stereo component system, and so on.

We all get a great deal of enjoyment from this, with Ray claiming that his fish is worth at least one speaker and Roel swearing like a trooper, as is his wont. He does it in a very attractive Dutch drawl, eyes twinkling, so that no-one takes offence. Ian, on the other hand, has picked up the habit, and when anyone he doesn't know comes to the compound they are confronted by a small nude boy glaring at them furiously and snarling '**** off!' in a loud voice. He has had, to be fair, some unnerving experiences with Africans. In some West African states, Helma told me, the children would surround him in droves, pulling at his hair and tugging his clothes, pinching his skin and jeering at him. Eventually some resident whites told Helma and Roel that the only way to get rid of them was to lob a stone at them or chase them with sticks. This, at first, was exactly what Ian did with any of the cheerful, welcoming youngsters who hang about here, and they ran off startled but not overly offended. They'd come to peer at him because they thought at first that Ian was Cameron, who also has silvery hair and also runs about naked shouting for Musa. One tubab looks pretty much like another, so they come shouting Cammy-RON, Cammy-RON! and get quite a shock at the shrieked expletives. They're beginning to realise it is a different small boy, and Ian's beginning to realise that they are friends, not foes.

The other day I found him doing roly-polys and hand-stands and catastrophic cartwheels with Elimman and Modou. Elimman misses Cameron a lot but, like me, he feels that having another little blond boy about the place streaking among the bananas, is better than nothing. As to Ian's tantrums, which are usually brought on by something of gargantuan importance like our having run out of mustard or his not liking the colour of his tee-shirt, and during which he kicks and screams and stamps and it takes me huge resources of self-control not to slap his bottom hard . . . as for these, we're all getting used to them, but the Gambians find them completely incomprehensible. Gambian kids don't have tantrums. They wouldn't dare.

I have the occasional tantrum myself, mind you. But when I do, I always tell Ray I'm merely expressing, volubly, a very valid and important point of view. He looks at me and mutters something which I think is the Wollof equivalent of 'Aye, that'll be right!'

Unhinged but Undaunted

I have just spent two hours crawling round Serrekunda in the 2CV trying to find hinges and door handles for the new hut we've been building. The carpenter, a large, jolly chap with a laugh like a chainsaw, disappeared off the site for twelve days.

Everything ground to a halt. Empty window sockets gazed at me dolefully. Half-finished door-frames lounged against walls. This is a common phenomenon. Builders, brickies, electricians, plumbers and carpenters will come and work for you with great gusto for a few days or even hours, then suddenly, simply disappear. Usually this is because they have asked you, with great persuasiveness and promises of redoubled efforts on your behalf, for an advance on their fee.

You comply; they pocket the advance and go off to their compounds and sit in the sun, or find another client and start work for him, so that they can ask him for an advance too.

Ebou, the master mason, went to the carpenter's house in Sukuta and told his wife to inform her husband that if he didn't come next day, he, Ebou, had a friend in the gendarmerie who would come and arrest him and carry him off to the Half Die prison. So he came the next day, beaming widely.

'Hey, it's good to see you people! I was waiting for you. Every day I waited for a message to say you had the things I needed to continue the work.'

What things?

'Hey, the things for the door, you know? The hinges. Every day I waited . . .' I was tempted to yell at him that the ceilings were to be put up, the windows were to be put in their frames and the mason wanted him to make shuttering so that he could get on with HIS work. But with commendable self-control I kept quiet. 'I'll be back at dawn tomorrow, so you be sure you get me these hinges so that I can work hard for you all day', he commanded briskly, and sailed off back to Sukuta, laughing merrily as he went.

So this morning I was up before dawn. Ray is in Casamance with our latest group of tourists in the Land Rover, and Musa is away sleeping and sulking and trying not to smoke during Ramadan, so there are just a few little things I have to do before I buy hinges. Like hauling up enough water from the well to water all the seedlings. Since I read one hut-dweller's postcard home, which described our garden as 'a dusty field', I am very sensitive about our attempts at growing things.

One reason the garden wasn't exactly flourishing, we discovered, was that Musa had given up watering in the mornings. It's a long time since the last rain, and I swear all my baby plants lift up their heads and sing with joy as I trudge round with my watering-can. The black bucket for the well is leaking like a sieve again, so by the time you pull it up most of the water has dribbled out. Sometimes, if Caroline's staying the night, she helps me. She says it's splendid exercise, though I doubt if she'd be as enthusiastic if she had to do it every day.

We both have our own technique. She goes for the knees-bent, back-stooped, hip-swivelling style. My own approach is straight-backed, swinging the torso from the waist, right-left, right-left, which I consider to be more stylish.

Until three days ago, my next job was sweeping and mopping out the loos and the breakfast hut. But I have enlarged our workforce by two pubescent schoolgirls, Awa and Adama, who now do this for me, when they remember to arrive on time. Adama is a bright little thing, but Awa is lumpish, and I have doubts as to how long she'll last.

I give them lessons on loo-cleaning. Their own toilet arrangements at home involve African loos – simply a hole in a concrete mound, over a deep, wide pit. It is perfectly functional, but doesn't encourage a girl to grow up knowing about Vim and U-bends. 'You have to sprinkle this powder in here,' I explain, 'and rub all round the inside and outside of the basin with this cloth, you see? If a tubab defecates' – you will recall that Gambian English is extremely formal – 'and something gets on to his hands and into his body, he will get sick and he may die and it will be your fault,' I utter dramatically. They look suitably awed, and occasionally scatter a little scouring powder down the lavvy-pan.

I make revolutionary suggestions, like taking the chairs and boxes of books and magazines OUT from the breakfast room before sweeping and mopping it, instead of brushing around them. This confuses them a little, but they're getting better every day. I have bribed them by telling them that when they leave school I will be able to give them references for possible jobs in hotels or other tubab households. They think, poor mites, that this would be a wonderful career-move.

Helma, our Dutch friend, comes with me to Serrekunda to buy the hinges. We stop to buy cement on the way. The Mauritanian shopkeeper looks appalled when I hint that he might lift it into the back of the car for us, so we find a bevy of urchins who don't even ask for a dalasi. Yesterday I became quite scared outside the supermarket, because I gave out a handful of coins to some of these ragged, hollow-eyed little boys and another twenty appeared from nowhere, clutching at my arms and clothing with talon-like fingers.

Their 'Koranic' teachers have a lot to answer for. My friend Monica, the born-again Christian, takes bread for them, because she says they'll just give money to their teachers and still be hungry. They are like the unlovely flotsam washed along the Victorian streets of Dickens' London. Everyone, black and white, gives them coins, but it's a stingy kind of conscience-salving compromise, when what's needed is to get them off the streets and into a decent well-fed, adequately educated way of life. One day, automatically, I said: 'What do you say?' – meaning, 'Say thank you'. Very patronising of me, I realise. I was bombarded by a dozen little voices all chanting Koranic verses at me like parrots.

Talking of parrots, I almost bought one the other day, from the two muscle-bound boys who have come to clean the worst of the weeds from the garden. It sat on a stick and looked cute but the asking price was too much, and how would I keep it away from the cats? Anyway, after Helma and I bought the cement, we went in search of a stall that sold hinges and got lost in the maze of back lanes crowded with goats and kids and women with huge bundles on their heads. A big crowd was gathered outside one Mauritanian shop, yelling and then darting away when a gendarme appeared. I think someone was being arrested for something. The Mauritanian was one of the local money-lenders, who often have altercations with their clients.

Finally we met the muscular parrot-owners, Yancobi and Ibrahim, and asked them to go into the market and buy hinges, door-locks and handles. 'If they see your white face they'll charge you too much,' they assured me. A bush-taxi – a large white mini-bus – had slewed across the road. There was an ugly dent at the front and a pack of passengers standing around it analysing the cause of the accident. I negotiated a passage through them as bicycles and motor-bikes swung across my path and teenage boys banged on the windows shouting 'Hullo! How are you? What country you from?'

'Demal! Du ma tourist!' I growled at them. You'd think they could suss out for themselves that a dusty woman with a two-year tan and a bag of cement in the back seat wasn't a holidaymaker worth chatting up. The Wollof growl doesn't help. 'Ah, you are a Gambian! That is good! Where is your compound? What is your husband's name?' Oh, sod off!

I bought mince in the supermarket. I use it to make kefta – meatballs packed with fenugreek and cummin and chilli and onion which seems to go down very well with the tourists.

I bought another bucket for the well. The boys appeared at last with the hinges and door-fittings, at about half the price I would have paid. Several hours had passed. The sun was high in the sky and as usual, sweat was running down my face and dripping down my frontage.

When we got back home, the builders had packed up and left. 'The carpenter didn't come, so they couldn't work,' explained Elimman. I didn't say anything. The doors still lean against the wall, dozing gently. The windows still stare blindly, but what's the use of grumbling? No-one takes any notice.

When Ray comes back from Casamance, he won't see much change in our building project. But he'll be gobstruck at the garden. My two strapping parrot-lovers are scything their way through the dry, prickly, thorny three-foot-high weeds with gusto. The flowers on the official plant-life underneath are well-watered and now visible to the naked eye. And it is now possible, from time to time, to flush the loos in the visitors' lavatories. I co-opted a squad of little boys from the village yesterday to form a human chain and pass buckets of water from the well up to our temporary tank (the big battered oil drum on top of the concrete tower) and fill it to the top. It should last at least a day and a half. I paid off the kids in cassettes of Van Halen, Alexander Brothers and the Groundhogs, something I feel more than a mite guilty about but they all seem delighted with their booty.

Modou has been up the baobab tree gathering the fruit, large lantern-shaped pendants. It is hard and white inside and very sweet, with black seeds. Ray says people use it to make ice-cream. The leaves are packed with protein and minerals when dried and used in soups and stews. I know this because Caroline has found a book on nutrition to help her set up informal sessions for the ladies of Tanji on how to get the best out of local foodstuffs.

Smoked bongo fish are, I read, absolutely jam-packed with nutrients. Domada, the peanut sauce or soup made with pounded groundnuts cooked in onion, garlic, tomato paste and water, is splendidly endowed with protein. All manner of leaves and plants which grow locally can be used to provide extra vitamins and minerals. Unfortunately, the women tend to look askance at them, and long instead for the hidden delights of our several recently established supermarkets. These are patronised by tubabs and rich Gambians, but no village woman could afford to pay, for example, £3 for a wee tin of Nescafe or £2.50 for a tin of corned beef. The village diet is 'coos' – ground millet with sour milk – for breakfast, and variations on rice for all other meals. Sometimes they add 'sooppa', that disgusting glutinous occra-based gunge; sometimes domada, but green vegetables never appear on the menu, eggs hardly ever, meat only a few times a year on feast days. I took Elimman into a supermarket a couple of times and he was mesmerised. He had never seen so many consumer durables in his life; his eyes almost popped out of his head. When I bought him some nasty fizzy sugary soft drink of the kind British kids love, he eyed it suspiciously.

He's familiar with Coke and Sprite, but as for the many elaborate new concoctions, not to mention things like chocolate biscuits, jam, baked beans, Brie, cat food and mortadella which he saw in abundance, they are as out-of-this-world for him as quail's eggs and caviare for the average small resident of Ruchill.

Indeed, it's only in the last few months I've begun to take them for granted myself. I don't buy many Western luxury goods, but I confess that I enjoy looking at them! Crazy prices, sometimes. Imported Scandinavian shrimps sell at about four times the prices of the fabulous local ones you can buy fresh at the market. The highly-paid European and American expatriates, working for the ODA, the UN, the various embassies and some local big businesses, wallow in it all, and the mostly Lebanese owners prosper and buy swimming pools and giant dishes for their cable TV systems.

But the wee boys who filled my water-butt reckon they're well-off today. I doubt if even the UN representative or the Senegalese ambassador own their very own Alexander Brothers' or Groundhogs cassettes!

The Bartered Bride

Ray's brother Lamin is a lanky likeable young man. On occasions I have seen him dance like a whirling dervish to the music of the drums, his long legs folding and unfolding and kicking the air, his arms pivoting. But most of the time he is a shy, sleepy soul who would drop into a deep slumber if you propped him against a tree for twenty seconds.

He has fallen mightily in love with a Bakau girl called Fatou. They hold hands under our baobab tree and last time we were in Banjul I caught Lamin coyly buying a piece of exotic parrot-patterned fabric to hang over the door of his room in the family compound. I always thought Lamin would fall for a sweet, placid girl from the village, but Fatou is a stunner and not at all placid.

Her hair is a lavish sculpture of braids woven and twirled in intricate bas-relief close to her head. Her eyes are deep and wide and flashing, and she wears clinging dresses with elaborate shoulder frills and fish-tailed hems, or sometimes mini-skirts even shorter than the tubabs wear. She is fond of shimmering green silk, the colour of the lily-leaves that cover the surface of the sacred crocodile pool near her home in Bakau. She is a cracker.

It has not escaped the notice of her parents and her senior uncles that she has spent more than a few nights behind the swirls of red, yellow and green parrots that shelter Lamin's doorway. Lamin's mum, my mother-in-law, likes her a lot. A new young able-bodied woman in the compound would be very useful to help with the cooking of the rice, the drawing of water from the well, the pounding of millet and groundnuts and the washing of clothes, not to mention the gossiping on the low chairs in front of the huts, where a new voice is always welcome.

At least two other young men, possibly more dynamic than Lamin, which wouldn't be hard, have asked for Fatou's hand in marriage, but Fatou has set her sights on Lamin.

Approaches have therefore been made by Fatou's family to the Imam of Bijilo suggesting that Fatou and Lamin have been 'playing' long enough. Gambians, as a matter of etymological interest, do not make love, they play love. It was high time he made a decent woman of her, said Fatou's mother, a woman of powerful voice and personality but a certain acquisitiveness. The Imam, as the religious teacher of the community, not to mention the fact that he is Lamin's uncle (brother of my mother-in-law) agreed, and entered into the negotiations.

The only stumbling block is that the Bakau family, which has seemingly well-connected offshoots in Senegal and considers itself a bit above our lot in Bijilo, has demanded 1000 dalasi, one cassette-player, a bed (made of carved mahogany, with a proper foam mattress, not a local sackcloth-and-straw job), and a watch, as a suitable compensation for the loss of their lovely daughter and an indication of Lamin's honourable intentions. The theory is that the bed and other items will rest at Fatou's mother's house so that, should anything ever go wrong with the marriage – if it ever takes place – she will have property there and not be destitute. The truth, I suspect, is that her mother will appropriate the lot.

Fatou has now been sent back to Bakau while negotiations proceed. The parrot cloth flutters before nothing more sensuous than Lamin's troubled dreams, while the haggling over the eventual satisfactory purchase of a new sister-in-law for me takes its slow, tortuous course. Gambians being what they are, I assumed that the deal would eventually come down to 500 dalasi, a transistor and a chair but Fatou's family seem to be tough bargainers, and things have reached deadlock.

Her senior uncle, her guardian, is in Senegal, and members of the family have gone to consult him. Lamin trudges about looking even more morose and half-asleep than usual.

His mother frets, working her way round family and friends pleading with them to contribute a loan or a gift which will help her find the loot she needs to seal the deal. The Imam acts as banker. As the owner of a proper bank account in Banjul, not to mention a motor-bike on which to travel there when necessary, he is relied upon locally as a kind of central bank of total trustworthiness (which is more than can be said of some of the employees in some of the banks themselves, but that's another story).

I have chattered cheerfully to Lamin about Scottish weddings, at which it is the father of the bride who has to dig into his pocket for a couple of hundred bottles of Asti Spumante and like numbers of prawn cocktails, chicken supremes and chocolate gateaux, while the bloke just pays for the car to the kirk. This just makes him sulkier than ever, so I've given up asking: 'Any news?' All I get is a grunt in answer.

Certainly I'm a bit of a dead-loss as a Gambian daughter-in-law. Here I am in my own compound, running after tourists and frying doughnuts for Ray, instead of in the extended family under the parental eye, collecting their firewood and stirring the benachin. But they seem to like me anyway. Ray's mum brings round left-over rice from the Day Centre where she works. It's for the dogs, hot as hellfire. She occasionally says touching little prayers to Allah thanking Him for His benificence in providing a tubab wife for her elder son.

Our little brother Elimman has been in the local private clinic having a vast swelling on his neck lanced and drained. I never thought I'd find myself supporting private medicine, but as I've said before, I have severe reservations about the Dickensian conditions at the Royal Victoria Hospital. Plump Gambian wives of prominent business people, and chubby Lebanese children are the main clients at the Kololi Clinic, where I forked out the price of Elimman's treatment. A holidaying doctor told me if it wasn't dealt with properly TB could develop. The various ju-jus and noxious potions applied by grannies and grandpas hadn't worked.

Elimman wasn't grateful for my intervention. In fact he hated me for it, lying there cocooned in crisp green cotton with needles being jabbed into his bottom, missing his mammy like mad. One night, the old lady in the next bed died. Elimman cried and cried for his mum, until she told the rest of the family they could manage without her, grasped a large bowl of rice and a sheet to wrap round her at night and went by bush taxi to the clinic, where she stayed till her son was ready to go home.

I felt like a monster, but his neck is better now and he doesn't hate me any more. He is ten and I love him better than any Gambian male apart from Ray. When I'm pulling up water from the well he pushes me away with an ever-so-macho swagger and says: 'Stop! I will do it, Mariama.' He waters the flowers and feeds the dogs and brings huge cans of drinking water from the ITC. I feed him on bread and jam or garlic sausage (beef, not pork) and tubab tea.

He is a little skelf of a thing, but of a sweet disposition and very protective of me, shouting at other boys when they line up on the wall, teetering like blackbirds in the breeze, to watch the strange antics of the white lady. I force him to write letters to my daughter, who loves him also and sends him story books. He writes: 'I hope this finds your body in good condition . . . your lovely friend Elimman.'

There are three brothers and three sisters altogether. That is to say, full-blood brothers and sisters, 'same-mother-and-father' as they say here. There are many other brothers and sisters with less solid affiliations.

There was a knock at the door this morning and I found Fatou on the doorstep. Not Lamin's Fatou, another one. 'Hullo, I am the sister of your husband,' she smiled shyly. 'We've never met because I've been training to be a nurse up-river in Bansang, so now I am here to visit you.'

She was in fact a cousin, but in Bijilo, a second-cousin-four-times-removed is still your brother or sister. We chatted and I gave her coffee, and hoped I would be able to recognise her next time we met. I try hard but often I fail to remember that the person we've bumped into in the lane is the guy we met in Uncle Dembo's three weeks ago. I don't feel too guilty about it, because, as Ray will tell you, all white people look alike too.

Ten minutes after Fatou left, Abdul came to call. I didn't recognise him either. This is because the first time I met him he was dressed in full Baye Faal gear, dreadlocks, vivid tunic and trousers made of tiny patchwork squares of coloured cloth, and a calabash for collecting charitable donations. The Baye Faal, as you may be aware, is a kind of hippie beggar-monk movement from Senegal. Abdul used to work for the Gambia Passenger Transport company, when Ray was a clerk in their office. He just dropped out one day and grew his hair. But today he was wearing a bunnet over his woolly locks and was looking for work before going back to the commune over the border.

It is lucky that most of the tourists have gone home now, what with these unexpected visitors and also the fact that Adama has done a runner. Well, she's gone to Dakar to find her mother. She is thirteen years old and endears herself to me and infuriates me at the same time.

Awa, the other girl who used to help with dish-washing and floor-mopping soon fell by the wayside. A lumpish girl who would turn up so late that I'd done all the work myself. But Adama stayed during the school holidays, arriving at dawn to rattle pots and clatter brushes and staying all day demanding to wash my clothes, clean my windows, draw my water. Sometimes she and Elimman almost come to blows over who should have the honour of supplying me with water.

Guests probably thought I was a big bully, but it's very hard to get Adama to sit down and relax.

She has been fiercely unhappy at home. Her mother dumped her on her granny when she was a baby and went to Dakar to live with another man, by whom she had several more children. Adama says her grandmother never gives her any rice and steals her clothes. I'm not sure if it's true but I shovel bread and jam into her and give her cast-off tee-shirts and jackets four sizes too big for her skinny little shape.

'I am not strong. I have never been healthy. I am too small. I am a very sick person,' she intones in a plaintive dirge, meanwhile heaving huge tubs of washing on to her head and fighting Elimman for the privilege of pulling up yet another bucket. I tell myself she's a hypochondriac with a dramatic imagination and a need for attention, but then I hear her coughing like an old woman and mix up honey and lemon and hot water for her. She banks her small wages in a jam-jar on my bookshelf. 'If I take it to the compound my grandmother will steal it', she said dourly. But suddenly she came and took all her savings and said: 'I am going to Dakar to find my mother.' She added confidently: 'She will buy me a new dress'.

Then she burst into tears. 'You don't get anyone else to work for you! I'm coming back. I just want to see my mother.' I hope she returns. I miss her resentful little face. And I'm fed-up doing my own washing.

Pretty Polly and Patter Merchants

Did I mention the baby parrot? The one Yancobi and Ibrahim tried to sell me?

People are always trying to sell me animals. The owner of the white horse has given up parading it past our gate, but wee boys keep turning up with terrified rabbits, and the other day a man with a monkey on his shoulder tried to sell it to us for almost as much as the horse would have cost.

So far I've managed to say no. I have enough problems with Maradonna and Stanley, especially since Stanley started biting people's bums. But we spent some time admiring the baby parrot and saying: 'Who's a pretty boy then?' It looked at us with its little green head tilted sideways and every now and then it jabbed at us with its indignant beak. That was when it managed to claw Helma's arm. It was her own fault; she was teaching it to walk up and down from her elbow to her wrist.

Within a few days, the small scrape-marks had turned into big nasty suppurating sores and I had to drive her to the Kololi Clinic. I've already expressed my views on the medical services in the Gambia, so I won't go on about it again, except to say that, generally speaking, I'd rather have a local witch doctor than some of the public health care I hear about.

Kololi Clinic is fine, though, if you don't mind queuing for a long time. Helma, aching bravely, took her place in the queue with a number of heavily pregnant ladies in elaborate dresses. People seem to get togged up in their best clothes to visit the doctor here. After the first hour, she moved out of the waiting room and sat on a bench outside, because there was a man howling and groaning and rolling round on the floor. I don't think there was anything serious wrong with him, but as I may also have hinted before, Gambians don't thole pain very well.

To pass the time while she was waiting, I went to buy a bucket for the well. We go through a bucket every two or three weeks, because the hand-stitching on the rubber inner-tubing doesn't last for very long. I wandered through the surging side-streets by the market helplessly peering into the dim recesses of shops containing kerosene, plastic potties, flour, mentholatum, corrugated iron and cement.

At last a cheerful young man in a straw hat told me to follow him and he beat a path through the crowds until we found a Mauritanian who sold buckets of various sizes and broad oiled cotton tape, which is much easier on the hands than rope which tears the skin off the inside of your fingers.

I have become obsessional about the numbers of items to be watered, counting them regularly and arriving at a different total every time. Sometimes whole saplings just seem to disappear, while other things I didn't know were there – like two baby guava trees – just appear out of nowhere. But at the latest tally there were over forty bananas, five small lemon trees, half-a-dozen mangoes, a patch of hot red pepper plants, numerous tomatoes, and about 150 flowering shrubs, so you can imagine how much water we have to pull up morning and evening, even before we start replenishing the contents of the buckets in the toilets and in the kitchen. The company who sold us the water pump in Britain looked at it dismissively when Peter from Prestwick took it home to them. 'Sorry, you've been trying to fix it yourselves, so you've broken the guarantee,' they said smugly. Since we can't afford a new one at the moment, we could be relying on bicep-power for some time to come.

Musa WAS back for a while, after three weeks off for Ramadan. He had intended to spend Ramadan with us, but I got so irritated at shouting in his ear at full volume while he snored on blissfully, that I exploded one day and Ray told him to go home and sleep in his own time and at his own expense. Let me explain Ramadan. The idea is you don't eat anything or drink anything – even a small sip of water – between sun-up and sun-down. After that you wash and pray and eventually stuff yourself with as much food and drink as you can take. After that, in my opinion, you should go to sleep (by this time it's very late at night) and snatch a few hours before getting up for early praying in the morning and another day's fasting. But Musa, like many of his mates, spends the night chattering, drinking attaya, and moaning about how hard it is to observe Ramadan. The result is he is totally knackered when he comes to work, and when he is awake, goes about sighing and shaking his head and grunting bad-temperedly at everything you say to him.

During his enforced absence, therefore, we began doing our own gardening and watering, and found that, for the first time in ages, the garden looked neat and the plants flourished. I think this time he's made himself redundant once and for all. I know I've said that before, but this time . . .

Back to the bucket. I bought two, and some oiled tape, and went back to the clinic. Helma was still in the queue. A clerk was laboriously writing down her particulars, including a Dutch surname full of syllables and glottal consonants which gave him almost as many problems as it gives me. 'So you were clawed by a parrot?' he asked calmly. Obviously it's not an unusual thing to happen here. The head doctor, a large black bearded gentleman in an expensive suit, wafted past with some important visitors who'd come to see a nursing mother. They were delivered in a long black government car, so he spent the next fifteen minutes shaking hands and slapping backs and generally making sure that the people who count got the four-star treatment.

Not that Helma could complain of the quality of her treatment when it took place. She was led to a trolley and given a large jab on her bottom, and another on her arm, one for tetanus and one an antibiotic. Her wounds were rubbed assiduously with antiseptic and painted with gentian violet. 'Don't play with any more parrots,' said the man who counted out a course of penicillin tablets for her.

Myself, I haven't had any parrot bites, but I keep getting attacked by ants. Not the big red ones, nor the tiny black ones, but the middle-sized black ones, which march around the tiled floor by the score, and, when stood on or slapped away, sting like wasps. Ray found one in a very personal part of his trousers last night and jumped around the living room yelling blue murder.

I brush them out every morning and swab the floor with a solution of strong bleach. Insect spray has no effect. I think they get high on it and bite even harder.

The other local pests are the tourist taxi drivers. Some of them, of course, are our best friends. But some of them are a pain in the neck. When we bought our Land Rover intending to take tourists on excursions to the bonny fishing and farming villages in the south, they blew a gasket and glowered at us, or ran after us demanding to see our papers. When we registered the company – tiny as it is – Ray took great delight in thrusting the impressive-looking document under the nose of the taxi *chef*, which stopped the rumpus for a while. It's a grand-looking document allowing us to open up hotels, motels, restaurants and heaven knows what, when in fact all we have is a small group of huts and one Land Rover! But if the tourist taxi-men leave us alone, it doesn't mean they relax their vigilance on other fronts. Tourists who wish to travel on local bush-taxis – which they are perfectly entitled to do – get chased and harried by the tourist drivers telling them they must use their vehicles. The other day some of them beat up a bush-taxi driver because he picked up tourist fares. The gendarmes came and investigated, but it still happens from time to time.

Peaceful co-existence between the various forms of transport might be easier to enforce if there were peaceful co-existence between the law enforcement organisations themselves. As it is, a state of overt hostility bubbles up regularly between the police and the gendarmerie. Once, the gendarmes stormed a local police station because one of their guys had been taken into custody. All hell broke loose, and the station officer was taken to hospital with serious injuries. A big debate ensued, about whether it was the fault of the police, who come under the authority of the Ministry of Justice, or the gendarmes, who come under the Minister of Defence – who happens to be the President.

It's probably fair to say there are faults on both sides – or to put it another way, both can be extremely bloody-minded.

Not long after I started writing this chapter, Musa came back yet again to plead for reinstatement. Now he's here on sufferance, desperately trying to make himself indispensable. Flapping about in his ragged cut-offs, with the seedy underpants hanging through where the zip should be, he whisks empty plates and glasses from the table under the baobab, where the guests eat omelettes and drink beer. He produces a dirty rag from some unspeakable recess and wipes the tables with a flourish, gabbling all the time in Senegalese Wollof. I think he overhead Peter, before he left for Scotland, saying: 'How's the managing director today?' and the joke has gone to his head. I don't think I can cope with an energetic Musa; it's even worse then a soporific Musa.

Tales of engaging chicanery continue to reach our ears. Sometimes they're more than just hearsay. Ray naively agreed to buy some steel reinforcing rods from a sad chap who said his family had swindled him out of all the money he'd brought back from Europe to build a house. He just wanted to sell what materials were left and go back to Germany. When Ray went to the arranged meeting place with the money, another man was there, who swore he was the brother of the first, and that Ray was to give the money to him and collect the goods next evening. Ray went to the first man's compound next day; he was wailing and sobbing and calling the cops. The 'brother' had nicked the money and everything else he could lay his hands on, including Ray's steel rods. . . .

The newest nightclub in Kairaba Avenue closed down after a few weeks because the Gambian partner did a bunk with the money. A man who offered to sell us cement at less than the going rate was arrested ten minutes before Ray arrived with the Land Rover. Three dock officials were nabbed for hiving off thousands of tonnes of imported rice provided by the Americans. It is alleged that much of it went to very prominent people in government and civil service who had businesses on the side selling commodities.

Ray's brother Lamin has just had his cassette player and speakers snaffled from the taxi he drives. One day we gave a lift to a Fula who'd bought a freezer at an auction sale in the docks in Banjul. We dropped him off and were shouting our goodbyes when we witnessed the astonishing sight of a freezer, which had been lifted from the back of our vehicle seconds before, simply vanishing into thin air with the Fula galloping furiously down the road yelling 'Stop, thief!'

When my son was here, he and his three friends waited trustingly at Uncle Dembo's for two hours for the bright-eyed and bushy-tailed young lad who'd promised to bring them motor-bikes to hire. They had, of course, paid him a deposit. He never appeared. Which was probably just as well, as the thought of them all bouncing around on Gambian roads with no crash-helmets (they are not obligatory here) had terrified me. The more I think about it, the more I realise that it's just like Glasgow! Full of charming con-men, lugubrious hard-luck stories, goods falling 'off the back of a lorry' (or maybe a donkey-cart) and always a gullible customer to be found if you spin your yarn convincingly enough.

But honest business is conducted too. In our case, it's the ferrying of wide-eyed passengers to the colourful beauty-spots they feel they should see. To be honest, many of the recognised spots are pretty boring, very dusty, and full of hustlers. But we try to pick out-of-the-way places where they really will find baboons, birds of every hue and empty beaches just like the ones on the postcards.

They all *ooh* and *aah* at the sight of monkeys trapezing through the trees, cashew nuts growing like little boomerangs embedded in the orange flesh of the cashew-fruit, and women pressing the palm-nuts to obtain the golden-red oil in which rice is cooked locally.

There are bad days as well. The fan-belt fell apart halfway to Tendaba, on a road as long and empty and barren as a politician's speech. The passengers went for a pee behind some dusty thorn-bushes, and looked into the hot, misty, unbroken distance, wondering when the vultures would gather. It always tells you in books to use ladies' tights in such emergencies but, as no-one wears tights in this climate, we used the strap from my daughter's camera-case, and made a makeshift belt, then limped slowly to Tendaba, stopping every ten minutes to pour water into the radiator.

The passengers said later it was all part of the fun and excitement of being in Africa. Ha ha. They come home with hair like straw, pale dust all over their clothes, and cheeks ruddy with the remorseless sunlight, and they insist they've enjoyed it. Being on holiday changes your perspective on things, I guess. Me, I'd rather stay here and watch the butterflies flicking through the flowers and the weaver birds yattering on the wall behind the kitchen. On the wall is as near as I need my birds to be. And Helma seconds me in that. As for the parrot, I think Yancobi and Ibrahim found a buyer. Good luck to him, I say.

Stolen Cows and Stolen Hearts

Ray's aunt, the builder's wife, came to see us yesterday. 'Now they've stolen another of my cows,' she moaned, tears welling up in her soft round eyes. 'Please take me to see your marabout.'

The reason we happened to have a marabout, the way you might have a hairdresser or a plumber that you recommend to your friends, is that we were burgled last week. There are several things you do, in the middle of a moonless night, with the wind cackling through the palm-fronds, the dogs yapping like hyenas and your eyes bleary from sleep, when you discover you've been robbed.

First, you trip over each other looking for candles and shoes, stubbing your toes and burning your fingers on the matches. You shout for Roel, who comes lurching over from his hut, wild-eyed and anxious, still hung-over from copious quantities of Julbrew before bedtime, brandishing a large club and looking a bit like Hagar the Horrible. The club is actually a wooden pestle for grinding millet. He looks, as we do, at the gap on the verandah right under our bedroom window, a metre or so from where we'd been sleeping minutes before, the empty spot where a couple of hours ago the stereo had been playing Ba Ba Maal's latest hits.

The dogs are growling and whimpering and jumping up and down in frustration. So am I. Roel and Ray plunge about among the bananas. Ray is waving a cutlass. He flashes his torch around frantically and realises that the corrugated iron door of the generator-house has a splutter of splinters where the hinge used to be. Someone has peeled the bottom upwards, cut through the flex and extracted our Honda 2.2, our source of light and music and power for the water-pump (if only it was working, but that's hardly the point . . .)

Ray is on the brink of tears. I am flaming mad. Roel is swearing in Dutch. 'These fooking teefs!' Ray sobs. 'I will kill them!' So will I. But how to catch them? I chug and shudder along the rutted road to the village in the 2CV. Dogs howl, babies cry and an old man gulps soundlessly and clutches the ju-ju at his waist when he sees Ray and Roel, weapons waving, eyes rolling in the darkness. It is 5 am.

Serrekunda cop-shop smells of urine and is full of mosquitoes. A thief (not ours) is lying on a bench, muttering and gasping and begging to be locked up. He was caught by the locals at London Corner, who threatened to hammer four-inch nails into his head (a method alleged to be used by people from up-river when they come across criminals pilfering their sheep and goats).

The police have no transport. If you require motorised assistance, you have to fetch them and take them to wherever they need to go in the pursuit of their investigations. The next few days are a bit of a blur. We meet Baius, the Gambia's answer to Dirty Harry, dashingly rigged out in technicolour cotton and dark glasses, the star of the CID. He even has a motor-bike.

Aunties and grannies gather on the verandah to offer sympathy and advice, and I produce endless cups of tea and coffee. 'You must get a marabout. You must buy a ju-ju, Mariama.' Baius and his henchmen slouch around looking tough and tracking footprints.

It is learned that our Finnish neighbour across the bush had fired his gun at an intruder the same night . . . his watchman had tracked three men to Bakoteh village . . . the schoolteacher's six sheep had been slaughtered and stolen from his compound the night before, only blood and entrails remaining.

From the footprints, various dents in the undergrowth and tyre tracks beyond the school football field behind our house, it is deduced that there were indeed three men, and they had escaped in a waiting car. Our Land Rover, with Ray and Lamin deputised as honorary CID super-sleuths, is driven past the suspect compound in Bakoteh, pronounced by Baius to be an obvious lair for all the most criminal elements in West Africa. A raid was planned for next day at dawn.

Meanwhile, accepting the advice of an earnest young police constable, we called in the marabouts. 'They helped us catch three thieves last week,' he informed us. 'Their magic is very strong.'

Two gentlemen of dignified bearing, in stiffly-pressed immaculate cotton robes, sat on the verandah looking wise and competent, drinking the coffee I made for them. It was a bit like calling in a crime prevention officer or a lawyer.

'Someone has brought bad luck to your compound . . .' You can say that again. 'He has buried something in your garden to bring you misfortune. You must come to us tomorrow and we will undo the spell. Then everything will be fine. You will be happy again.' They gave me professional handshakes and left. Next morning Ray and Roel went to visit them at their consulting rooms.

Roel was sent to buy a chicken. One marabout stared at the unfortunate bird and muttered incantations over it, over and over again. Suddenly, the chicken keeled over and died. A bottle of greenish-brown liquid was given to Ray and he was instructed to take it home, add perfumed water to it, and bathe in it once a day. He used his Chanel Pour Monsieur which I gave him last Christmas. I doubt if Chanel has ever been put to such challenging use before.

'I can see . . . three men . . .' intoned the chief marabout. 'They live in a village not far from you . . . 'one of them is known to you . . . they will be caught. Your goods will be restored to you . . .'

Jolly good show. A consultation fee of 450 dalasi changed hands. The raid took place next morning. Ray, whom I had expressly instructed to stay in the bloody Land Rover out of sight, leapt over the wall with Baius and Lamin and several sidekicks. Two armed, uniformed policemen covered the escape routes. In a small room a box-bed was found to contain various items – tins of paint, a metal safe, plumbing materials, and our generator. The cassette-player had already been sold to the old man, who, it was alleged, had arranged the Renault Four taxi, the getaway car!

Two of the 'teefs' were arrested during the raid. The third was spotted crouching behind a car near the police station and cliped on by his mates. Ray and Lamin (Batman and Robin, Starsky and Hutch, the Bijilo Bill) grabbed him in a citizens' arrest. A triumph for the forces of law and order. Ray is still splashing his magic water-plus-Chanel all over him, assured that it will give us good business next season.

Meanwhile, Ray's aunt's cows have been abducted, so naturally she turns to us, as experts in the being-robbed business. The return of our goods is the talk of the neighbourhood. It is ascribed neither to the acumen of the police nor the derring-do of Ray and Lamin but to the evident powers of our marabouts. Can they help auntie?

Most of the cows in the village are owned by Ray's uncle, the Imam. But other people, like auntie, keep a few beasts in the herd which is tended by a man called Ibrahim. In recent weeks, nothing has been safe. Not just cows, but sheep, goats and chickens have been disappearing in droves. Two cows were taken from Ray's dad's compound and slaughtered on the road to Brufut. One had been in calf and the unborn baby was discarded and left in a ditch. I keep sending Ray round to Uncle Alieu's to check that my sheep is still safe.

There is a suspicion that Ibrahim may be in cahoots with the rustlers. The marabouts do impressive things, like telling auntie that if she digs in a certain corner of a certain field she will find a certain object. She does, but she never gets her cows back.

Once, when Ray was a schoolboy in Sukuta, he tells me a local shopkeeper had a cow nicked. The thief, not knowing whose cow he'd taken, approached the shopkeeper the next day and offered to sell it to him. 'You ****!' bellowed the honest trader, and he and all the schoolboys in Sukuta set off in pursuit of the thief. 'Did you catch him?' I asked Ray. 'Oh, yes!'

'What happened then?'

'The shopkeeper tied him to a tree and everyone who went past gave him a slap or a kick,' said Ray with relish. Rough justice rules in the Gambia. Sometimes too rough for tender tubab stomachs.

Two of our own thieves are still on the run, having managed to escape while released from their cells for urination purposes, the police explained. Every so often we bump into Baius, the dashing detective, and he says: 'Don't worry. This is the Gambia. It is very small. We will get them.' But I have my doubts. There are bush-taxis to Casamance, and beyond, to Guinea Bissau. And it hardly seems worth calling in Interpol, I tell myself.

I suspect, meanwhile, that Ray's aunt has a secondary motive for calling on us so often to discuss her vanishing cows. Every time she comes, she brings grapefruit and coconuts and lemons, and her delicious little daughter, Yandi, always with her hair elaborately twirled into tiny plaits and wearing her best frock.

It was to Yandi that my three-year-old grandson Cameron gave his heart and his hand when he first came to the Gambia in the spring. The two of them toddled together among the bananas, little white head and little black one bobbing along, Yandi's enormous dewy eyes wide and subservient. It's my theory that auntie and uncle have visions of an engagement. A tubab husband would be a good catch, worth waiting fifteen years or so for . . . She would, from a chap's point of view, be the perfect wife, for she never utters a word, and docilely does absolutely whatever he tells her. 'Gimme that ball!' instructs Cameron. 'Push me on my bike!' 'Carry my toy jeep!' And she does, more fool she.

Meanwhile, our young brother Lamin is still chewing his nails, waiting to know whether his proposal to the fair and fickle Fatou from Bakau will be deemed acceptable. Her uncle is ill in Senegal and nothing can go ahead without his approval. Ray's mum is in a state of nerves, borrowing and begging where she can to produce the price demanded for this delectable bride, which seems to have gone up in direct relation to the desire of the suitor.

Seeing how distressed my mother-in-law was about this need to raise money to 'buy' a daughter-in-law, I asked naively if she would waive all this materialism should the situation be reversed. Would she let my little sister Mariama go for free to the right man? Ray translated for her and she looked shocked. 'Of course not,' she said witheringly. 'It is the custom here.'

You may recall that my own price, when I was married in Bijilo these two years or so ago, was a mere 300 dalasi. I suppose as a middle-aged, divorced mother-of-three it was a case of second-hand goods being worth much less . . .

Under the Baobab Tree

One thing is sure. When, or if, Lamin and Fatou get married, they won't be short of advice and discussion about their behaviour and problems. Marital discord is viewed with sympathetic tolerance. Forgiveness is very big in the Gambia. The other day I thought Mariama, wife of Mulai the new watchman, might bash his head in with her rice-pot. I could hear her screeching from the doorway of her hut, waving her hands and uttering what Ray told me were imprecations concerning Mulai's habits, selfishness, boorishness, family history and general entitlement to call himself a man. We didn't mean to hire another watchman after Musa, but, after the theft of the generator, Ray's dad brought Mulai along, with Mariama following close behind. I don't feel very optimistic about them, but only time will tell. And all these other Mariama's are becoming very confusing.

'What started all this?' I asked Mulai, who was doggedly pulling up water from the well, allowing the tidal wave of abuse to pass over his head. 'I asked her to make me some food. Everything I ask, she takes ten, fifteen minutes before she will move and do what I tell her. What kind of wife is that? If I tell her to do something, she should do it at once.' I took a deep breath and joined the fray. We women must stick together. 'What are you talking about, you big bully? For a week now, you have been leaving the compound every morning to dig the well you forgot to tell us you promised to dig before you took this job. All the time you're away, your poor wife is opening and closing these big heavy gates, pulling up water, hoeing round the plants, doing YOUR work. She is tired! You should be ashamed of yourself!'

Ray raised his eyes and Mulai went on hauling up buckets from the well. 'Women!' I could hear them thinking.

I found these words, by a Gambian poet, the other day.

'I would not argue with you tonight over salty food and half-cooked rice
For the moon is too hostile and I do not want to add to the madness of this hour.

I would just eat cassava. And fried geckos wriggle on the cinder-coated walls of our patient kitchen,

While the glittering fireflies teach you the silent grace of marriage.'

I still haven't learned the silent grace of marriage. Just ask Ray. But I have learned to take the generator thieves and eccentric watchmen in my stride, not to mention the poet's salty rice, the ubiquitous cassava, and geckos on the walls.

I am brown as the burnt sand and my feet are leathery. I can draw water up from a well and recognise five different West African tribal languages. I typed most of this by candle-light in the hours when the Gambian moon lies like a silver cradle in a sky festooned with stars I never saw before.

But one of them must be shining especially for me.

188